NAMING THE GODDESS

Naming the Goddess is a delightful read  raising them, from a variety of per personal experiences, often in years (Goddess and Goddesses. There is son for those new to the Goddess and fc especially liked the reflections with which the book begins and appreciated the catalogue of Goddesses written by different people who understood the different Goddesses from their different standpoints.

Carol P. Christ, author of *Rebirth of the Goddess*, leader of Goddess Pilgrimage to Crete

Naming the Goddess is an amazing combination of the practitioner's voice alongside the scholar, while addressing many of the important issues within Goddess Spirituality today. Within the pages of *Naming the Goddess*, Goddess Spirituality comes of age as it manages to strike a healthy balance between honoring the old beliefs yet reclaims the Divine Feminine in a more contemporary context for modernity. Great new voices carrying the torch for understanding and embracing The Great She for the future of our world!

Karen Tate, author of *Walking an Ancient Path*, *Goddess Calling* and *Voices of the Sacred Feminine*

This collection of writings is so rich and diverse, it could be of interest to anyone seeking the essence of the divine, whether polytheist, pantheist, monist, or otherwise, and whether their principle understanding of deity is gendered female or otherwise.

Indeed perhaps it is in that very diversity, in the cracks of divergence, that the sacred is most potent, accessible and enthralling.
Emma Restall Orr, author of *Kissing the Hag, Living With Honour* and *The Wakeful World*

This fabulous overview of modern Goddess spirituality includes not only 13 thought-provoking thealogical essays, but also a gazetteer of goddesses from across the globe. Written by over 85 professional writers and spiritual practitioners, this meaty and vibrant guide to the Goddess is one you'll want to add to your library ASAP.
Jeri Studebaker, author of *Switching to Goddess*

A must read for those old and new to Goddess. With new and known authors, this book gives an interesting and varied view on Goddess and feminine spirituality, and how that effects both spiritual paths and society. Brilliant!
Annabell Alexander, Founder of the Goddess Foundation

Naming the
Goddess

Naming the Goddess

Edited by

Trevor Greenfield

Winchester, UK
Washington, USA

First published by Moon Books, 2014
Moon Books is an imprint of John Hunt Publishing Ltd., Laurel House, Station Approach,
Alresford, Hants, SO24 9JH, UK
office1@jhpbooks.net
www.johnhuntpublishing.com
www.moon-books.net

For distributor details and how to order please visit the 'Ordering' section on our website.

Text copyright: Trevor Greenfield 2013

ISBN: 978 1 78279 476 9

A CIP catalogue record for this book is available from the British Library.

Design: Stuart Davies
www.stuartdaviesart.com

Printed and bound by CPI Group (UK) Ltd, Croydon, CR0 4YY

We operate a distinctive and ethical publishing philosophy in all
areas of our business, from our global network of authors to
production and worldwide distribution.

CONTENTS

Epilogue – Emily, Goddess of Forgiveness

Preface

When Moon Books began, at the beginning of 2012, we determined from the outset that as well as publishing books from authors, both well-known and new, we would endeavour to develop a community of readers and writers, bloggers, poets and critics. *Naming the Goddess* is one of the results of that commitment. In this book over seventy five writers come together to honour the Goddess and produce a book that above all is a celebration of Her and their creativity. The book is in two parts; the first is a series of critical essays reflecting upon contemporary issues, the second is a spiritual gazetteer featuring Goddesses from across the globe. It was a pleasure to be involved in the book's creation. I hope you enjoy reading it.

Trevor Greenfield

Foreword

Nearly 40 years ago, I was setting off for a holiday on the Greek island of Lesbos. Just as I was leaving, a friend thrust a book into my hand and said: "I've just received this from America – I think you will probably enjoy it". I put it into my suitcase, and when we arrived in Lesbos it was raining, and continued to rain solidly for three days. So I sat down to read what looked like quite an academic book, and found myself absolutely enthralled. It was as if all the things that I had believed in all my life without knowing it had validation and precedence. The book was *The Goddesses and Gods of Old Europe* by Marija Gimbutas (1974), a Lithuanian-American archaeologist and anthropologist who had excavated at a number of sites in Europe and had found a wealth of Goddess figurines, images and iconography at a time when such finds were deemed to be of no particular significance. From this Gimbutas developed a theory that there were many cultures throughout Europe from the Neolithic, Chalcolithic and Bronze Ages that were Goddess-celebrating and matrifocal in their beliefs and practices. This was revolutionary stuff, and if ever a book changed my life that one did! Later Gimbutas was to develop a theory about the universal "language" of the Goddess encoded in the iconography and visual symbolism from these societies, which she published as *The Language of the Goddess* (1989) and *The Civilisation of the Goddess* (1991); two magnificently illustrated and well-argued books.

Marija Gimbutas encouraged me to research my own native Cornwall (UK) and Britain and Ireland, looking at prehistory through the same Goddess lens that she had used, and the result was a number of books that I wrote and have been published over the years. Since those early days, there has been an explosion of research and writings on the Goddess, from many approaches and viewpoints. Just the ones that my partner and I possess fill two complete full-size bookcases along a complete wall of one of our rooms! Of course, there has been the inevitable backlash to her ideas and assertions (the notion of "Goddess" seems to touch a raw nerve in many people), as well as a more moderate and reasoned modification of some of her ideas, but the seed that she planted 40 years ago has now grown into a healthy, full-blossomed tree, with many branches bearing rich fruit. This book is the latest one of these, and, to my mind, one of the most important to have come out in recent years.

The book falls into two parts, both distinctive in their own way. The first part, entitled "Writing the Goddess", consists of a number of essays, looking at how Goddess is experienced and celebrated in society today. The writers of these essays raise pertinent and relevant questions for those who have just discovered Goddess as well as those who are seasoned and experienced practitioners of Goddess research and belief. They talk about the specialness, the uniqueness, of Goddess belief, and of how the beliefs of ancient societies can be of relevance to us today. They ask questions about what "Goddess" means, and how that is different from "God" or "spirit", and they challenge both our ideology and our concept of what "Goddess" means. They stimulate our personal arguments and ideas of what is "Goddess", and engage us in a process to re-think, re-establish or re-affirm our personal beliefs. They cover a wide range of topics, including gender, nature, politics, energy, meaning, belief and practice, and ask fundamental and important questions, such as "what does belief in a Goddess, or many Goddesses, mean to me?" and "how can this belief best manifest in my life and in my world?". These are significant and meaningful essays, and it seems to me that they should be required reading for anyone with a Goddess-focused spiritual belief or interest today.

Then, in the second part of the book, there are nearly 70 individual Goddesses featured from cultures all over the world. Each writer gives the mythology and meaning of his or her chosen Goddess, and also writes enthusiastically and inspirationally about who that Goddess is, how that Goddess manifested to the culture from which she arose, and what that Goddess means to the writer of that piece. This is not just an encyclopedia of Goddesses (though it can certainly serve as such) but a bringing-alive of the whole ethos and significance of that Goddess. These Goddesses are experienced by the writers as a living presence in their lives, and they vividly show how that particular Goddess continues to live and have real presence in the world today, sometimes long after the culture that named and celebrated her has disappeared. It also shows that all individual Goddesses are but aspects of the One Goddess, with attributes that have as much meaning and relevance for us today as they did for the people who originally worshipped or celebrated them.

I have been producing and editing a magazine all about Goddess and Goddesses now for some 15 years. It has always aimed to reflect the diverse community of Goddess spirituality both reclaimed from the past and alive in the world today. This book does the same. It has information and research aplenty, but it has something more as well: a love of Goddess, and a celebration of her multifaceted significance for women and men in the world today. While there are so many people who relate to Goddess and bring her into their lives, Goddess will never die out, nor be just a passing phase. She has the ability to empower people to connect with their inner selves, and strive for a better, more harmonious and peaceful world. The seed that Marija Gimbutas planted all those years ago nowadays bears wondrous fruit. She would have been very proud of the writers and readers of this inspirational book.

Cheryl Straffon is the Editor of *Goddess Alive!* magazine (2000-present) www.goddessalive.co.uk. She is the author of *Pagan Cornwall: Land of the Goddess* (1993/2012); *The Earth Goddess* (1997) and *Daughters of the Earth* (2007).

Introduction

Pathways of Goddess and Goddesses

Since ancient times, the Sacred Feminine has been part of religions and cultures the world over. Now in the twenty-first century, Goddess spirituality is flourishing in many places and in many ways the world over, both within contemporary Paganism as well as in other world religions. There is a variety of ways of connecting with The Goddess and/or Goddesses. I have identified six pathways of Goddess spirituality drawn from Goddess workshops I have presented over the years across the US, Canada, UK, and in other countries. My own path of Goddess spirituality is multifaceted and includes experiences with each of these ways. May this overview of Goddess pathways guide you in your own Goddess studies and spiritual practice.

Path of Universality

On this path, Goddess is The Goddess. Also known as All-Goddess and the Great Goddess, She is the embodiment of all Goddess forms, and every Goddess is a facet of Her. For many on this path, She also is the Divine Universal, not only embodying all Goddesses, but also all Gods, Nature Spirits, and other Sacred forms. For some, The Goddess is the same eternal, all-powerful, all-knowing, creative Divine force that others call God or Great Spirit, and still others know as Mother Nature. However, for many, She is not only transcendent and beyond the boundaries of human comprehension, She also is immanent, and therefore, indwelling, omnipresent, and personally accessible. As She-who-is-All-that-Is-and-Is-Not, The Goddess is the union of creator and creation; form and void; time and timelessness; life, death, and rebirth... Infinite Mystery.

Path of Particularity

Journeying on this path involves coming to know and work with a particular Goddess or Goddess aspect. In contrast to the broad scope of the universality approach, this focused way involves in-depth study, invocation, worship, shrine keeping, and alignment with a specific Goddess and Her symbols, stories, attributes, and cultural roots. For some, a single Goddess is the only form of the Divine worshipped; for others, She is primary. The particularity approach may come from being part of an area, family, group, and/or community where a particular Goddess predominates, such as the worship of Athena by Athenians in ancient Greece and the attunement with Diana by some contemporary Dianics. For many on this path today, developing an alignment with a particular Goddess occurs as a result of a powerful spiritual encounter with that Goddess in a dream, vision, or ritual. For others, the relationship develops more gradually as part of spiritual studies.

Path of Dyadicy

Those who walk this path relate to the Goddess as part of a Divine Pair. For many Wiccans and other Pagans, this is in the form of a Divine Mother and Divine Father, commonly known as the Goddess and the God. In some traditions, the Goddess and the God also have special sacred names known only to initiates. Attributes and symbols associated with the Goddess and the God vary across Pagan paths. Some honor the Goddess as the Moon Goddess and the God as Sun God, but others honor the Sun Goddess and Moon God. Another form of the Divine Pair is Mother Earth and Father Sky. There are other sacred Pagan Dyads as well, including that of Divine Mother and Daughter, such as Demeter and Persephone, and the Divine Mother and Holy Son, such as Isis and Horus. Most working with a Sacred Dyad not only align with each but with their Unity.

Path of Triplicity

On this path, the Goddess takes the form of a Sacred Trinity. Many Pagans today know Her as the Triple Goddess — She who is Maiden, Mother, and Crone. Some Pagans work with a Goddess with three domains, such as Brigid, the Celtic Goddess of Inspiration, Smithcraft, and Healing. Sometimes, the Triplicity is a grouping of Three Goddesses, such as Hygeia (Health), Iaso (Healing) and Panacea (Cure-All), the Divine Daughters of Asklepios, the Greek God of Healing. Other Triplicities in Pagan religions include the Three Fates (Rome), Three Norns (Scandinavia), Three Graces (Greece), and the Three Mothers or Matrones (Roman Germany). In addition to developing relationships with each of the three forms, most Pagans on this path also connect with their Unity.

Path of Multiplicity

This approach involves work with Goddesses as part of a pantheon, or community of Deities. For example, among the Olympian pantheon of the Greek religion, the Goddesses include Hera, the Queen of Heaven; Athena, Goddess of Wisdom; Aphrodite, Goddess of Love; and Artemis, Goddess of the Moon. However, a pantheon for some practitioners today may be multicultural and include Goddesses from many times and places that have touched the practitioner. My own work on the path of multiplicity includes work with a multicultural pantheon of Goddesses now honored across spiritual traditions such as Bast (Egyptian), Libertas (Roman), Brigid (Celtic), Yemaya (African), Holda (German), Kuan Yin (Asian), Mother Earth, and Mother Nature.

Path of Inclusivity

This is the path which combines work with all these paths and ways of knowing The Goddess and Goddesses. Those who journey on this path of paths focus on experiencing and understanding both Unity and Diversity.

Selena Fox is a priestess, environmentalist, interfaith minister, and holistic psychotherapist with a Masters in Science in counseling from the University of Wisconsin-Madison. She is author of *Goddess Communion* and other works, and is founder of Circle Sanctuary which has been serving Pagans and other Goddess Spirituality practitioners worldwide since 1974. She teaches through a weekly podcast and travels internationally presenting workshops and facilitating ceremonies.

www.selenafox.com;

www.circlesanctuary.org;

www.facebook.com/SelenaFoxUpdates

Prologue

The Maiden and the Moon

When all is dark and the moon plays
hide-and-seek with the land, the maiden
practices seeing with the eyes of a cat
watches the field mice scurry, her lithe
little hands graze the back of a deer
who leads her to the water; where
she sees herself for the first time:
Her eyes are round as an owl's.
The maiden screeches a wild cry
and is rewarded with Owl's answer.

The flowers she wove into a crown
fall into the water and create ripples.
Her hair spirals down her young form.
She notices her hands and feet, good
for climbing trees, dancing, and leaping
with the deer through the woods.
Her stomach digests wild mushrooms
onions, and herbs; it gurgles, she giggles
and pats it like a drum to the beat of heart.

Her arms grow stronger and longer like her legs.
Her hips curve out like flowers she picks.
She makes skirts to match her favorite petals.
The moon brightens with the maiden
and every night they dance until the sapling
she first climbed as a girl teaches her
how to build her first bow and others
besides the moon ask her to dance.

The Mother and the Moon

A wisp of light curves like bow
in the dark cradle of the moon.
The autumnal geese aim their V
south for the winter, and so
she knocks an arrow in her own
bow which has weathered
many seasons; no longer
a maiden she needs to eat.

Sometimes it is a deer or a boar
which falls beneath her arrow,
as the field mouse is swallowed
by the snake and fills the fox.
As are the cycles of seasons,
so are the cycles of life and death.
The wisp of life curves inside her
growing arms and legs good
for climbing trees and dancing
beneath the waxing moon.

She births the babe as nature
has long birthed the hills, the lakes,
the animals, and set the stars
deep in the cloaked night.
The mother names these stars
between tight breaths until
in the warm cradle of her arms
she holds her first-born child.

The mother watches as her babe
waxes like the growing moon.
She teaches her child what
the seasons have taught her,

and when her babe's legs have
grown long enough to outrun hers,
the mother smiles at the full moon:
a loving face to guide her child.

A wisp of light curves like bow
in the dark cradle of the moon.
The autumnal geese aim their V
south for the winter, and so
she braids her silver hair,
shining like moonlight on snow.

The Crone and the Moon

The waning crescent flickers
behind swaying branches
of a twisted old oak tree.
The crone's knotted fingers
unbend the boughs of silver
loose from her long braid.

She screeches a shrill sound
which echoes into the night.
Owl twists his head around
and answers her, wide eyes
reflecting memories of yore.

The sapling which taught her
how to use her feet for climbing,
how to use her hands to curve
a bow: has taught her the wisdom
of flexibility, of life and of death:
has taught her the wisdom
of being firm, the shaping
of a staff the way old bones

age into sturdier stuff.

She has wrought the paths
in the fields and over the mountains.
She knows the way. The secret:
There is more than one path.
Her ancient body charts
the seasons, the scars, the stars,
each wrinkle a rivulet of mastery.
She adds more every day,
especially when her bawdy
laughter howls with the winds.

When there is only starlight
in the dark sky, the crone
will walk the long walk
striking the land with her staff,
building mountains, steadying
the legs of mothers as they tremble,
making corn dollies for the children.

She is the revered one, all falls
silent beneath her mantle. If,
you should find her crooked finger
pointed beneath your nose, do not
ignore her wisdom or knock-knock
jokes, or you should find yourself
as the start of her newest riddle.
She is a fierce sight to look upon,
but her smile rivals starlight,
brings back the light of the moon.

Tiffany Chaney is an artist and writer residing in North Carolina, USA. She holds a Bachelor of Arts in creative writing from Salem College and is Founding Editor of Recto Verso Review, serving as Art Editor of Thrush Press. She is the author of *Between Blue and Grey*.

Part 1

Writing the Goddess

Strangers in a Strange Land: Ancient Goddesses in a Modern World

Morgan Daimler

Many people in today's world seek to connect to Goddesses from the ancient world, often by seeking out their stories and looking at how their historic root culture understood them. This is a good way to understand who these Goddesses were and that there is beauty and power in the old myths and folktales that certainly deserves to be honored. The history of each Goddess is the unique story of her life and, in many ways, the lives of her worshippers, and yet history only takes us so far. Relating to Goddesses in the modern world can mean bridging the gap between the past and the present, between knowledge and experience, in powerful and meaningful ways. Human culture is a fluid thing that changes and the Goddesses change along with us, keeping the core of who they are as they move with us into the future we are shaping.

The first place people start looking when seeking to understand a Goddess they feel drawn to is the past. Many of the Goddesses that are honored today have been revived from ancient cultures and the myths and stories of these cultures form the bones of what we know about the Gods. People read and study until they know every story, every version, every nuance. They take apart context and tone and search for meaning in every detail. They seek out archeology and any appearance of their Goddess in the writings of other cultures or sources. Even a single line can provide powerful clues to add to the story of who that Goddess was. The stories shape our vision of who each Goddess was and what she did; we build a relationship out of the pieces of the past. And yet, the old stories can only take us so far, the old lore can only create a partial connection. To relate an ancient Goddess to our world today we have to bridge the gap of time and culture, we have to bring the image of that Goddess into our world and our modern reality. We must cherish the past and preserve the old stories, while making new stories and new visions. There is a continuity to the divine that keeps it always present and vital while simultaneously being solidly part of our history.

There is a saying that that which isn't growing is dying, and it is true of the Gods just as it is of anything else. Although we tend to see them as fully formed and realized Beings, they are as much in constant flux as we are. Looking at the past shows you the beginning of their story and we can watch the way they changed with their cultures. Hekate has been a Titan, a virgin Goddess, a mother, a psychopomp and queen of witches at different points in Greek mythology. With every age and shift in culture she changed too, staying modern and relevant for each new generation, creating layers of personality and power. So it is with every ancient Goddess, as the modern world is reflected in them and changes how we understand them.

Do deities evolve? The world of our ancestors and our world are vastly different places in many ways. While the broad strokes of life, death, love, and health remain the same, some of the things ancient Goddesses oversaw are less applicable in our world and some things we live with every day didn't exist back then. In order for ancient Goddesses to remain relevant and vital to each new generation we must not only connect to them but we must feel also that they connect to us. Goddesses became associated with specific things because the people realized that a certain deity seemed more disposed to handle it or willing to quickly respond. Flidais was associated in myth with milk and abundance, so it's logical to see her as the one to pray to when you need your cow to give more milk. Brighid was a Goddess of the hearth fire, so people prayed to her when building their fires up in the morning to warm their homes and cook. But what do these things mean for us today? We have changed, our needs have changed – and our Goddesses have changed with us. When our sustenance comes from a store not our own barn we can still pray to the same ancient Goddess of abundance. When our home is heated by a furnace not a fireplace we can still kindle devotional fires in our hearts to the same ancient Goddess of inspiration and flame. We must be willing to look at the ways that the Goddesses we know from the old stories relate to our modern world, not because the Gods need updating to stay relevant, but because it is the nature of the Gods to grow and change with the people who worship them.

Understanding Goddesses in the modern world, as we move beyond the old myths and stories, relies on personal gnosis and on shared gnosis. Personal gnosis is born from experience and inspiration; it is the knowledge of the Goddesses that we gain from interacting with them and actively seeking them. Personal gnosis can be a vague feeling or a complex theory, it can be the way we visualize a Goddess with a certain hair color or mannerism or the way we create new stories of the Goddess out of our own lives. Personal gnosis is powerful because it is personal, it is that which connects us to the deities we honor on the most visceral level. We all have different degrees of personal gnosis which act to connect us to these Goddesses; sometimes we share our personal feelings and knowledge about a Goddess and find that other people, on their own, have the same feelings and knowledge.

Shared gnosis is a slow process that we, as modern pagans, are only just beginning to nurture, as we share our personal beliefs and begin to create a new understanding of the old Goddesses that is viable for our communities. This will not be a single homogenous vision, but a series of small community understandings that reflect the same diversity the Goddesses existed in long ago, when every community had its own ways and beliefs. This then becomes shared knowledge, and over time shared knowledge becomes modern belief. An example of this shared knowledge might be offering strawberries to Freya, because many individuals came to believe that this was something she liked as an offering. As more people believed it and shared the idea it spread and became a more widely accepted idea.

What we offer the ancient Goddesses is strongly influenced by our personal knowledge and our instinct, as the options we have today are so wildly different than what our ancestors may have had. The traditional offerings are still valuable and important, we can still give milk, honey, and bread, but we can also offer coffee, chocolate, and exotic fruits. We can offer poetry, song, art and the skill of our hands as well as donating to charity or doing things to serve a greater cause in honor of the Goddess we are offering to. In the ancient world the people offered the best of what they had and we still do the same today, but our options are so much wider now. We have access to things unknown in the ancient world that can make for successful and meaningful offerings. As time goes on we build a new under-standing of modern offerings, of what our Goddesses like and want, and this strengthens our relationship with them.

Often we continue to see the Goddesses the way they were seen in the ancient world – in dresses, in armor, in cultural costume – but there is an increasing movement by artists and writers to re-envision the ancient Goddesses in modern settings. Just as the way we relate to the Goddesses has changed as what we need in our lives has changed, so too the ways we imagine the Goddesses looking are changing. People may still see the Morrigan in bloody battle armor, but some also see her in jeans and a leather jacket. Freya may appear driving her cat-drawn chariot or she may be driving a Jaguar race car. Today when Goddesses appear in dreams and visions they are as likely to be wearing modern fashion as ancient garb, but their personality still comes through. How we view them changes because their appearance has always been a reflection of our expectations; the Goddess appears to us as a mirror of our own assumptions and needs.

Each Goddess we love walks in the ancient world, but her footsteps are here too, today, in our forests and cities, our shorelines and homes. The ancient stories are still told, but new stories are being told as well, woven from the threads of the old. The Goddesses that were beloved and revered by our ancestors are still loved and honored today and they move as easily in our modern world as they did in the ancient one. The Goddesses still light the fires of our hearths and of our hearts but they also listen to our prayers about computers and commuting as we reach out to them from a modern world.

Morgan Daimler is a Druid in the Order of the White Oak and dedicant of Macha. She has had her poetry and prose published in seven anthologies, Circle magazine, and Witches and Pagans magazine. She is the author of *Where the Hawthorn Grows* and *Fairy Witchcraft*.

The Nature of a Nature Religion

Hearth Moon Rising

I am Isis, mistress of every land...
I laid down laws for mankind and ordained things that no one may change...
I am she who governs Sirius the Dog-Star...
I am she who is called divine among women...
I divided the earth from the heaven
I made manifest the paths of the stars
I prescribed the course of the sun and moon
[From *Aretalogy of Isis from Kyme*, circa 200 CE, trans. Sophie Drinker]

We live in a created, creative, and continually re-creating world, and thus a highly feminine one. The many creation myths starring anthropomorphic male Gods notwithstanding, we know that a male cannot give birth to a single child, let alone a whole universe. The ancients certainly understood this, before patriarchy confused the meaning of creative power. The best of the male bards have understood this, drawing on feminine spirit in muse or human form to infuse life into their words. Modern biology has also recognized this, and so refers to parthenogenic entities as female.

The trend in Pagan thought over the past five years has been to reject feminine creative power – in word and concept – in favor of gender neutral constructs which divorce our creator from her capacity to give birth. These constructs ignore sex and reproductive capacity and so are at odds with biology, nature, and our history as a nature religion. While advanced as more "progressive" or "equality minded," these constructs end up reinforcing patriarchal paradigms and marginalizing the female sex.

Arguments in favor of a gender neutral reconception of Goddess hinge on the assertion that "God is neither male nor female," "God is beyond male and female," or "God is both male and female." Saying "God is neither male nor female" reduces the deity to an "it." The "neither" argument neuters Goddess and so separates her from progeneration, sex, and creative functions. The "beyond male and female" argument also carves a piece out of the whole. Surely Goddess includes male and female, embraces both, and disdains neither. The "both" argument I would agree with, though not in the spirit it is usually intended. The unspoken premise in the "both" argument as it is usually advanced is that God and Goddess, male and fe(male), are opposite, or at least separate, entities. This takes us back to the problem of fragmentation. If the divine couple are creative, what is the generative or creative power of the two as a whole? Not neuter or "it," not something apart from them, but a creator of both, which would be female. This is not strictly a linguistic problem, but a symptom of deep cosmological underpinnings that have become embedded in language. Conceptions of creation are intrinsically tied to ideas of sex, motherhood and birth – and therefore to the female. We could rename our Goddess "Goddert," emphasizing that the word contains both God and Goddess, yet this would still be just another name for a Goddess giving birth to a God.

Manipulating language is the strength of the postmodern generation, and no doubt the great minds of this era are equal to the task of linguistically severing the description of creator and creative force from anything suggestive of "female" without taking us back to the ludicrousness of the male birth. Whether the *concept* of creator as female can be broken is another thing entirely, but before we proceed too much further down this road we do need to ask why the pressure to de-emphasize the feminine nature of the divine has become so intense. Why exchange the intellectual convolutions of a male birth for convolutions that make a non-female birth sound convincing?

The answer comes back to male supremacy, the need to delineate or deny the feminine in order to control. The religious right is too conservative for feminine power and the left is too progressive, although both have declared women "equal" and thereby irrelevant as a sex. Fear of feminine power crosses all religious boundaries: Christian, Muslim, Jewish, Buddhist, fundamentalist, liberal, atheist – and yes, even Pagan.

What is it about feminine power that is so frightening? Is it the connection to the female human, to those scary, scary people called women? Is it about the realities of human birth – the broken waters, the blood, the pain, the screams, the torn vagina, the harried bustle in the delivery room, the fears of mortality for infant and mother? Does recognition of feminine power put all of us, male and female, in touch with the messiness, the unpredictability, the uncontrollable nature of Mother Nature?

The primacy of feminine creative power is simple even if unsettling. It is reflected clearly, not in our constructs – which are almost always patriarchal – but in the natural world. It is the mother who births the egg, the acorn, the cub. Are we a nature religion or aren't we? The Pagan religions as a whole are at a crossroad. There are some who argue we should abandon the Goddess, or redefine her in ways less threatening, out of a sense of progress or political correctness or "equality" as understood within patriarchal frameworks. The laws of the natural world become defied and denied to make room for this. Are we a nature religion or aren't we?

It is no accident that the concept of a feminine creator is being questioned within Paganism at a time when redefinitions are obscuring the very existence of the human female. In the terminology being forced on the Pagan communities by adherents of Queer Theory, it is no longer correct, or even framed as bigotry, to associate "woman" with menstruation, birth, and the womb. When women defer to these dictates by redefining themselves as "women-born-women," "female," "genetic female," or "biological female," they are told that this, too, is unacceptable, that any identity or designation referring to the female body type will not be tolerated. To class those with female bodies as an identifiable group has become politically incorrect, subject to derision and censorship if not outright death threats. In this frame of reference the female body – her blood, womb, eggs, placenta – has again become too dangerous to be named. Yet we deny nature, and our Great Mother, when we deny the existence and significance of the female body. Denying the feminine creator, denying the existence of human females – twin handles of the new patriarchy.

On a metaphysical level, encompassing all of our greater selves in all the worlds they inhabit, we can argue that every person is female. But on an earth level, humans are divided into female and male, and it is the female of the species who holds the womb. A nature religion does not deny the physical, the biological, the sexual. Our creator is our Mother, with all the sexual correlations that implies. If we dismiss her significance we cannot work with living energies – only sterile abstract variables and constructs. To come back to nature as a religion we must affirm life, the power of the womb, the human female holding the womb space, and the womb of the Great Mother Goddess. She has ordained things no one may change. No one's discomfort with feminine power can change this.

Hearth Moon Rising loves exploring the multidimensional stories of animals and trees. Her book *Invoking Animal Magic: A Guide for the Pagan Priestess* takes an experiential and historical approach to understanding the powers we share with our furred, feathered and scaled friends. Hearth is a Dianic priestess and a priestess in the Fellowship of Isis. She has taught magic for more than 20 years. Hearth is a licensed outdoor guide and lives in the Adirondack Mountains of upstate New York.

She of 10,000 Faces: Monist Thealogy and Goddess Worship

Susan Harper

In one of my favorite scenes in Neil Gaiman's *American Gods*, the Norse god Odin (cleverly disguised as a human) asks a diner waitress which Goddess she worships. The waitress – an admittedly unsympathetic character – replies, "You know, the feminine principle." Odin clearly doesn't think much of this response. In the two decades in which I've been answering similar questions with a similar answer, I've also gotten my share of eye rolls. The idea that one chooses to worship or venerate a deity simply known as "The Goddess" is confusing to many of my fellow Pagans, especially because to many it appears as though "The Goddess" is what one of my dear friends terms "Yaweh in drag." Why, the argument goes, reject the worship of one dysfunctional parent in the sky only to adopt the worship of another?

The Goddess I know, however, is not just the female version of the angry Judeo-Christian sky God with whom I grew up. In finding Feminist Thealogy, and particularly Feminist Witchcraft, I found a communion with the Divine Feminine that moved me far beyond the shame and fear-based theology of my childhood. In finding The Goddess, I found a recognition of my own sacredness, of the holiness and power of women and women's bodies – I found, in the words of Patricia Lynne Reilly, "a God who looks like me." When I look to Goddesses from the world's culture – the Greek Artemis, the Norse Freyja, the Aztec Xochiquetzal – I see them as reflections of that fundamental Sacred Feminine. I see those Goddesses as a new symbolic language which I can use to relate to the Sacred, both within myself and in the larger world.

One, Many, None, All?

So exactly who is this "The Goddess" that I know? What do I mean when I say "The Sacred Feminine"? My understanding of The Goddess and the Sacred Feminine has evolved and changed over the two decades I've been practicing Feminist Witchcraft, and I fully expect it to continue to do so. When I found Feminist Witchcraft and Feminist Spirituality, what fundamentally appealed to me was the assertion that all women are reflections of The Goddess – that we all hold within us a spark of divinity and sacredness, and that this spark deserves to be recognized, to be honored, to be celebrated. I also resonated with the idea that worshiping a Goddess, a female and feminine divine, was a radical and transgressive act. If I wanted to reclaim my own inner sacredness, seeing God as female was fundamental.

And yet I was drawn to, fascinated by, moved by, the stories of Goddesses from around the world and across cultures. Diana, Juno, Isis, Spider Woman – since childhood these stories have spoken to the deepest part of my soul.

What I sought was a way to blend, to marry, these two understandings – of the Divine as all-encompassing, a multifaceted jewel that reflected truth in myriad ways, with my love for the many different Goddesses I encountered through myth, through ritual, in my dreams. I could not imagine myself worshiping just one Goddess, though for a time I tried – I couldn't be thealogically monogamous. I wanted to know all the Goddesses, to experience them all. I wasn't a monotheist – the idea of telling anyone that their God/dess didn't exist is completely foreign to me – yet I am not cut out to be a classical polytheist, either. Surely, surely there had to be an answer.

There was, and it came to me not through study of Feminist Witchcraft or Pagan thea/ology, but through the unlikely conduit of a graduate class in religious studies. When my professor presented the idea of *monism* – a theology which recognizes the existence of an Ultimate Truth which is reflected in a multitude of ways – the lightbulb went on. Much like when I discovered Feminist Witchcraft itself, I realized that I now had a word for what I was – I was (and am) a monist.

One Goddess, Many Faces

The Goddess is, to me, one way of envisioning a Truth that is far bigger and more complex than human understanding can grasp or human language can communicate. As I've grown as both a religious practitioner and a religious scholar, I've become firmly convinced of the fact that all spiritual traditions contain glimpses and pieces of this Truth – no one theo/alogy, doctrine, or path has a monopoly on what is real, good, and True. I am equally convinced that as humans we have an inalienable right to know a Divine that looks like us. I consider it spiritual violence to tell any group of people that they are not a reflection of Divinity, that they don't have God in them. After all, one of the reasons I sought out and was drawn to Feminist Spirituality was its assertion that women were reflections of the Divine. It may seem contradictory to hold these two ideas in tension – that my own spiritual path and practice are a reflection of Ultimate Truth, and that at the same time all other religions and spiritualities contain that Truth – but it is what makes the most sense to me. And part of that is being able to hold in my mind and my heart the idea that, as one of the first Feminist Witches I knew said, "All Goddesses are One Goddess."

I see the many Goddesses that have populated cultures across time and space as reflections of the greater Truth – that Divinity exists, and that it can (and should) be envisioned as feminine. While I don't work with masculine deities in my own spiritual practice, I recognize the validity of envisioning Divinity as male – and as genderless, and as any gender that might lie between male and female. From my monist standpoint, all Gods and Goddess are valid ways of approaching the Ultimate Divine. The sacred stories of the Goddesses and Gods of cultures both ancient and contemporary represent the myriad ways in which people have grappled with human dilemmas, explained human experiences, and encountered the Divine. Each Goddess I read about, meet in ritual, or hear stories about represents to me a piece of the larger Ultimate Truth – call it Spirit, Divinity, God/dess, or The Source. All Goddesses exist simultaneously and equally, and represent aspects of the larger Universe which people have called forth – the nurturance of the mother, the fierceness of the warrior, the gentleness of the maiden, and wisdom of the crone, and so much more. We put names and faces on these aspects and qualities so that we may approach and know them, and yet they are all part of a larger, complex whole.

The Goddess I know has 10,000 faces – indeed, She has faces beyond number and beyond knowing. I often think of The Goddess, and larger Truth of which She is a reflection, as a vast and multifaceted jewel. Depending on the direction from which you approach this jewel, on the angle of the light, on the time of day, the light will refract through it differently. The colors and images you see will change, will shift, will dance their own dance. If you approach from another angle, on another day, at another time, in other frame of mind, what you see will be qualitatively different. And yet the jewel remains the same, and the light reflected and refracted is fundamentally the same light. Each Goddess is, to me, one of these unique reflections and refractions of light – born from the same source, channeled through the same Ultimate Truth, and yet unique in form and color and movement. I approach the jewel that is The Goddess from a different angle depending on what I need at a given moment, and what is reflected and refracted back to me is different each time, yet always what I need.

Monism in Action

The way I approach The Goddess is, as for many or most practitioners of Goddess religions, through ritual. Ritual is, for me, monism in action – Goddess as a verb, if you will. Whether in private prayer, a small women's circle, or a large public moon or Sabbat, I use ritual as a way to recognize and call upon specific aspects of The Goddess, to bring the energies of sacred stories and specific faces and forms of The Goddess into my life, my ritual, and my magicks. At the Spring Equinox, for instance, I invoke Ostara, Goddess of Spring; Kore, the Greek maiden whose return to the Upper World marks the beginning of Spring; and Demeter, Kore's mother and Goddess of the grain and the greening earth. At Samhain, I welcome Persephone, as she descends back to the Underworld; Cerridwen and Hecate, powerful crones and guardians of the crossroads; and the Morrigan, who guides the souls of warriors through the veil. When I plan a ritual, one of the first things I do is research the Goddesses associated with the holiday, season, or purpose of the ritual. Not only does it help me choose which faces of The Goddess to invoke, but it also helps me grow in my knowledge of The Goddess.

One of my favorite ritual practices when working with a group is to invoke The Goddess – by the name – and ask those in circle to call out the names of specific Goddesses they wish to welcome. It is powerful to hear the names spoken, and to hear the chorus of names grow as each person speaks and reminds others of Goddesses they know and love. It also brings each person's energy into the ritual space, as he or she names The Goddess as he or she knows her. It creates a ritual that is truly collaborative, truly communal – and truly powerful. I have heard Goddesses invoked in circle whom I had no knowledge of, and yet felt pulled to research when I heard their names spoken in sacred space. Some of those Goddesses now feature regularly in my own devotions and rituals.

Working with The Goddess in this way, through her many faces, produces a beautiful syncretism in my rituals and my life. While I understand the reasons why some practitioners of

Paganism prefer to work with one Goddess, or to stay within one specific pantheon (Norse, Greek, Sumerian, and so forth), I find deeper connection through swimming in the intoxicating brew of diverse Goddess images I gather around myself. There is something about finding The Goddess in images seemingly so disparate – The Morrigan and the Virgin Mary, or the Orisha Yemeya and Persephone – that has been intensely healing and intensely powerful for me. Being able to see the spark of Divinity in images of Goddess and powerful female spirits from all around the world and all across time has better enabled me to see the spark of the Divine in other women and in myself.

Calling upon Goddesses from cultures and heritages not my own also brings up complex issues about cultural appropriateness and privilege, which are vital to recognize. I believe that working within a monist thealogy has made me a better feminist and social justice activist – not just a better Feminist Witch. For it is through this monist approach to The Goddess that I've come to see the way in which all humans, like all Goddesses, are connected and part of an intertwined, complex, and interdependent reality. If I can resonate with a Goddess from a culture not mine, then I must recognize the fundamental humanity of the people from that culture, that path, that place and time. And if I can recognize the fundamental humanity of others, then I must recognize that an injustice done to them is an injustice done to me. Once I recognize that my liberation is tied up with the liberation of others, then I cannot stay silent – I must work for our shared liberation and against injustice.

We are all faces of The Goddess, after all.

Susan Harper, Ph.D is an educator, activist, advocate, and ritual facilitator living in the Dallas, Texas area. She holds a doctorate in anthropology and teaches courses in anthropology, sociology, and women's studies, as well as facilitating rituals in the Feminist Spirituality and Feminist Witchcraft tradition.

The Queer of Heaven: Goddess Culture and the Empowerment of Gay Women and Men

David Salisbury

For I am divided for love's sake for the chance of union. This is the creation of the world, that the pain of division is as nothing, and the joy of dissolution all. For these fools of men and their woes care not thou at all! They feel little; what is, balanced by weak joys; but ye are my chosen ones.

[AL 1.29-31, *The Book of the Law*, Aleister Crowley]

When I was trained in American Wicca as a kid, I learned very early on that everything has its holy place in the world and universe. I was taught that everything on Earth has a correspondence that matches some things in the world of spirit. Red is for love, green is for money, and ground pepper keeps thieves away. Part of learning correspondences meant learning about what natural things represent the Goddess (the Divine Female) and the God (the Divine Male). Most often these were things that went together, usually in a procreative way. For example, the witch's knife, the athame, is always to the male as the chalice cup is always to the female. It was understood early on that we do this because the regenerative powers that the Goddess and God bring forth through their union is the most holy mystery in the Craft. I agreed with this for several years.

As a couple of years passed in my training, I started to grow up and change. As always happens in the teenage years, I discovered all kinds of things about myself. One of them was that I had an attraction to the same sex. I realized very quickly that I was gay and that my whole life would be a little more different because of that. The unique part of that process was that I wasn't concerned about what my family thought or even my friends at school. Instead, I was worried and confused about what that meant for my relationship with my Gods. After all, the Goddess and God have to be heterosexual, right? It didn't seem to fit well within my new worldview, but I accepted that as much as I could. I figured out that if I just removed the idea of my physical nature from that picture, then I could resolve to still love my Gods and see myself in them.

Years went by throughout my teen years when the thought of removing myself from the cycle of the Gods felt comfortable enough to me. But that all changed the older I got and the more deeply I experienced the gnosis of the divine first-hand. I realized that everything isn't as black and white as I assumed it was. And, most importantly, I realized that in this ecstatic experience-based practice I call Witchcraft, it was no longer possible for me to remove myself from the image of the Gods. So I set out to resolve my queer physical self with the powers I adored.

If you look up information about "queer" Gods and Goddesses for the first time, you may be surprised at what you find. I certainly was! While I was expecting a couple of queer Gods scattered throughout the abyss of our world's history, I instead found a rich collection of what might be referred to as the "Queer Mythos." I use this term when I talk about any Goddess or God that, while not necessarily homosexual in their myths, displays some kind of attribute that resonates with the queer heart or thought process.

It's actually quite easy to discover and learn about queer male-identified Gods. The ancient world is filled with myths of Gods who sport with other male Gods, come to Earth and have affairs with mortal men, or transform themselves into women for a time for a tryst with a mortal man. But what of the Goddesses?

The mysteries of the queer Goddesses are a bit more elusive, hidden within the shadows cast by moonlight, as is her signature method of wisdom delivery. The first place to look is her ancient forms and human followers. The Goddesses Artemis, Ishtar, and

Inanna all had cults dedicated to them where both queer women and men were commonly priests. Inanna in particular is a Goddess who embodies the independent woman, refusing to simply be a pawn in her husband's kingdom and taking the throne for herself. It is her alignment with wisdom and power, rather than her subservience to an opposite-gender partner that gives her the status of "Queen of Heaven."

In the Aztec people we find Huastecs, transgender or lesbian priestesses protected by the Goddesses Tlazoteotl and Xochiquetzal. Tlazoteotl is known as the "Filth Eater" who turns suffering into gold – surely a powerful display of sovereignty and championship over the downtrodden.

In Haitian Voodoo we find the Lwa Erzulie Fréda Dahomey, who reigns over the powers of love and passion. I have been told by friends in the Voodoo community that the men she "inhabits" during her rites will sometimes display homosexual traits and actions, regardless of their usual sexual orientation. Erzulie Fréda is thought to correspond to gay men while Erzulie Dantor is connected to lesbian women.

The classical myths of Greece present us with a plethora of stories relating to the queer Goddess. Above all stories stands Aphrodite, Goddess of the love of all people, including those attracted to the same gender, along with her accompanying Gods Eros, Himeros and Pothos. The writings of the Greek poet Sappho identify Aphrodite as having particular guardianship over lesbian women. Aphrodite is so famous in queer myth that she later takes on a mostly-male image in the form of Aphroditus, her male form worshipped on the island of Cyprus.

In the modern-day western world with its newfound acceptance and respect for lesbian, gay, bisexual, and transgender individuals, it's easy to find queer followers to the Goddess in all her guises. The Dianic tradition of Wicca, founded by Zsusanna Budapest, is a Goddess-based tradition that welcomes both lesbian and straight women to worship the Goddess in her many facets, including sometimes her queer nature (depending on the coven or line you speak with). For men, the Minoan Brotherhood and Brotherhood of the Phoenix are two well-known traditions for gay men that fully embrace the concept of a queer Goddess and a queer God. They explore the mysteries of the Gods by working with each other, other queer Goddess-worshippers. The idea being that the divine is firmly present within the self and is reflected out of every individual identity, including queer identity.

The Feri tradition of witchcraft, founded by the late Victor and Cora Anderson in the United States, is an interesting example of a tradition where queer divinity is highly present and obvious. In the Feri mythos, God Hirself gazed into the black void of space and fell in love with her perfect, holy nature. Upon the height of her pleasure, the universe erupted in a cascade of ecstatic power, rippling through time and forming the other divine reflections of her beings, the other Gods. The Blue God is the first male emanation of this Star Goddess. He is called a "he" often for convenience sake, but shares very obvious ambiguous traits. He is youthful and playful, often seen with both an erect phallus and the newly-forming breasts of a young woman at the same time. He is as queer as the Goddess who birthed him, for she is him and he is her. And out of their holy creation, we are born from the same qualities.

This idea that the Goddess can be queer because many of us are is the banner point made mostly by queer practitioners of modern-day Wicca and witchcraft. Original Gardnerian Wicca was sometimes seen as homophobic because Gerald Gardner was often insistent on the idea that the power must be passed from man to woman and from woman to man. There is no evidence to suggest that Gardner took this idea into the area of human sexual relationships as well, but the debate still rages on today. In any case, the typical Wiccan coven spent many decades under the influence of a male High Priest and a female High Priestess, without any other option. But things are much different today. Today, most Wiccans will tell you that the power can be passed through any individuals who can possess and receive it. Why? Because we each have traits of the two within us. In some circles, having a queer nature is thought to grant one a special relationship to the Goddess and God simply because the queer Wiccan is thought to embody the traits of both so strongly. This is an old idea and is portrayed beautifully in the concept of the "Two-Spirit" people of some Native American tribes.

I end this short musing on the queer Goddess where we began, with the excerpt from *The Book of the Law* from the Thelema religion. These words are spoken by Nuit, the Star Goddess who is divided unto herself, for the chance of union. Gendering and sexualizing the Goddess can be a helpful way for our human brains to understand and take part in her holy mysteries, but only if we avoid falling into the trap of limits and constraints. If the Goddess is truly the limitless expansion of the All, then it must stand that her divine love and lust is just as limitless. She is "divided" but only for the sake of love. The dissolution of her being is truly the reunification of her presence in all things. The great alchemists of the Middle Ages knew this, and so are the Goddess-worshippers of the modern day remembering this now.

If the resurgence of the Goddess in the present day has taught us anything, it could be that the downtrodden and misunderstood will never fully retreat when the forces of oppression are thrust upon them. The queer Goddesses in all their forms seemed for a moment to be lost to the mists of time, frozen in place by the violent uprising of patriarchy. Just as her queer devotees have risen up out of the ashes of defeat to claim their rights, so too is she making herself known once more.

David Salisbury is Wiccan clergy within Coven of the Spiral Moon, a coven based in Washington DC and author of *The Deep Heart of Witchcraft* and *Teen Spirit Wicca*.

Maiden, Mother, Pensioner: The Role of the Goddess in Accepting our Self and our Life-Stage

Rachel Patterson

Firstly I want to add a category to this… and make it four stages – maiden, mother, matriarch, crone. I think as we now have much longer life spans and the way that we live is very different from that of our ancestors we need that extra stage, otherwise the jump from mother to pensioner seems too long.

The Triple Goddess is a familiar term within the pagan world; she is usually three facets of a single Goddess or a triad of Goddesses and also represents the moon phases – waxing, full and waning.

These phases in life are rites of passage, but sadly we don't seem to celebrate them as such. We tend to mark the "big" birthdays, but we don't really have definitive celebrations to mark the passing from one phase of life into the other – although I definitely plan to have a croning ceremony when I reach that stage.

Let's start with the Maiden Goddess. She is spring, new begin-nings, youth, vitality, innocence, being carefree and your inner child. There are many Maiden Goddesses such as Artemis, Rhiannon and Persephone. The Maiden is usually thought of as a virgin too. How does that relate to our current times though? You don't usually see fair maidens with flowers in their flowing hair dancing down the high street … at least not where I live. I guess the modern-day equivalent would be a group of teenagers walking home from school carrying their books in fashionable handbags, mobile phones in the other hand, wearing makeup and talking about who is seeing what boy and what the latest gossip is. That isn't to say the youth of today is bad, I have a teenage daughter myself and am a very proud mother.

My own youth was in the eighties, a time of ra ra skirts, leg warmers and electronic pop music and I loved every minute of it. My teenage years played a huge part in shaping the person that I am today (although I no longer wear the leg warmers).

To me the Maiden Goddess isn't about floaty dresses and running through fields of corn with gay abandon, it is about remembering that you were young once, reminding yourself that you made rash choices based on all sorts of outside influences, but also that you had fun. You had few worries (apart from what to wear to the Friday night disco), looking back life was totally carefree, although it probably didn't seem so at the time – ask my parents... I had my fair share of dramas! Although I wouldn't want to go back to being 16 (I like being a grown up and being able to make my own life decisions) and although I wouldn't mind the figure that I had then, I know I learnt very valuable life lessons from those years. It is good to look back and remember how I dealt with certain situations and how good it felt to just dance, laugh and let those situations just sort themselves out without getting involved in all the drama.

I guess the period from maiden to mother can vary greatly now. Our ancestors would have had children at quite a young age – yes, I know that happens now and it worries me greatly when I see or hear of teenagers having children. I do feel that they haven't had time to grow out of being a child themselves, but everyone has their own journey. I came to motherhood fairly late really, in my early 30s, and actually it was the right time for me. I had no desire to be a mother until I hit the milestone of 30 and then panic set in as the biological clock started to tick incessantly loudly.

The Mother Goddess is a provider and a nurturer, she is summer, loving and giving and does whatever she can for anyone who needs help. Again, there are many Mother Goddesses, such as Brighid, Demeter and Hathor. When I think about Mother Goddesses I am probably visualizing the stereo-typical mother figure, slightly plump and wearing an apron with flour on her hands from making bread... yes I know that is so outdated! For reference, my mother is very smart and fashionable, but also a wonderful cook. When I first became a mother I also worked in an office and believed that to be a mother I had to be perfect – a perfect wife, perfect mother, perfect home maker and also perfect at work. Believe me, it doesn't work. There just aren't enough hours in the day, trying to do it all is incredibly stressful and there has to be some compromise. The key (for me anyway) in the mother stage is to not beat yourself up, having a dust-free house is not a high priority when you have small children. I suspect that although they didn't have the same outside influences even our ancestors sometimes found motherhood stressful, worrying about the cold or the damp and whether there was enough food to feed all the hungry mouths. Sadly that still happens in parts of the world today too. I also don't think to connect with the mother stage in your life that you necessarily need to have your own children. This part of your journey is perhaps just about being comfortable, feeling secure and knowing that you are working towards being happy with yourself and who you are. You may not have children, but you may have those that are dependent on you – dogs, cats, partners, friends or relatives.

I have put the matriarch stage in because I do feel that from mother to crone is such a big leap. If you are a mother you will always be a mother even when you are of crone age and even then, what age do you class as crone? If you have a child at 20 you could say you move out of the mother stage at 40 perhaps, which seems way too young to be a crone. This is where I see the matriarch stage fit in. The official meaning of matriarch is a leader of a clan or group, one who is a respected elder. I am not sure if there are any dedicated lists of Matriarch Goddesses anywhere, probably not, but the main one that springs to my mind is Gaia. She is an Earth Mother, yes, but maybe just a bit more experienced than a mother?

I think of this as the autumn stage in your life, when you have achieved goals that you set in your early years. Maybe you have a job that you have worked hard for, a nice house, nice car and all the material things, if that is how you measure success. But also, from a spiritual point of view, I think that it is a stage when a woman may be at her strongest point; she isn't young but isn't old, she is mature and knowledgeable, with good long-standing friends, confident in herself and able to deal with situations as they arise with wisdom and dignity… well hopefully anyway!

This is perhaps also the period in a woman's life when she has a bit of spare cash and some time to herself to follow her dreams and wishes, to take up hobbies and maybe travel to places she has always wanted to see and discover more about herself in the process. On the downside, this stage of life sees the menopause, but even then perhaps it should be something that is celebrated as a rite of passage?

And then on to the crone phase; she is the wise woman and the sage. Our ancestors would have revered the crone for her wisdom, knowledge and possibly the actual fact that she survived to old age! Sadly, I think the pensioners of our modern age don't always get revered or even respected, which is a real shame because they have so much knowledge and insight to share. Although as time moves on the pensioners now, the people in their 60s and 70s, are possibly more likely to be riding Harleys and taking holidays in the South of France than retiring to the seaside to sit in a deckchair and eat fish and chips.

The Crone Goddess is the winter phase of life: wisdom, knowledge, experience, guidance and transformation in the guise of destruction and death, which brings the circle around again to new life and new beginnings. My vision, possibly the archetypical one, is that of an old woman with white hair, a hunched figure and a wrinkled face. Our pensioner generation today, those in their 80s and 90s, may fit that image but those just starting under the pensioner bracket (60/65) may still be fighting the battle of hiding the grey hair under hair dye (hey I am in my 40s and I am fighting that battle!), be dressed fashionably and still be rockin' the "live life to the fullest" idea. But it is the phase in your life journey that maybe gives you the most time to yourself. Retirement offers days free to follow pursuits or just to potter about in the garden, reading, relaxing and perhaps spending time with your grandchildren. Not so relaxing if you are grandparents though, because our generation relies a huge amount on grandparents looking after the grandchildren so that the parents can still go to work!

There are many Crone Goddesses such as the Cailleach (my own personal Matron Goddess), Kali and Macha. A lot of the Crone Goddesses are also linked with death and destruction and to me that makes sense. There must come an age in your life when you think, "I must have fewer years left in my lifetime than those I have already lived" and that can be pretty scary. I believe that part of the crone phase in your life is to accept that life is a circle, a never-ending one, one of birth, life, death and rebirth. Thinking about death is not pleasant, but it is a reality and one that should hopefully make us think about how we are as a person, what kind of life we live and how we have treated others. The crone stage is also one of introspection and maybe even one of making amends. Do you get to the crone stage and think about all the decisions you have made, all the people you have helped... or not helped, those you have hurt or cared for. It is an interesting exercise to do when you are in your 20s, 30s or 40s, but I would imagine it would be extremely eye opening to look back over, say, 80 years and review every part of your journey, good or bad.

The question is... when you get to the crone stage what will you think and feel when you look back over your lifetime?

Life is precious and no matter what stage, phase or age you are I urge you to treat others as you would like to be treated yourself, make time for the important things in life, be respectful to the planet and all the creatures that live on it and make sure you live life to the fullest.

Rachel Patterson is High Priestess of the Kitchen Witch Coven and Team Leadership member of the Kitchen Witch School of Natural Witchcraft. She is the author of *Grimoire of a Kitchen Witch*, and three books in the *Pagan Portals* series – *Kitchen Witchcraft*, *Hoodoo* and *Moon Magic*. She lives in Portsmouth, UK.

The Warrior Way: The Goddess as a Role Model for Women in Politics

Laura Perry

What is feminine power? What does it mean to be a warrior following the path of the Goddess? Women have been asking themselves these questions with greater and greater frequency over the past few decades. In the second half of the 20th century the shifting of gender roles in western society toward greater equality for women coincided with a renewed interest in Goddess spirituality across a broad spectrum of the population. Together, these two forces have inspired several generations of women to take action, to become warriors of a sort, fighting for change in the world.

Socially acceptable aspects of the Goddess, like the docile and submissive Christian Virgin Mary, have long been easier to access than Her darker aspects. For centuries the male-dominated (and male-deity-dominated) monotheistic religions demonized or dismissed the stronger faces of the Goddess, but those darker aspects have a formidable attraction for women seeking to identify their own power. These deities include the fighting, warrior and destructive faces of the Goddess as well as Her shadowy Underworld aspects. Acknowledging the fierceness within the Goddess – in Her faces such as Kali, Sekhmet, Oya, The Morrigan, and Athena – allows women to accept that same quality within themselves and draw on it for the strength to fight the battles, literal or figurative, that will change the world.

There are many ways a person can fight for what they believe in without invoking violence or militarism. The pen and its analogue, the human voice, are still mightier than the sword, and those who wield either in service to their beliefs are indeed warriors. Women who have turned to the Goddess for inspiration have found a fresh vision of ways to make the world a better place through political activism of all kinds, from nonviolent protests to petitions to the holding of public office. How does a focus on the divine feminine inspire this kind of action? It has to do with the basic values of Goddess spirituality.

Though there are many different faces of the Goddess and many individual paths toward the feminine divine, this multiplicity of traditions holds a set of values in common. Among these principles is the concept that the earth is a living thing, a sacred source of life and not a dead ball of dirt to be exploited at will by the greedy who seek to take advantage of its resources for their own profit and power. In this view, each generation must weigh its use of the earth's reserves against the needs of future generations, ensuring that the environment is left in good enough condition to support those who have not yet been born.

For many, this concept also includes the idea that spirit (the divine) and matter are not separate, but are interconnected parts of a greater whole. Though James Lovelock did not intend his Gaia hypothesis as a spiritual treatise, many women have taken inspiration from it and support the notion that the earth itself (Herself) is a Goddess. This principle inspires women to join environmental groups, or start their own, in order to safeguard resources and protect the earth we all live on. They lobby their governments for changes in laws to protect endangered wildlife and habitats. They speak out against practices that damage the environment over the long term in exchange for short-term profits.

Viewing the divine as fully feminine, as well as fully masculine, empowers women and gives them an emotional and psychological place in the world that male-deity-only religions do not offer. Throughout history religious paradigms have been used to reinforce the place of those already in power (the divine right of kings, for instance, including ancient kings and pharaohs who claimed to literally be Gods) and exclude certain others from power. Allowing the divine to have a feminine as well as a masculine face permits women to enter into positions of power based on that paradigm.

Some women, both professional scholars and amateurs, have chosen to examine ancient cultures and societies in which women had high status equal with men, to offer examples of how modern women can fight to achieve a similar position in current society. Consistently, we find that ancient cultures in which women had equal rights and power with men revered strong Goddess figures as a central part of their pantheon. Merlin Stone's watershed book *When God Was a Woman* details such cultures and outlines the subsequent eradication of women's rights along with the demotion of powerful Goddesses from their positions at the heads of pantheons to simple maidens or even demons. Ms. Stone's work demonstrates, from a historical perspective, that spiritual traditions have clear political ramifications.

Anthropologists such as Clifford Geertz and Mary Douglas have stressed the power of religious symbols not just to express the values of a society but to shape them as well. In order to create "heaven on earth" or follow an "as above, so below" philosophy, people shift their social behaviors to emulate the relationships and activities of their culture's Gods as described in their spiritual traditions. If a religion depicts an authoritative male God dominating others in the absence of female deities, the society that follows that religion will tend towards family structures and political institutions with men in domineering positions and women poorly represented, if at all. In contrast, a spiritual tradition that depicts male and female deities in equally powerful roles encourages a society to shape itself with parity between men and women in business, politics and family life. The re-emergence of Goddess spirituality in modern western society, which has been dominated for so long by male-only monotheistic religions, has given women not only symbolic permission but also the motivation to take action in order to bring society into balance with these spiritual concepts.

The archetype of the warrior Goddess has inspired such women as earth-based activist and writer Starhawk, a leader in the feminist Neopagan movement. Her book *The Spiral Dance: A Rebirth of the Ancient Religion of the Great Goddess* has provided many women with a doorway into not only the Goddess movement, but also the concept of social and political activism as a way to express their spirituality. Like many women active in the Goddess movement, Starhawk works to replace structures of power and domination with those of consensus, equality and co-operation. She founded Reclaiming, a spiritual collective that combines feminist Goddess spirituality with political activism, concentrating especially on the peace and anti-nuclear movements, but including a broad variety of progressive social, environmental and economic issues. Reclaiming has communities worldwide that offer workshops focusing on Goddess spirituality and earth-focused values.

Though cultural historian Riane Eisler is not a public follower of the Goddess herself (she keeps her spiritual views private), she has inspired many women to approach Goddess spirituality as a motivator for political activism. Dr. Eisler has explored the historical shift from partnership societies, with Goddesses holding a prominent place in the pantheon, to dominator cultures, in which Goddesses are demoted or removed altogether. Her book *The Chalice and the Blade: Our History, Our Future* focuses on the ancient Minoan culture on the Mediterranean island of Crete, a society whose spiritual traditions were crowned by the Goddess Ariadne and in which women held high status compared with contemporary and later European cultures. Dr. Eisler has inspired women to take action to change modern society on many different levels, especially the improvement of women's rights through action in local and national politics. She has demonstrated that the Goddess movement, as an integral aspect of feminism, leads to the rise of women in the workforce and politics. A social activist herself, Dr. Eisler co-founded the Spiritual Alliance to Stop Intimate Violence, an organization that focuses on the role of spiritual communities worldwide in finding practical solutions to domestic violence.

Carol P. Christ, a scholar who focuses on feminism and theology, has said, "The simplest and most basic meaning of the symbol of Goddess is the acknowledgment of the legitimacy of female power as a beneficent and independent power." This quote is from *Why Women Need the Goddess*, a keynote address Dr. Christ gave at the Great Goddess Re-emerging Conference at the University of Santa Cruz, California, in 1978. The idea of the Goddess being a politically empowering symbol for women was so radical in the 1970s that Dr. Christ's speech was reprinted and shared widely in ink-and-paper format, and even now it makes the rounds on the internet as a new generation discovers the force of deity in feminine form. In the intervening years Dr. Christ has written extensively about the political ramifications of the divine feminine as a template for women's power in the world; her book *Womanspirit Rising* is a classic in feminist theology. Like Dr. Eisler, she often focuses on the ancient Minoans as an example of a culture whose spirituality and social organization reflect each other: when Goddesses hold high status, so do women.

Goddess spirituality has become mainstream enough that we now find journalist and Wiccan priestess Margot Adler speaking as a regular correspondent for National Public Radio in the U.S. on its morning and evening news programs. In this capacity Ms. Adler focuses on the intersection between spirituality and politics. Author of *Drawing Down the Moon: Witches, Druids, Goddess-Worshippers and Other Pagans in America Today*, the classic study of Paganism and nature religions, Ms. Adler demonstrates through her journalistic investigations that religious beliefs have a strong motivating force on those who hold them as well as those who oppose them.

Many of the women who draw on these spiritual resources for political activism do not consider themselves to be warriors. Others identify specifically with warrior-Goddesses as they fight for change in the world. Whatever they call themselves, these women are following the path of the Goddess in an effort to make the world a better place for everyone.

Laura Perry is a Wiccan priestess, and long-time pagan and shamanic practitioner. She is also a Reiki master, herbalist, naturopath (N.D.) and the author of *Ariadne's Thread: Awakening the Wonders of the Ancient Minoans in our Modern Lives*.

All the Goddesses who are Independent – Throw Your Hands up at Me

Joanna van der Hoeven

Most of us are familiar with this popular Destiny's Child song about independent women. In this essay, I would like to look at independent Goddesses and how we relate to them, using my own personal knowledge, experience and intuition as an example.

For many within Paganism their deities are paired under a myriad names, titles and associations. The generic Lord and Lady, for example, encompasses a plethora of Gods and Goddesses into one association that can be used in group ritual language, where specific deities may not be applicable to all participating. It can also help when one is beginning in their spiritual search but has as yet to enter into any relationship with a specific God or Goddess.

Others may find a paired God and Goddess within a certain tradition or pantheon – Odin and Frigge, Isis and Osiris, Zeus and Hera. Sometimes these pairings are marriages within the religious framework of the culture and worldview that follows it – other times these pairings are created through unverified personal gnosis, later becoming tradition.

Often these pairings explain the polarity of male and female, expressing in myth and symbolic references the union of the two and the resulting expression of that union. For many fertility deities it is necessary. However, for the purpose of this essay, I will be looking at those deities for whom no "other" is necessary – Goddesses that are whole in and of themselves, who have no need or desire for union or prolonged relationship with another deity in order to live their true soul songs. For me, these are the Goddesses that really shine, often seen as Maiden Goddesses.

I first became entranced by the singular Maiden Goddess, Artemis. I had a children's book of Greek myths which I read and reread, over and over again. Artemis with her bow, running through the woods and hills, patroness of wild animals and utterly free – wow. What a Goddess. As an eight-year-old girl, I saw who I wanted to be. She loved animals, she loved archery, she loved the wilds. A deer was often her companion under the waxing crescent of the moon. Though the references to her were simple and not delving into her story in any great detail, it was enough to go on for the rest of my life.

Later study of Artemis revealed her power – those who tried to rape her were thwarted by her and punished. She was a Goddess of midwives and childbirth. She was associated with the bear and loved hawks. At Epheseus, in Ionia, Turkey, her temple became one of the Seven Wonders of the World. This was one powerful lady.

What was it that made her so powerful? I think it was in her uncompromising attitude to the direction her life would take, as well as her principles and beliefs. She guarded her chastity as well as that of her handmaidens, for this was of great importance to her. She was truly an entity unto herself, with no need for a male God to validate her existence. She simply was who she was, and venerated the world over because of it.

I later came to explore deities nearer to my natural heritage – closer to home, if you will. I spent a few years researching the mythology of the Germanic peoples and, in doing so, found quite a few independent madams. Many people know of Freya, the often portrayed promiscuous Goddess of love. I do have a deep abiding for Freya, of her strong love and lust, given and taken only where and when she sees fit. Yet for me, another Goddess in that pantheon called out to me – Skadhi.

Perhaps it was because I grew up in a climate where the cold winters were similar to that which my European ancestors knew and dealt with, year after year. We would have snow for at least four months of the year. I had my first pair of skates and skis at the age of four. Every weekend we went cross-country skiing as a family in the woods behind our house. Every night after supper my brother and I would head down to the ice rink at the bottom of our road and, while he played hockey with his friends, I gave some music to the caretaker and he played it on the loudspeakers while I did figure skating. I keenly remember the cold winter nights, listening to the tinny music coming from those old metal speakers, letting my body dance on the ice and express all that I could not say with words. The sound of the skates on the ice, the calls and thwack of the hockey puck on the other rink, the smell of wood smoke on the wind, the contrast of the darkness waiting just outside the circles of light; it was a very good time.

When I learned of a Goddess who loved outdoor winter pursuits as much as I did, I was thrilled. I would head out into the wilds with my skis or my snowshoes, saying a prayer to this Goddess in order to connect with her. I felt a kindred spirit in my heart with Skadhi. The more I learned of her, the more this grew into a deep and long-lasting relationship.

Skadhi was not a Goddess who could settle down. She did have an attempt at marriage, after she was tricked into thinking she was going to marry the most beautiful God and instead got the god of the sea, Njord. They tried it out for a while, she spending time by the sea, he spending time in her mountain home. However, eventually they just couldn't make it work. She hated the cries of the gulls and longed for the mountains – he hated the cries of the wolves and longed for the sea. And so they split up, returning to their respective homes, perhaps a little wiser for the experience.

Skadhi loves skiing and snowshoeing. She loves the wild places. She is etin-born – giant kin; her elemental blood mixing with her godhood to create a Goddess who is of both worlds. She demanded reparation for the death of her father as she strode, alone and unaided, into the hall of the Gods. She is strong and willful, often seen as very serious, yet she shows she has a sense of humor, as when Loki makes her laugh. She is also vengeful, placing the serpent above Loki's head when he betrays the Gods one time too many.

I found a deep connection with this Goddess that I love and hold dear to my heart to this very day. She is an inspiration to me, her soul song reflecting melodies that I can understand deep within my heart. I think this is what is most important to a religious person – finding that relationship that both witnesses and supports the things in life we go through, as well as inspiring us to continue on the journey.

Even more recently, I have come to know the Brythonic Goddess, Elen. Similar in many ways to my childhood heroine, Artemis, Elen is a Goddess of the forest, of the wild and untamed. Her roots are believed to date back to when reindeer roamed Britain and so she is connected with reindeer. Now that the reindeer are extinct in Britain, I see her as the patroness of all deer, red and fallow, muntjac and even the most recently emigrated Chinese water deer.

Not much is known of Elen – a few artifacts may allude to her, as well as place names. Her name in parts of Europe translates as "deer" and so that connection is reinforced. Other than that, it is up to the seeker to come and find her themselves – this is why I love her so very much.

When there is very little written about a deity, personal experience becomes the main driving force behind establishing and maintaining that relationship. It requires a lot of effort to seek out a deity like Elen – she cannot be found in books, or in the mind. She must be sought out on the wild heaths and woodlands, on the trackways that bear her name. She is wild and she is free; she is most certainly alone.

When I first began on this Pagan path, I held a ritual alone outside in one of my power spots. I asked for a Goddess to make herself known to me and, in a very powerful encounter, was introduced to Morrigan. Another singular Goddess, this lady is beholden to none and I am quite glad to have had a relationship with her as my first patron deity. My current patron deity is Nemetona; with her I have learned how to be both strong and vulnerable in my role as a priest. She has taught me about sanctuary and sacred space, both my own and that of others. Some try to pair her up with another British or Roman deity, but for me, this lady acts alone. She teaches me of solitude. It is in solitude that we can hear most clearly the words of the Gods, of the ancestors and the spirits of place.

Why do I feel that pull towards these singular Goddesses? I could say that I am attracted to their strength of character, however there are many paired Goddesses such as Frigge or Isis who are strong in their partnerships. Strength is not determined by marital or relationship status. I think that it is more in their wild freedom, in their choices that they make and their self-knowledge that inspires me. They are remit to no-one and will not allow anyone to tell them what to do, think or feel.

Being childless by choice, these deities resonate within me, acknowledging my choice and respecting that choice. Through their own actions and stories they tell me that it is okay to not have a desire to have children. They tell me that what I want most, I should go out and seek instead of waiting for it to come to me. They are young and they are ageless. They are strong and they are determined. They flow in the waxing energy of the moon towards the full; they are full of their own integrity. They need no other in order to be respected; they are Goddesses in their own right. They show us that polarities are not necessary in life; that we do not need the push and pull of masculine and feminine in order to find spiritual structure and inspiration in our lives.

They show us that it's okay to just be yourself, whoever that is. They tell us that it is okay to have a failed marriage. That it is okay to remain a virgin. That it is okay to find our wild selves. We see ourselves in them, and they in us. In this relationship, we are all inspired and, after all, is that not the point of a spiritual path?

May the blessings of these wild and free Goddesses be with you.

Joanna van der Hoeven is a Druid, the director of Gypsy Dreams Belly Dance and the author of two books in the *Pagan Portals* series: *Zen Druidry* and *Dancing with Nemetona*. She lives in East Anglia, UK.

What's Love Got to Do with It? Abduction and Seduction in Linguistic and Cultural Context

Robin Herne

Some 2,500-plus years ago the philosopher Xenophanes found himself ill at ease with the religion of Ancient Greece. One of his numerous complaints was that the myths, such as those told by Homer and Hesiod, portrayed the Gods and Goddesses as fairly awful – lying, cheating, stealing, seducing, slaughtering people for petty reasons etc. Xenophanes felt that any divine force ought to be morally superior to humanity, and not indulge in our worst vices.

Our knowledge of how ancient pagans understood their religions is rather limited because the few written sources we do have almost entirely represent the views of a highly educated, wealthy (and mostly male) elite. How closely such views reflect the way poor, uneducated people (or, indeed, how wealthy but largely silent upper class women) viewed their deities is open to a great deal of debate. Critics of Xenophanes claimed that the myths were not meant to be taken literally, but were symbolic. Hermes stealing the cattle of Apollo was not a divine approval of theft, or an encouragement to the devotees of Hermes to go out cattle rustling, but a metaphor for something deeper. Whether or not this was how the workaday pagans of the ancient world understood these tales, we shall probably never know.

One of the challenges to pagans in the 20th and 21st centuries is to relate modern sensibilities to these ancient myths. Those stories featuring sexual transgressions are, perhaps, some of the most difficult for the modern mind to comprehend. The Victorians found the casual inclusion of same-sex passions particularly embarrassing and so glossed over the "unspeakable vice of the Greeks". For those of us born after women won the vote and began pushing for greater social reform, homosexuality is little or no shock – rape, however, is almost universally seen as unacceptable with the stigma being increasingly (though not yet completely) residing with the male attacker. This is not to ignore the role of women as sexual aggressors, but it still seems to be a mercifully rare event and practically all the myths that involve rape are ones in which the violator is male. If a pagan reverences a God who is supposed to have raped someone, or a Goddess who was somehow raped, how do they understand this?

One of the first issues to tackle is the limitation of language. Pretty much all of the myths we are referencing were written in languages other than the one we now speak, and so have had to be translated – a task in which there is invariably room for things to be lost and unexpectedly gained. The modern word rape stems from the Latin *rapere*, which originally meant abduction rather than its present connotations of brutish sexual violence. A better semantic understanding would be kidnapping. A number of ancient and some still current cultures have the tradition of a ritualistic kidnapping of the bride by the groom, who carries her off to his family home or sometimes the church for the wedding ceremony. The bride's family usually makes a humorous token protest, and sometimes the best man plays a role in the drama. Marriage by abduction is an acknowledged concept in many cultures, and is usually of this consensual type. Usually, though not always – there are current as well as ancient cases of horrendously violent abduction-marriages which must have been living hells for the women involved. Arguably, the jocular ceremonies known today may have their origins in past warfare and the brutal kidnapping of girls and women (and sometimes young lads) to be forced into sexual and domestic servitude to invading warriors.

Many of the sacred stories from older cultures are perhaps best understood in this context of abduction, the carrying off of a woman to a new world or the transition of a Goddess into a new aspect – such as Kore's abduction into the underworld by Hades and her subsequent transformation into Persephone, or Leda being whisked away by Zeus. There are other stories which are more distinctly about sexual violation. One Irish tale told of Áine (in some versions a fairy woman, in others a more Goddess-like figure) being assaulted by King Ailill Olom, in retaliation for which she bit off his ear and exacted various other vengeances. For those readers who see Áine as a Goddess, the notion that a divine being could be sexually abused needs some explaining. It could be seen as a metaphor for the exploitation of the land by an inconsiderate monarch, or an attack upon a human priestess who represented the Goddess.

As previously mentioned, attitudes to rape have changed over the generations and understanding how our pagan ancestors viewed the act cannot only help us understand the stories they told, but also help us reflect on our own views upon the matter. For example, the Egyptian story of the prolonged warfare between Heru (Horus) and his uncle Setekh (Set) includes the attempted rape of the younger deity by the older one, and the almost as revolting retaliation, which doesn't bear repeating here. Setekh, too drunk to realize that his rape attempt had failed, denounced Heru before the divine court as unworthy of the Pharaoh's throne because he had been raped. Clearly the burden of shame was upon the victim and not the person freely admitting to having engaged in an odious and incestuous act. The story is played rather for laughs, which itself says something about attitudes of the time, and rape as a tool for political ends is accepted as a matter of course. Sexual violence as a tool for establishing dominance is used the world over, sometimes at a small-scale, individual level but often as a socially sanctioned weapon of warfare.

Even though Egyptian women enjoyed more legal freedoms than a great many other women in the world at that time, some laws suggest they were regarded almost as a form of legal compensation to cuckolded husbands. The *Instruction of Ankhsheshonq* stated that, "He who violates a married woman on the bed will have his wife violated on the ground."

In Roman law the concept of rape hinged not upon the consent of the woman but of her husband or (if unwed) father or other male guardian. The concept of *stuprum* (non-consenting sex) did not distinguish between a brutal assault and a consensual coupling where the woman in question was going with a man without her male guardian's consent. Adultery and elopements were as much *stuprum* as violent sexual abuse, because all such situations involved a man having sex with a woman without the consent of her male guardian. The notion that the woman herself should have the right to give or withhold her consent came fairly late (in Britain it only became possible to prosecute a husband for raping his wife in 1991). Later Roman laws separated adultery out as a distinct crime from other forms of *stuprum*.

It is possible that the laws of the Insular Celtic tribes may have run along similar lines, if the Irish Brehon laws (whose earliest written form stems from the period of increasing Christian conversion) are anything to go by as indicators of what earlier generations believed. The Brehon laws perceived family units as being headed up by a representative (the *ceann fine*), usually a male elder, who was both held accountable for the misdeeds of family members but also received compensation for crimes committed against the members under his or her jurisdiction, sexual offenses included. In this culture people were not so much viewed as individuals as they were viewed as members of a tribal collective. Attacks upon the individual were attacks upon the tribal unit, and the notion of legal consent to an act of any sort was one in which the group itself (personified by the *ceann fine*) was the power that gave or withheld consent, rather than the specific individuals involved.

The majority of modern pagans were not born to their religions, but converted to them from a Christian, Jewish, agnostic etc. background. Even those coming from non-religious upbringings are likely to be "cultural Christians", to borrow Richard Dawkins'" clunky term. So a question arises as to how much the attitudes of distant ancestors to women in general and sexual abuse in particular really have much influence on people of the 21st century following those shared deities. At first consideration, probably little – we are more likely to be influenced by Christian and secular values. However, as Colette Dowling observed when writing about the Cinderella Complex, frequent exposure to specific stories, religious myths, legends etc. will tend to steep the mind in the values and ideas of those tales. It's also worth bearing in mind that mainstream Western religions acquired many of their ideas from older sources anyway.

In recent years sociologists, psychologists and other commentators have begun talking about the idea of a "rape culture" – that is, sets of social values, norms, presumptions etc. that inform many men that they have a right to force sexual demands on others, whilst simultaneously informing women that this is simply what men are like and that any woman (or man) who gets raped is somehow complicit in what has happened to them. Do the contemporary followers of the old ways challenge the wider culture on matters of sexual domination, or are we complicit in maintaining the culture in which sexual aggression is seen as a norm to be expected? Clearly amongst so large a group of people there cannot be a universal attitude, but some approaches may be more common. Some pagan traditions, such as Dianic Wicca, are explicitly feminist in approach and so encourage considerable thought to issues which so directly impact upon women's role and wellbeing. Not all traditions are particularly feminist, though this does not mean that they are indifferent to suffering or negligent of the causes of dishonorable behavior.

Pagans tend to view sexuality as sacred and the erotic act as a reciprocal gift between the people involved, an approach that sits ill with the notion that sex is something that ought to be demanded with menaces or insisted upon as recompense for a meal out or a few drinks at a club. A key fact for us to consider is that we should not merely hold this as a nebulous notion or see sex as only sacred if it is between initiated pagans wreathed in incense smoke and candlelight. Rather, if we see sex between any people as sacred (regardless of gender, religion, or photogenic status) and, more importantly, teach this to our children, to people finding paganism for the first time, and live it in our own lives by not devaluing our own or other people's sexuality, then the attitude may spread by domino effect and increasingly become the norm. The more value attached to sexuality, hopefully the rarer acts of sexual exploitation and violence will become.

Robin Herne is an educator, poet, storyteller, poet, artist, dog-owner and Druid. He is the author of *Old Gods, New Druids*, *Bard Song* and *A Dangerous Place*. He has also written numerous articles for pagan magazines and has appeared in television documentaries. He lives in Ipswich, UK.

My Goddess, Myself: The Role of Goddess Energy in Ritual

Tim Lord

As magicians, we work with many different ritual tools. We use the wand, athame, and a host of other items to represent individual elements and their association with our specific need; these tools help direct our magickal energy. Similarly, we sometimes invoke a Goddess in our ritual. Generally, a Goddess chosen for inclusion in ritual is carefully selected because of her connection to our desired outcome. For instance, a magician might choose to call upon Aphrodite for aid in the working of a love spell. As we recognize the role of the Goddess in our rituals, we must also recognize that the Goddess is merely a tool, like the chalice, that we use to help manipulate energy.

In order to realize the Goddess as a tool, we must reconsider two beliefs about her; we must change our cultural and personal understanding of the Goddess. When the Goddess Athena is mentioned, whether one has an image of her or not, we think about her wisdom, her ingenuity, and her role as protector and matron of Athens. We think about her in this way because this is what culture has taught us. Each Goddess is imbued with certain characteristics and sometimes physical qualities; these are relatively immutable as they are steeped in history and help to create an energetic archetype. In the cultural description of a Goddess, the attributes ascribed to her are both personal to individual deities and representative of types of energy, such as love energy or inventive energy. Essentially, because Aphrodite has been identified as the Goddess of love, she is representative of the whole of love energy in our culture. Other Gods and Goddesses represent all imaginable types of energy. Every form of energy from the lightning in the sky to death itself is represented by a deity. Following this logic, we know it is useful to work with a Goddess who represents our goal because she will be able to provide the appropriate type of energy for our spellwork.

It is not surprising that personal beliefs and understandings about a Goddess are influenced by the cultural perception of her, but it is important to point out that the cultural perception is also influenced by personal belief. In previous generations, this was possible. If someone expressed an idea about the physical characteristics of a Goddess in a painting or statue, the new or augmented characteristics might become popular. The same is true for her character; if a poet such as Homer included a description of a Goddess or spoke of a given characteristic or capability, it may become a permanent part of the cultural heritage. These personalized inclusions about a cultural figure have transformative power. This has not changed. Now, it is even easier to alter one's perception of a Goddess. It can be done by simply publishing an illustration on a webpage. If the illustrator's vision is popular, it can change society's ideas. A recent string of Hollywood-enhanced Pagan deities, including the characters of *Xena: Warrior Princess* and the *Thor* comics and films, have tremendous opportunity to change our cultural perspective because they reach such a wide and accessible audience. The characters portrayed here come from a mixing of the cultural heritage handed down over generations and a contemporary influence on costuming, ideas of sexuality, potential capabilities, and so on. While the work of a screenwriter, an actor, director, costume designer, and even a production designer has the power to change our beliefs about deities, personal beliefs are more important.

When it comes to communing with a matron Goddess, it is the personal that is accentuated. While we recognize a shared cultural image of a Goddess, each of us individualizes her. One practitioner may see the Goddess Bast in full cat form while another might view her as having the body of a human with the head of a cat. Not only is the image personal, but her symbolism and potential are individual. The first practitioner may see Bast as the warrior Goddess and call upon her for protective energy; the second may choose to see her as the mother figure and summon her power for fertility and parenting skills. No two people will see any deity the same way, and this potential for a personal relationship with a matron Goddess is reason enough to seek her out.

There are two common ways of attuning with a matron Goddess, and they are related. The first way is to meditate. Some recommend meditating in a quiet environment or specifically in nature, but the general idea is that by meditating, the magician is able to feel the presence of the Goddess and have a sense of peace and wholeness wash over him/her. The second method, a more involved and time-consuming process, is by astral projecting. This is the process which, beginning with meditation, leads to a person's consciousness exiting their physical body and traveling to higher planes of existence, most notably the astral plane. Many Pagans believe that the astral plane is where magical beings such as faeries and angels reside and that one may closely contact a Goddess or God there. Believers in this practice explain a few advantages over meditation: by astral projecting, they are able to see their matron Goddess with their astral eyes, and they may be able to touch her and receive power from her in ways similar to an invocation. Rather than just feeling her presence, by visiting her, they may receive direct advice or assistance with a personal problem. There are too many potential advantages to discuss here, but this sampling shows the potential for great communication through astral projection.

Astral projection's more literal communication with the Goddess facilitates our understanding of the personal vs. cultural representations of the Goddess. The first thing that will influence our understanding of the Goddess is the need, if any, we are communicating. In the example of Bast, a magician seeking protection is likely to see Bast as being physically different from the practitioner who is petitioning her for the wisdom to be a good mother. Similarly, in these two situations, Bast is likely to speak differently, behave differently, use different mannerisms, and so on. Another reason these two Pagans see her differently is because they are not likely to have been exposed to the same sources. As we learn about different deities, we are exposed to different images and explanations of a deity's energy, interests, and areas of expertise. Ultimately, the experience of communing with a matron Goddess through astral projection is very personal.

Whether the magician prefers to meditate or astral project to attune with the matron Goddess, the result is the same: the magician is exploring the catacombs of his/her own mind. There are many guided astral projections that can be read or played through an audio system to facilitate this practice. In all of them, whether the author is trying to help believers visit Faeryland, help them meet a guardian angel, or help them communicate with deceased loved ones, the author stresses the point that every person will have an individual experience. The author offers enough detail to persuade the mind to create the world, but provides more general ideas so that the architect of this world, the practitioner, can make it personal and encourage the belief of the practitioner in its reality. This is the basis for Goddess communication. The practitioner creates an image of the Goddess based on personal and cultural beliefs and conjures that image before him/her using nothing more than an idea.

When we combine ideas, both cultural and personal, about our matron Goddess and energy, we can create her as a thoughtform. She exists in a personal and powerful way; we can communicate with her and call upon her for our needs, but she is also a part of us. This thoughtform Goddess is created from our energy and our ideas. She is a part of the practitioner that, for whatever reason, wishes to be profoundly felt and understood. Perhaps a matron Goddess is chosen because the practitioner feels as though the description of the Goddess describes him/her; perhaps a matron Goddess is chosen because the practitioner wishes the description of the Goddess described himself/herself. Essentially, the Goddess is chosen because of some inner connection on the part of the magician; he/she is recognizing something inside himself/herself as it is reflected in society through this deity. By giving this idea increasing amounts of energy, the practitioner is able to consciously or unconsciously summon the deity as a thoughtform, but because this Goddess is created from the practitioner, to attune with the Goddess is to attune with himself/herself. That is why attuning with a matron Goddess or a patron God is enlightening and reduces stress, bringing on sensations of euphoria.

If the practitioner understands that he/she attunes with himself/herself it is easy to see how bringing the Goddess into spellwork might improve its effectiveness. When we attune with a matron Goddess, we attune with an aspect of ourselves that she represents. To use that image again is to empower our magick by focusing a specific kind of energy on a specific need. A carefully chosen Goddess, like a wand, can help us manipulate our own energy and that of the natural world to better ourselves and others. That is what magick is all about. Perhaps, if we stop thinking of a matron Goddess in the traditional way and see her as a powerful thoughtform, we may be able to return her to our rituals and make her a bigger part of our lives and magickal workings.

Tim Lord is an award-winning writer and a student of the ways of nature. He has been studying Pagan beliefs for 15 years.

Christian Wisdom, Pagan Goddess: Reclaiming Sophia and the Saints from the Judeo-Christian Tradition

Simon Stirling

They were once a pair, the Goddess and her consort. Throughout the ancient world Goddesses were worshipped alongside their male counterparts, and the further we go back, the more it would appear that the Great Goddess took precedence.

Thus, Osiris had to be pieced back together by Isis, who then mated with his reconstituted body. Inanna-Ishtar, the Sumerian Venus, escaped from the Underworld (where her sister was queen) and then condemned her own consort, Dumuzi-Tammuz, to death.

In her complex role as mother-daughter-bride, the Great Goddess presided over birth and death, growth and decay, and so she wielded supreme power: she could breathe life back into the scattered remains of her sacred partner and strike down others without mercy.

She was Nature itself, embodying the inspiration and expiration, the expansion and contraction of all creation. Her forms were multifarious; she could appear in three aspects – Maiden, Mother and Crone – or with a face of two halves: one lovely, the other hideous.

More than anything, perhaps, she personified the exchange of spirit and matter (or, to be slightly more scientific, "energy" and "mass"). As Venus, the brightest of stars, she reminded mankind that we are all descended from the celestial sphere. The chemical elements which make up material things were formed when stars exploded, and this transformation of star-energy into atomic matter was the original descent – the condensation of spirit (energy) into matter (mass).

"The soul comes 'from the stars'," wrote C.G. Jung, "and returns to the stellar regions" – which is as much as to say that our spiritual essence takes on its physical substance when the atoms created by dying stars constellate, and our corporeal bodies eventually release their constituent molecules back into the cosmos. The Great Goddess governed this alternating concentration and dissipation of energy, the endless cycle of material creation and dissolution, the descent of the spirit into matter and the corresponded ascent of mass into energy.

The Goddess therefore had a binary function: she presided over the coalescing of atomic matter (birth) and the dispelling of material existence (death), these being the "downward" and "upward" phases of the energy-mass interchange or the periodic transition from essence to substance and back again. But her image was also three-fold. She was youth, maturity and senescence.

It has become customary to file New Age interests and ideas under the category of Mind, Body and Spirit. This is a useful shorthand, although a better designation might be Soul, Self and Spirit – for various ancient cultures, including that of the Egyptians, acknowledged the existence of three essential "selves". One of these we might now recognize as the Freudian *ego*: the Self as it perceives itself. Related to the Self, though, were two complementary essences, one of these being a form of body-double, a "ghost-in-the-machine" that was thought to reside in or around the solar plexus. The other was the true spiritual essence of the individual and was associated with the head. If the former represented the life-force which animates the body, the latter was the eternal expression of a person's spirit.

On either side of the Freudian *ego*, then, there existed a ghostly *id* and a disembodied *superego* – or, if you prefer, each person comes fully equipped with an inner daemon and a guardian angel.

The "lower" of these two essences – which we might call the

Soul – had its infernal qualities. It was the individual's animal nature or "child within". When the Greek hero Odysseus summoned up the "mindless disembodied ghosts" of his fallen comrades, it was the detached lower self with which he conversed. In the Polynesian tradition, this low self is an ever-willing, if somewhat literal, helper – like the Sorcerer's Apprentice. It is also the repository of memories, personal and ancestral, and when it detaches itself from the physical body it can appear as a phantom or wreak chaos as a poltergeist.

The "higher" essence (which we might call the Spirit) belongs to an eternal family of higher selves which guard and guide their embodied, living forms, towards which they exhibit nothing but unconditional love. The Spirit is therefore our heavenly aspect, to which we should aspire, while the Soul is our internal child-of-nature which, if damaged by abuse or neglect, will tend to hold us back.

We could say that every person has his or her spiritual connections with the Underworld ("Hell") and the Upperworld ("Heaven"). The "middle self" or *ego* inhabits the material world while the "low self" or *id* belongs to the infernal, nether region and the "high self" or *superego* resides in the celestial realm of discarnate eternity. And – an important point – *the Great Goddess ruled all three of these realms.* She was the Queen of Heaven, "Heavenly Venus", her infernal counterpart being the Goddess of the Underworld. She was the youthful child-of-nature, the matronly Mother and the hag-like personification of wisdom, age and death – which was simply the dissolution of bodily substance (the star-stuff of which we are made) and its conversion back into primal energy.

What should be apparent is that the seemingly simple division of the Goddess into complementary opposites (her beautiful-hideous face) or her three-fold appearance is, in fact, anything but simple. For, if the "beautiful" half of the Goddess was symbolic of her life-giving qualities (youth, love, growth, reproduction) then her beauty was also symptomatic of the descent of spirit into matter, the freezing of energy to form mass. In other words, the lovely Maiden aspect of the Great Goddess represented the *downward* motion of creation, while her "hideous" Crone aspect suggested the *upward* motion of matter as it returned to the stellar state of liberated Spirit.

It follows that the Goddess was at her most beautiful when she was heading in the infernal direction and most hideous when her trajectory was celestial. Or, to put it another way: the loathsome Crone was implicit in her lovely aspect, as she turned spirit into matter and descended, just as the beautiful Maiden was implicit in her hideous aspect, as she converted mass back into energy. Her totality was therefore undeniable, because when she was at her most life-enhancing she was simultaneously repellent, and when she was in death-dealing mode, she was inherently lovely.

So how did the Goddess of Complete Being (as Ted Hughes described her) become so marginalized and forgotten?

The answer has to do with trauma on a massive scale and can probably be traced back to the Babylonian exile of the Jews. Prior to their captivity in the 6th century BC, the Canaanites had worshipped the god El as the father of all things (the Semitic root of *El* also gave us *Allah* and *Elohim*, the latter meaning "God" and "Gods" in ancient and modern Hebrew). Notably, El had a wife – Asherah – who, as the Queen of Heaven, took her place alongside those other Mesopotamian Goddesses, Ishtar and Inanna. Asherah was a Great Goddess, the Venus of her people.

It was only after their enslavement in Babylon (modern Iraq) that the Jews rejected their traditional polytheism. The exclusive worship of Yahweh was instigated. Statues of Asherah were destroyed. By the 2nd century BC only one God was tolerated by the Jews – and he was decidedly male.

The trauma of their Babylonian captivity altered the relationship between the Canaanites and their Gods. The feminine principle was displaced (symbolized by Lilith, the first wife of Adam, whose sexual dominance led to her being cast as a demon and a new, more compliant woman being created in the form of Eve). This could only have been the consequence of a schizoid split in the psyche and a retreat into the logical, law-making side of the brain, which then began to wage war on the feeling function represented by the pattern-forming and connection-seeking right-brain hemisphere.

Or we could say that the damaged (brutalized, paranoid) inner child began to avenge itself on a supposedly uncaring mother-figure. It did this by transferring its affections to a jealous and wrathful Father and breaking the Goddess of Complete Being down into binary opposites: the idealized virgin-mother and the man-eating whore.

The Judeo-Christian tradition has maintained and perpet-uated this schizoid imbalance, repeatedly traumatizing its children in order to disrupt the natural sense of wholeness embodied by the Great Goddess of old and substituting a violently polarized set of mutually exclusive opposites ("good versus evil", "male versus female", "us versus them", etc). The outcome had been the triumph of masculine "logic" or "will" – patriarchy, bureaucracy, law and order – along with its side-effects: technological mastery and the rape of the natural world. At the same time, the dominance of ego-driven left-brain thinking has suppressed, often with stunning brutality, all expressions of feminine potency: sensuality, relatedness, empathy. Rather than being part of an endless cycle, life and death have been separated into binary compartments – life is "good", death is "bad"; "they" must die so that "we" can live.

We can best appreciate the extreme one-sidedness of all this by considering those feminine figures which have been tolerated by the Judeo-Christian tradition.

One such is "Wisdom" (Latin *Sapientia*, Greek *Sophia*) whose form, in Gnosticism and Christian Mysticism, is generally female.

Wisdom was invariably an attribute of the Great Goddess, even as she was being demoted (Athena/Minerva being a watered-down expression of the Goddess of Complete Being). But with Sophia we encounter a divinity of sorts which has been relegated to just one end of the spectrum. She is a manifestation of "Mind" (Greek *Nous*), which we might think of as the higher self or Spirit in its celestial environment. There is no accompanying body, no *ego*, and definitely no hint of an infernal or animal Soul.

Sophia has clearly been trapped by the dichotomy of either/or thinking: she is energy without mass and, therefore, symbolizes only one half of the cosmic process. She is "light" and "love" without the blood and tears of childbirth – heavenly wisdom without the darker knowledge of the Underworld.

The pedestal occupied by Sophia was similarly used to defuse the tremendous power of the Goddess by converting her into one or other of the saints. A classic example is Brighid (Latin *Brigantia*), the Venus of the Celtic world. The "beautiful Brighid" was a Maiden, Mother and Crone whose face was half-lovely and half-hideous. But Christianity confined her to the status of virgin. A legend was concocted which saw the girl transported by angels from her home on the Isle of Iona to Bethlehem, where she became midwife and foster-mother to the Christ child. Thus, the Great Goddess of the Hebrides was limited to her Maiden-Mother function (Brighid became the "Mary of the Gael") and honored as a patron saint of Ireland. Her former totality as a Goddess of Complete Being (she also presided over the battlefield) was denied her.

It is impossible to overstress the psychological damage that has been done by this insistence on disempowering the Great Goddess by dividing her into positive and negative opposites. Women have paid a dreadful price for this since they have been required to conform to the positive qualities of the Goddess and punished for reflecting any of her negative aspects. Men, too, have suffered, for they have been forced into believing that there are "good" and "bad" women, and that their beloved mothers and lovers hide a terrible Lilith behind their outer Eve. And this is not to mention the internal feminine – Jung's *anima* – which is possibly the low self or Soul in every man, and which, informed by misogynistic indoctrination, sulks and rages at the injustice of it all.

Beyond the individual, we have the feminine in its broader manifestation. The Goddess of Complete Being is also the receptive, fertile earth and its life-giving waters, both of which we have poisoned and pillaged through our left-brain arrogance, with its insatiable greed and dogmatic belief in a male God who made us do it. Our relationships with the women in our lives, our own souls and our Mother Earth have been soured and rendered dysfunctional, distrustful and destructive, by the paranoia which comes from the false dichotomies drilled into us by Judeo-Christian teachings and their obsessive, psychotic hatred of the all-encompassing, mothering-and-smothering arms of the Eternal Feminine.

There is a way back, of course. Though most of us will have been damaged in childhood, raised to take our place in the divide-and-conquer, winner-takes-all world of polarized thinking, it is up to us whether or not we inflict the same psychological violence on our own children:

- Whether we embrace the cosmic totality of the feminine or break it down into a predatory vagina and a soothing breast;
- Whether we see the Earth as our marvelous (though temporary) home or a treasure chest to be plundered for short-term gain;
- And whether we view death as a natural return to the stars or a terrifying negation.

Everything depends on whether we wish to enjoy our lives and pass on to our children a healthy, inhabitable planet, or whether we would rather live in pain and fear. The Great Goddess is ready to accept us, nourish us, delight us and – sooner or later – to transform us back into that original state of pure energy, but only if we recognize her for what she always was: the Goddess of Complete Being and the Queen of All That Is.

Simon Stirling trained as an actor at LAMDA before turning professional as a writer. He has written for several hit TV drama series, as well as adapting an opera libretto and providing scripts for the Open University. An avid historical researcher, he is the author of *The King Arthur Conspiracy: How a Scottish Prince Became a Mythical Hero* (The History Press, 2012) and *Who Killed William Shakespeare? The Murderer, The Motive, The Means* (The History Press, 2013). He lives in Worcestershire, UK.

Evolution, Revolution... The Transformation of Kali Ma in Western Society

Avi Lago

"J'ai mata di"... ("All hail the great mother"). As the aarti commences the statue of Kali Ma glows as I pour oil into the *"diya"* (an oil lamp still traditionally made the way my own ancestors would have, from clay and using a cotton wick to illuminate our inner consciousness). With the intense swaying of incense, I am suddenly swept into a meditative experience and, once again, I'm taken into an embrace with our Dark Mother. The energy intensifies and I'm taken within. The flow is so strong as I close my eyes, I begin to lose control. I can hear many people chanting and becoming one with the Devi's love.

Who is Kali Ma? Why from such a young age has my family worshiped the glorious Dark Mother, whose tongue sticks out with her grimace and fearsome pose, holding the demon in her hands? As a child and even to this day Kali Ma has always drawn me. From Indian films to songs devoted to her, I always wanted to seek out who Kali Ma really was. Kali means Black One, she is fertile like the ground and the primal mother, the absolute void. Many say that to know her is to know the entire understanding of life and one becomes free from Maya (the illusion of life). Compared to many other Hindu deities, she speaks volumes and has never been in the background.

Her story stems from the *Devi Bhagavatam* (ancient scriptures based on the Goddess and the epic battle of Mahisasura and Durga, the fearsome lion-riding Goddess). The story goes back to when the Trimurti (the Hindu Trinity) Brahma (the creator), Vishnu (the preserver) and Shiva (the destroyer) were created from the mother herself; primal Shakti (life-force). As Brahma stepped out of this bubble he saw he was about to be attacked by two demons. He panicked and began to shout, but the sleeping Vishnu, who he was coming out of, couldn't hear him. He screamed louder and, like all children, he called, "MA!" The primal Shakti, also known as Mahaesavri or Adi-Shakti, came and granted him safety as each aspect of the Hindu Trinity was formed. In Hinduism, each God has a counterpart. Brahma's wife is Saraswati, Vishnu has Lakshmi and Shiva has Parvati (Gauri).

Let's explore Ma's creation story (there are a few, some overlapping, so let's keep this one simple). Kali comes from the word Kala meaning "time" in Sanskrit, named after her spouse Shiva the destructive transformer and beholder of time. She is known as a crone in western Paganism, but in India she is the grand Matrika or Maha Dakini (Queen of Witches). The story I was told as a child was from the *Devi Mahatmya* (known as the Glory of the Goddess). As mentioned above, this is one of the most popular stories in Indian Devi scriptures. It is about Devi taking the form of Kali to kill Mahishasura. Originally written between 400 CE and 500 CE, this is a tradition known as "patha", which involves reading spiritual scriptures with song, dance and sometimes fasts. These are observed all night and during them one would be given visions of the Goddess on her journeys. Even today there are festivals known as Jagrans (vigils where practitioners sing and dance all night in the streets and constantly praise the mother).

Demons don't specifically feature as evil in Indian mythology. When the Devas (Gods) and asuras (demons) battle, it is for attaining one goal, spiritual attainment or enlightenment. Long ago a being prayed to the Gods; attaining his siddhis (spiritual austerities by practicing extreme yogic exercises), he obtained the Gods' attention and impressed them so much that they granted the being his wish. He asked for one thing, to be invincible so that no "man or God be able to harm him". From that instant, the Gods granted him his wish and this created chaos. The demonic entity started killing all the beings on earth from humans to demi-Gods. Life on earth got out of hand, and the Gods realized their mistake. No followers meant no offerings and the Gods couldn't live without the humans just as the humans couldn't live with the Gods. The Trimurti (male trinity: Brahma, Vishnu and Shiva) and other minor Gods (elements) discussed the problem. They created a Yagna (holy fire) and then created a beautiful woman who stepped out of the fire. She had the most dazzling eyes that glowed like embers, hair dark as the night, glowing skin and 16 arms. Each God gave her their weapon (power). This Goddess is called Durga (the invincible one). She then arrived at the battleground and, with deep fury, unleashed from her brow Kali. Some say that she was so angry and fearsome that she turned into Kali. The fearsome form of mother Kali was terrifying to her onlookers as she had her tongue out and uttered a blood-curdling scream. Holding a sword in one of her hands she ran towards the demon. She began to fight him but noticed that each time she cut off his head, where his blood fell it created another duplicate form.

Like all wise mothers, she undertook the task of sacrifice out of true love. As she fought, more and more forms appeared and, realizing the task ahead would not be easy, Kali Ma began to drink the blood of the demon, known as Raktabija (Blood Drop). As she drank, she screamed out in madness and lost control. In a frenzy, she began to kill anything in sight. All the Gods panicked and wondered how they could control Kali in her blood lust.

There are two stories that describe how Kali was calmed from this state of mind. The first is that Shiva appeared, but in two different ways. In one story he appeared as a child and when Kali Ma heard the cries of a child, the innocence melted her heart and the purity brought Kali Ma back to her form as Gauri (Ma Parvati). In the other story, Shiva lay amongst the corpses. As Kali Ma stepped on him she realized that it was her husband and life partner. This calmed her down and she stuck her tongue out in embarrassment. (This explains the metaphysical side of Shiva and Shakti)... without Shakti, Shiva would be Shava (corpse or dead) and when Shakti is out of control they need body and spirit, one without the other doesn't work. This is an example of divine polarity or yin and yang.

This is only a short explanation of why Kali Ma is so deeply loved as a mother. In life it relates to our relationship with our own mother, not just microcosmically but also macrocosmically. It shows many themes; the Gods can't live without the Goddess, just as humanity can't live without the Divine Mother.

Hinduism is polytheistic and pantheistic. Depending on which part of India you are from, and even which city and which village someone is from, the Devi takes on various forms. This would be known as folk shaktism. As I grew up with various forms of the Devi, our Kuldevi (ancestral deity) is Kali Ma. Stories of Kali Ma are still strong despite how long this tradition has survived; she is so ancient some people say she is the original Devi. This is why she has no name, only Ma. When you explore her life and history, Kali is marginalized yet misunderstood in a society which was always misunderstood. My own background is Punjabi (in Punjab north India today she isn't popular, although her worship is well known in Bengal, in east India). There are problems when someone says they worship Kali Ma because it is still a taboo. It is like someone in medieval times in Europe saying they were a practicing witch. You have to be cautious about how you approach the Goddess, as Tantra in India isn't what those in the west think it is.

As Kali traveled into the western imagination, films like *Indiana Jones and the Temple of Doom* portraying the infamous thugee bandits in India, the TV series *Charmed*, and many other fictional stories have distorted her as a demonic blood-thirsty mother. But, just as times change, so do attitudes towards our Dark Mother. Kali Ma is misunderstood, though conceptions of her are always changing. She is a popular feminist, a vampire, a seductress and a symbol of taboo. We keep hearing that the return of the Great Mother is on a rise, but knowing Kali Ma isn't at all different. With changes in attitude to woman in religion, to cultural diversity, and sexual freedom (gay rights) it is obvious Kali Ma is creating a new age (in India this is known as Kali yuga, the age of Kali). As more people feel drawn to their inner voice, it is obvious that this is their inner Shakti (source) making us all aware of the changes within us and around us.

Kali Ma is direct in her attitude and wants us to appreciate our life, a mother who creates and destroys. This doesn't mean she would destroy us, as might be imagined from images that show her holding the head of a demon as a lifeless Shiva lies beneath her foot. This is a powerful symbol of letting go; dancing and feeling the movement around us allows the kundalini to rise. Embrace her, touch her and allow your own appreciation for the divine to awaken. No longer do we need to stick to the cultural confinements of our past. Whether this relates to a fundamental ideology, relationship, career or anything holding us back, when Kali calls it means it is the time for change! It can be hard, but Kali Ma, like any Dark Goddess, will allow you to grow from your pain and become stronger. In a society where racism, homophobia and sexism are prevalent, Kali cuts this out, smashes it and shows that diversity is the beauty in our practices.

Working with and knowing Kali Ma, she teaches us the beauty in the darkest moments of life, for there are many, but her magick isn't known as dark or light. She wants us to surpass this simplicity, for there isn't white or black. In her eyes it is both day and night, for even the dark shows us the most beautiful things. Like a moonlit night, Kali is the Milky Way, full of beauty, smiling with her teeth sparkling and eyes twinkling. The moon and stars show this. Oh! How our mother is prevalent and very much returned, and it is up to us to listen and take her hand. I can only say that once you do, you'll never regret it, for this mother is very protective, and will never let her children down.

No matter what situation you're in.

Oh, mother you provide us with such beauty and love, knowing you is to know the deeper mysteries…!

I open my eyes as I return from the meditation, I finish chanting and singing praises to Kali Ma.

OM KALIKAYAI NAMAHA.

Avi Lago practices a wide range of divination techniques, gives readings using tarot and mediumship and is a member of the Theosophical Society. He writes articles and hosts workshops in Glasgow.

The Lady of Avalon: An Ancient New-Found Goddess and Her Impact in the Lives of Many who are Called to Become Her Priestesses and Priests

Kathy Jones

The Lady of Avalon is an ancient and new-found Goddess, whose name invokes feelings of magic and mystery. She is Nolava, Goddess of the Sacred Isle of Avalon, the mysterious Otherworldly Paradise, which lies far to west, across the Lake, across the Sea. Avalon means the Place of Apples and from time immemorial it has been regarded as a home of Goddess, where the Lady rules with Her sisters, the Nine Morgens. In the present time the Lady of Avalon is calling to many women and a few men to remember Her and to become Her Priestesses and Priests of Avalon once again.

Marion Zimmer Bradley in her inspirational novel *The Mists of Avalon*, published in 1983, first named *Lady of Avalon, Lady of the Lake* and *Priestess of Avalon* as Priestess roles in service to the Goddess in Avalon. It was over twenty years later, in 2006, in my book *Priestess of Avalon, Priestess of the Goddess* (Ariadne Publications), that I took this naming a step further, reclaiming *Lady of Avalon, Lady of the Lake, Morgen la Fey* and the *Nine Morgens* as ancient Goddess names and as emanations of Goddess, sometimes manifesting in human form. I reclaimed the title *Priestess of Avalon* for myself and those who dared to come with me on her magical journey of transformation.

For thousands of years in Brigit's Isles, and before we became a group of islands cut off from Europa's land by the sea, our communities celebrated the seasonal cycles of Goddess, the movements of the earth, moon and sun, of the stars in the heavens. We acknowledged Goddess as Earth, Water, Fire, Wind and Space, as Giver of Birth, Life and Death. We recognized Her in the shapes of the land, as Her paps (breasts) and womb hills, as Her body fleshed out in rounded hills, Her face carved out by wind and weather in rocks and mountains. The springs and rivers were known to be Her flowing menstrual streams and Her life-giving ovulation fluids. After the ice melted and the seas rose again eight thousand years ago we were one of the last indigenous European societies to lose our connection to Goddess and to our spiritual Ancestors.

Collectively we showed our love and respect for Goddess in Neolithic times by creating hundreds of small and large ritual sites dedicated to Her and to the Ancestors, who were born from Her body and died back into it. We built up great mounds of earth and stone shaped like Her body. We erected individual marker stones, and large and small circles of stones, wood and earth, where we honored Her and the cycles of Her seasons.

Over the last five thousand years different patriarchal cultures entered Brigit's Isles, coming in peaceful waves of change or through raiding and invasion, bringing war and destruction. They transformed over time what is believed to have been on the whole a peaceful, pagan, Goddess-loving society into today's crumbling bastion of Christian religious belief, which is based not in this green and pleasant land and its indigenous spirituality, but in a hot dry desert land which lies thousands of miles to the southeast.

The threads of Her memory in this land were cut, the traditions gone. We cannot know as fact, as received wisdom from our elders, as traditional knowledge handed down to us through the ages, how to be a Priestess of the Goddess and of Avalon in this land. There is no-one to tell us. We have to begin again to learn about Goddess in the same way as our ancestors, from experiencing Her many faces as they are revealed to us in the cycles of the seasons of Her nature.

Here in our Goddess community in Glastonbury, England, we

explore Goddess as She manifests Herself in the land here, where we live. Glastonbury is the physical Outerworld counterpart to the Otherworldly Paradise of Avalon, which lies just beyond the Veil. We work with the Sacred Wheel of Brigit-Ana/Britannia, the early tutelary Goddess of these islands, which first emerged in 1992, and with the Sacred Wheel of the Lady of Avalon. These Goddess-centered Wheels of the Year celebrate the many different faces of our indigenous Goddesses in Britain and Ireland, that are expressed in our landscapes, weather, folklore, traditions and culture. (See *Spinning the Wheel of Ana*, Ariadne Publications). On these wheels the elements of Her nature are in different positions to those used by Wiccans. For us Air is in the north, Fire is in the east, Water is in the south and Earth is in the west, similar to the Native American Wheel, as it happens.

Today, in this third millennium CE, a remarkable change is occurring within human spirituality, which is almost unnoticed in mainstream culture. Tens of thousands of women and some men, are journeying daily across the world, visiting the ruins of ancient Goddess sites, travelling to new Goddess Temples, seeking Her here and there, wanting to connect with other Goddess-loving people. Among these are a multitude of women and some men, who travel to Glastonbury, England, in search of Goddess. They come seeking the Lady of Avalon, Her Priestesses, Her Temple and Her land, as if returning to a Place of Origin, a place called home, where the Goddess lives and is honored today.

Priestesses of Avalon are returning to life with memories clouded by patriarchal conditioning, but re-membering our destinies. We are incarnating especially for this experience of bringing the Goddess alive once again in the 21st century. The Veil of Avalon is becoming more and more transparent as Her Paradise Isle, Her Motherworld of peace and love emerges from the mists once again.

When the threads of memory are cut much that is good is lost.

But there are also benefits. Old habits, outmoded ways of thinking and being, received rather than experienced knowledge, rigidities, corruptions, personal and collective resistances which cling to outworn ways of doing things, all are also lost in the tides of forgetting. When all that remains of the physical past are bones and stones, we begin once again to listen to the Goddess as She speaks directly to us in the whispering wind, in the crackling fire, in the crashing ocean waves, in the tinkling brooks, in the caves in Her body, in the songs of birds and calls of animals, in the voice of our intuition, our direct connection to Goddess. We begin to sense Her presence and hear Her speak to us. With no human mediator between ourselves and Her, no priest standing between us and the divine, no book that tells us what to believe, who we are and how to be, then we can each become truly creative from our souls, in the present. We call all our Goddess-given resources to the task of bringing our innate divinity into life on this Her beautiful planet Earth. We can truly incarnate.

In 1996 craftswoman Tyna Redpath and I organized the first international Glastonbury Goddess Conference. Our aim was to bring together Goddess – loving writers, artists, speakers, poets, performers and ceremonialists to celebrate our British Goddesses. Although not without challenges we were successful beyond our wildest dreams, and nineteen years later the Goddess Conference continues to grow stronger and more vibrant. Each year we focus on a different aspect of Goddess, creating a nine-day pilgrimage into the Sacred Mysteries of Avalon.

But it was in the first year of the Conference that I realized we needed properly trained Priestesses to hold energy in our ceremonies. In 1998, inspired by the Lady, I initiated the first millennial Priestess/Priest of Avalon Training in Glastonbury. It was something I did not do lightly. The title *Priestess of Avalon* is charged with magic and meaning. It speaks of ancient forgotten virtues, of the powers of women and the celebration of our mysteries, of hidden secret knowledge, of inspiration, enchantment, holiness and revelation. It speaks to a part of ourselves as women and men that longs to bring meaning back into mundane life, that thirsts for a true spirituality which is directly connected to the land on which we live, or have lived in the past in other lives. It is also a title which carries much glamor and I wanted to be sure that anyone who took this training was taking it for the right reasons, because they wanted to love and serve the Lady, Her land and Her people, and not because they wanted to be a princess.

The Priestess of Avalon training has now been taught for 16 years by myself and Priestess tutor Erin McCauliff. It developed into a three-year Three Spiral training, with additional optional trainings to enhance and develop Priestess abilities. Our teaching is based in feminist ideas and new-found Goddess spirituality. We explore Goddess in all Her aspects as they are lived here in Glastonbury Avalon. Priestess training by correspondence is also available. For further information about our Priestess training go to www.goddesstemple.co.uk.

Over many years my partner, Mike, and I visited the ruins of numerous ancient Goddess Temples throughout Europe and other countries of the world. These Temples are the remnants of a widespread Goddess-loving culture that was once alive everywhere in the ancient world. In 2000 we visited the wonderful Mount Olympus in Greece. As we stood in the ruins of another ancient Goddess Temple, I felt such an overwhelming sorrow for all that has been lost. I vowed that day to create a modern-day living Goddess Temple in my hometown, in Glastonbury. When I returned home I called together people who I thought might be interested in helping. We decided to rent a room for a few days, decorate it as a Goddess Temple, and hold seasonal ceremonies. We placed one of the large wicker Goddess Conference Goddesses in the center of the room and surrounded Her with veils. We held a wonderful ceremony, which ended with champagne and strawberries. We received donations which helped to cover our costs. We had such a great time we decided to do it again at the next seasonal festival.

Over the next eighteen months for every seasonal festival we would hire a space for a few days, decorate it as a Goddess Temple, hold ceremonies, and then take it all down again. In 2002 a room became available in the courtyard of the Glastonbury Experience, and we decided to take it on as a permanent Goddess Temple. We have now been there for twelve years. We are the first formally registered public indigenous British Goddess Temple, probably ever, but at least for the last one thousand five hundred years. We are open to the public every day for personal prayer, ceremony and meditation. Our income comes from donations of time, energy and money from our supporters, and from the Goddess courses that we offer.

In 2006 we bought our bigger Goddess Hall so that we can accommodate all the people who want to come to our public seasonal ceremonies. It's another beautiful Goddess Temple space in our town. It is also the venue for all our Priestess and Goddess trainings. We are growing organically from strength to strength in Her love.

In 2012 I received the vision of Her Motherworld, a renewed society which holds Goddess, the Earth, mothers and the values of mothering, of love, care and support for each, in the center of life, rather than being left out on the periphery. We grounded this vision in ceremony at the 2013 Goddess Conference. I hope that you will join us in expanding and committing to this Vision of Peace. You can find full details on the Goddess Temple website about this and all our work. See www.goddesstemple.co.uk.

Kathy Jones is a Priestess of Avalon. You can find details about her personal work, her writing and her books at www.kathyjones.co.uk and about the Goddess Conference at www.goddessconference.com.

The Goddess of Freedom: From Libertas to Lady Liberty

Selena Fox

The honoring of the Goddess of Freedom began more than two thousand years ago among the ancient Romans. They called Her Libertas, the Latin word for Freedom. Libertas signified freedom of action, freedom from restraint, independence, rights, and related forms of personal and social liberty.

The Roman religion had a large and complex pantheon with a great assortment of Goddesses, Gods, and other sacred forms. Ancient Romans revered and deified certain values, known as Virtues, and Libertas was one of the most important of these. A few of the more than two dozen other private and public Virtues were Hope (Spes), Justice (Justica), Piety (Pietas), and Courage (Virtus). According to their religion, Roman citizens were to uphold Virtues in their personal lives as well as in the culture as a whole.

Libertas as a deity usually took the form of a Goddess. A temple to Her on the Aventine Hill in Rome was dedicated around 238 BCE. Sometimes She merged with the chief Roman God Jupiter, in the form of Jupiter Libertas, whose feast was celebrated on April 13. Libertas also was closely associated with the Goddess Feronia, and some viewed them as aspects of the same Goddess, including the Roman scholar Varro, a contemporary of Cicero. Feronia is thought to have been originally an ancient agricultural and fire Goddess among the Etruscan and/or Sabine peoples. During the Roman Republic, Feronia's feast day was November 13. She was honored in central Italy as the Goddess of freedwomen and freedmen, and She was associated with the granting of freedom to slaves. Part of the passage from slavery into freedom in Roman society involved having the head ritually shaved, being ceremonially tapped by a magistrate with a rod, called a *vindicta,* and then wearing a cap, known as a *pilleus,* to symbolize freed status.

Some of the Roman depictions of Libertas have survived to this day on coins and other artifacts. Libertas is usually pictured as a matron in flowing classical dress. She often is shown holding both the Liberty Pole (vindicta) and Liberty Cap (pilleus). In some depictions Libertas wears the Liberty Cap or a crown of laurel leaves. Sometimes She carries a spear instead of the Liberty Pole. Sometimes the Goddess Liberty is shown with a cat at Her feet.

Although the Roman Empire is no more, the Goddess Liberty still survives. Over the centuries and across cultures, She has continued to signify Freedom in Her appearances in paintings, sculptures, songs, stories, poems, and other literature. In recent centuries, the form She has most often taken is that of Lady Liberty.

Libertas as Lady Liberty began emerging in America during the colonial era as part of the American quest for political independence from Britain. American patriot Paul Revere may have been the first to depict Lady Liberty in that context. In 1766, on the obelisk he created in celebration of the repeal of the Stamp Act, he used the image of Liberty with a Liberty Pole surmounted by a Liberty Cap. Another patriot leader, Thomas Paine, included Her in his poem, the "Liberty Tree," referring to Her as "The Goddess of Liberty." Freedom Goddess depictions not only emerged in America during its Revolution, but a few years later in France during its own Revolution, with the female symbol of the French Republic, the Marianne, depicted wearing the Liberty Cap, and often accompanied by Liberty's cat.

As the USA became a nation, Lady Liberty became part of the official symbology of some of its newly formed states. Holding Her Liberty Cap atop the Liberty Pole, Lady Liberty appears along with the Goddess of Justice on the New York State flag. On the obverse of the Great Seal of the Commonwealth of Virginia, created in 1776, Liberty holds the Liberty Cap atop a pole in Her right hand and is flanked on Her left side by the Roman Goddess of Eternity (Aerternitas) and on Her right by the Goddess of Fruitfulness (Ceres). In addition, the Goddess Liberty, also with a Liberty Pole and Cap, appears with Ceres on the front of the Great Seal of New Jersey, adopted in 1777.

As more states were formed in the United States of America in the 19th and 20th centuries, some of them also chose to include Liberty imagery as part of their iconography. In addition, Libertas and Libertas-inspired images appeared on coins, paintings, stamps, and in sculptures throughout the land, including the colossal bronze Statue of Freedom, which was commissioned in 1855 and in 1863 set on the top of the dome of the US Capitol building in Washington, DC, where it can still be seen today. It is interesting to note that during America's Civil War era both sides claimed Liberty and sought to use Her images to promote their own causes. Among abolitionists, Liberty was depicted freeing slaves, while states rights advocates used Her image to signify independence from the "tyranny" of centralized government. Today, Liberty images are used in connection with a wide range of political parties, candidates, and positions on various issues.

The most famous of the Freedom Goddess' American depictions, the Statue of Liberty, was a gift from France to the United States in honor of America's 100th birthday. Originally called "Liberty Enlightening the World," the Statue of Liberty was designed by French Freemason and sculptor Frederic-Auguste Bartholdi with the assistance of engineer Alexandre Gustave Eiffel. The head of Lady Liberty's statue wears a crown with solar rays, similar to the crown on the Colossus of Rhodes, a magnificent monument to the Sun God Helios that once stood astride a Greek harbor and was considered one of the seven wonders of the ancient world. The seven rays on Liberty's crown represent the seven continents and seven seas. The torch Liberty holds in Her right upstretched hand is the Flame of Freedom, and underneath Her feet are broken chains representing overcoming tyranny and enslavement. The tablet Liberty holds in Her left hand is inscribed with July 4, the date of the signing of the Declaration of Independence and the birth of the USA as a nation. Her flowing gown is similar in design to depictions of Libertas in ancient Rome.

More than a hundred thousand people in France contributed money to the creation of the 151 foot (46 meters) high copper clad Statue of Liberty. In the USA, in a grass-roots effort spearheaded by newspaper magnate Joseph Pulitzer, thousands of Americans contributed money for the creation of the 65 foot high granite pedestal to serve as the Statue's base. The Statue was completed in Paris in May of 1884 and shipped in pieces to the USA where it was reassembled. Work on pedestal construction began in August 1884 following the laying of the cornerstone by Masons of the Grand Lodge of New York in a traditional Masonic ritual. The Statue of Liberty was erected on top of Her pedestal in New York Harbor on Bedloe Island, which was renamed Liberty Island in Her honor seventy years later. Thousands of people attended the dedication ceremony held on October 28, 1886, including Suffragettes, who, while circling the island in a boat, loudly proclaimed through a megaphone their freedom demand that women have the right to vote.

A plaque was added in 1903 to an interior wall of the pedestal containing "The New Colossus," the poem written by Emma Lazarus in 1883 as a tribute to the Statue and to immigrants coming to America for freedom. In the twentieth century, in preparation for the one hundredth birthday of the Statue of Liberty, an extensive renovation project was undertaken from 1984-1986. On the weekend of July 4, 1986, a great centennial celebration was held and the newly restored Statue was re-opened to visitors. The Statue of Liberty continues to be one of the most beloved of America's civic shrines. The United Nations designated it as a World Heritage site in 1984. The Statue of Liberty receives over 3.5 million visitors each year.

Lady Liberty images can be found not only throughout America, but elsewhere in the world. She sometimes makes appearances at political rallies, usually in Her Statue of Liberty form. Such was the case in May, 1989, when She gained worldwide attention as She emerged as the Goddess of Democracy in student demonstrations in Beijing, China. Pro-democracy demonstrators erected a 33 foot styrofoam and plaster Liberty Goddess with torch image in Tiananmen Square, and this became a powerful rallying symbol of their quest for Freedom. Although, a short time later, tanks moved in and crushed this statue as well as demonstrators and their demon-strations, their vision and work for Democracy continues within and outside of China.

Images of Lady Liberty now abound in American popular culture. In addition to the variety of Statue of Liberty replicas, postcards, T-shirts, and other souvenirs at tourist shops in New York City and elsewhere, Lady Liberty imagery can be found in movies and on television, on postage stamps and posters, in books and newspapers, in art museums and theaters, in poems and songs, in cartoons and advertisements, in public squares and private homes, in pageants and costume parties, plus in many other contexts. Lady Liberty's biggest feast day in the USA is Independence Day, July 4, and many images of Her abound in connection with this celebration.

Lady Liberty is honored on other occasions as well. She often has Her own float in nationally and globally televised parades celebrating Thanksgiving and New Year's Day. For example, in the 2000 Rose Parade in Pasadena, California, the float, "Liberty for All," sponsored by the Family of Freemasonry, included a 50 foot high replica of the Statue of Liberty.

For many contemporary Pagans, Lady Liberty is more than a

symbol for Freedom. Pagans of many paths have invoked Her in rituals for personal and social liberation. Some include Her image in their household shrines and altars. Because of Her ancient Pagan origins, Lady Liberty is an excellent Goddess to work with in support of Pagan religious freedom. Lady Liberty League, the national and global Pagan civil rights network sponsored by Circle Sanctuary, is named for Her.

Libertas, now also known as Lady Liberty, is both an ancient and contemporary powerful Goddess who can guide, inspire, protect, and comfort. May attunement and work with Her bring more Freedom to the lives of individuals, communities, and the world — now and in the times to come.

Selena Fox is a priestess, environmentalist, interfaith minister, and holistic psychotherapist with a Masters in Science in counseling from the University of Wisconsin-Madison. She is author of *Goddess Communion* and other works, and is founder of Circle Sanctuary which has been serving Pagans and other Goddess Spirituality practitioners worldwide since 1974. She teaches through a weekly podcast and travels internationally presenting workshops and facilitating ceremonies.

www.selenafox.com;

www.circlesanctuary.org;

www.facebook.com/SelenaFoxUpdates

Part 2

Naming the Goddess

Aine

Aine (her name meaning "bright one") is an Irish Goddess. While originally she was a sun Goddess, she's also a Goddess of the moon, cattle, fertility, love, and fires. She's known as the Faery Queen of Munster and has appeared in the form of a red mare that no other horse could outrun. Her most sacred day is Midsummer, as it is the longest day of the year, but the first harvest festival, Lughnasadh, is another important day.

According to *The Battle of Mag Mucrama*, her father was the Faery King of Munster, Eoghanach. However, some sources say that he is only her foster father and states that her true father is the sea God, Manannán mac Lir. No mother has ever been connected to her. She has several sisters: Grainne (who may have been her twin), Milucradh (a sometimes vengeful lake Goddess), Oonagh (queen of all the faeries in Ireland), and Aoife (a moon Goddess and shape changer).

In the County Limerick, there is a hill named Cnoc Aine, which literally means "the hill of Aine." W. Y. Evans-Wentz called it "Aine's true dwelling place." There is evidence that Midsummer rituals took place there up until the early 19th century, which involved bonfires and torches of straw that were then carried around the land while asking for protection for the animals and a bountiful harvest. In *Celtic Myths and Legends*, T. W. Rolleston says that with a simple wave of her arm, Aine can show those on Cnoc Aine a glimpse into Faerie.

In County Louth, there is a large stone called Cathair Aine. Michelle Skye states in *Goddess Alive!* that if you sit on her stone, you may be "forever maddened by the intensity of Aine's emotions." According to Skye, herbalists and healers would honor Aine before helping the patient. It was an old superstition that she had control over individuals' life forces. Being a Goddess of the land, this power would include control over the flowers and herbs used to heal the sick and injured. Edain McCoy says in *Celtic Myth & Magick* that Aine is the one who gave "meadowsweet its delicate scent."

There are many stories of Aine in Irish mythology. According to Byrne's *Irish Kings and High-Kings*, she is raped by King Ailill Aulom. During the attack, she bites off a piece of his ear, disfiguring him enough so that he is seen as not fit to be king. A second story states that her husband was Gerald, a human and Earl of Desmond in the 1300s. However, their union may not have been consensual. She was found combing her hair by her sacred lake when he captured her. In the version Monaghan uses in *The New Book of Goddesses and Heroines*, they have a son who turns into a goose and flies away after Gerald breaks his promise by becoming shocked by their son's magical abilities. In MacKillop's *Dictionary of Celtic Mythology*, she exacts revenge upon her husband by either turning him into a goose or killing him, or perhaps both.

In some stories, she takes her brother-in-law, King Fionnbhar (Oonagh's husband) as a lover. In others, Manannán mac Lir was her lover instead of her father. Monaghan also tells of her love for Fionn mac Cool, and how it was not meant to be. Aine's sister, Milucradh, in a fit of jealousy enchanted a lake that turned his hair gray, while keeping his youthful appearance. As Aine had made a promise to never sleep with a man with gray hair, she sadly had to turn away from the hero.

There are many rites and rituals in today's world where Aine would be the perfect Goddess to work with. She is very much a protector of women. Women who have been abused and are looking for their attacker to be brought to justice should call on her for aid. For women who need comfort after an attack, I'd recommend contacting her through meditation. She is also very helpful in spells that aid in keeping promises.

I always invite her to join in my rituals for Midsummer, as this sabbat is her most sacred day. She's also a great Goddess to work with when doing any spells that are ruled by the sun. As she is also a minor moon deity, I've called her into an esbat, especially at the Hawthorn Moon. It is appropriate to call Aine into a ritual dealing with the protection of animals and the environment.

While there are many stories of Aine's various consorts, there are other stories in which she is the victim of assault. As she is a Goddess of fertility and linked with the land, the men who possess her against her will may be doing so as a way to possess the land. She has the ability to make a man a king or take the crown away. Despite these attacks, Aine is a powerful Goddess, not to be trifled with. She comes to the aid of women in need and celebrates the cycle of life. She is the land itself.

Andrea Burdette has been Pagan for over a decade, working mainly with Aine and Cerridwen. She runs a Pagan group, Pentacle Grove, near Washington DC.

Aphrodite

... there is nothing that has escaped Aphrodite:
none of the blessed gods nor any of mortal humans.
[Homeric Hymn to Aphrodite, translated by Gregory Nagy]

Perhaps the only thing Homer got right about Aphrodite is the above quote. He portrayed her as a rather empty-headed love Goddess a, "lover of smiles." Like many Goddesses her essential nature was lost when patriarchal societies began to dominate. What is often forgotten is the fact that Aphrodite caused the Trojan War, Persephone to be raped and the death of Psyche. The golden Goddess of love has a dark side.

Aphrodite came from the Orient. She was Ishtar, Astarte and Ilat. She was also, undoubtedly, the "great whore of Babylon," and maybe the Greeks did not know how to handle a Goddess as complex as she was. The oriental Aphrodite was worshipped as the bestower of all fruitfulness and as a Goddess of women. This last is a glimpse into her true nature. Seen in later times as another ideal of feminine beauty, she is not an enemy to women. She is the embodiment of feminine power.

In the Greek pantheon her birth story gives us a clue to the complexities of her nature. She was born through an act of extreme violence; a reminder to us all that love can have its dark, violent moments. Cronus castrated his father, Uranus, and threw his severed genitals into the sea. From the foam, a girl was born, (Aphrodite means "foam-arisen"). The drops of blood from Uranus' severed member gave birth to the furies. Aphrodite floated to shore on a scallop shell and alighted in Cyprus. Sappho, the great poet, referred to her constantly in her poems as "Cyprian." The Graces adorned her and she was led to Olympus where every God immediately desired her for their wife. She turned them all down, even Zeus. Zeus, however, saw there would be trouble and so married her off to the steady, ugly, hardworking smith of the Gods, Hephaestus. He made her beautiful jewels, including a magic girdle that made whoever wore it irresistible. However, she is the Goddess of love and was never going to settle down with just one man. She took many lovers including Ares, the God of war, and Hephaestus spent their marriage as a cuckold.

She is known as the Goddess of love but she also is the Goddess of death, Aphrodite *Tumborukhos,* gravedigger and Aphrodite *Androphonos*, killer of men. She stands beside the mourners, sharing their pain, as she herself knelt down and tore at her hair when her lover, Adonis, was destroyed by a wild boar.

Little is said of Aphrodite as a mother, and yet she raised Adonis, before becoming his lover. She has a close relationship with her son, Eros. When she took Ares to bed, Eros guarded them, playing with Ares' weapons. Her other children are important as well. Her daughter, Harmonia, brings peace to the world after the Trojan War. Hermaphroditos (born of the union with Hermes), is a being that is both sexes at once and therefore the perfect balance of masculine and feminine energies. But she is also the mother of Deimos, God of fear and Phobus, the God of panic. It isn't all love and light.

This extreme nature is shown by her sacred birds, the dove and the sparrow. The dove is a delicate, pure bird, whereas the sparrow is commonplace. Why these two such different birds? Because she is both *Aphrodite Urania,* of the heavens and *Aphrodite Pandemos*, Goddess of the people. She protects marriage, but is the patroness of prostitutes. She rides the swan of pure love but also a he-goat of wantonness. Extreme she may be, but above all she is a Goddess who feels.

In today's world Aphrodite is still a wounded Goddess. After years of being repressed and feared for her sexuality, it would be hoped that she has returned to her full power, but one only has to look at the media to know this is not so. Our attitude to sexuality is still warped. Women all over the world are raped and sex and female flesh are still used to sell and to entice us. We have come a long way from the Victorian values we once had, but we are also a long way from the sacredness of sexuality that was shown in her temples, by her sacred harlots.

Marilyn Monroe has often been cited as the modern Aphrodite. There is a story of how a taxi driver picked her up and, not recognizing her said, that if she lost a few pounds, she could pass for Marilyn Monroe. Turning to the friend she was traveling with she is quoted as saying, "Shall I do 'Marilyn'?" She "transformed" herself into the sex Goddess in the back of the car. The taxi driver almost crashed.

The trick to remember is that Aphrodite is a power we can all use. You may not be the most beautiful woman in the world, but by drawing on Aphrodite's energy, people will think you are. To have Aphrodite in your life is to feel alive. She is the space between kisses and the long golden moments of an orgasm. She is found in the beauty of a sunset and the wildness of a storm. She is *the* life force. When she envelops us there is no past, there is no future, only the moment. To have Aphrodite present in your committed relationship is to have a lifelong love affair. Homer was right; no one escapes from her and would we truly want to? But when dealing and communing with this Goddess of smiles, keep in mind this information: *Aphrodite and the furies are sisters.* Consider yourself warned.

Adrienne E. James trained as a priestess under Naomi Ozaniec. She chose Aphrodite (or rather Aphrodite chose her) as the Goddess to align herself with. She lives in the UK and teaches astrology.

Aradia

A teacher of the "Old Religion" Stregheria, Italian Witchcraft during the 14th century in Tuscany Italy. Also known as the "beautiful pilgrim", daughter of the Goddess Diana and Lucifer the God of Light. Aradia was taught Witchcraft and, by her mother's will, was made mortal to be sent to earth to teach her disciples the art of Witchcraft.

Aradia's rebirth came as the Goddess Diana observed the cruelty and suffering the poor had been enduring at the hands of the rich as they were enslaved, imprisoned, and made to go hungry as the great lords sat in their palaces, drank wines and ate lavish meals. Struggling to do almost anything to be free, the poor had become desperate at the hands of their oppressors. Some had even turned to crime as a way to survive and escape slavery; they hid in the mountains and the forests as robbers and assassins. This enraged the Goddess and she told Aradia that she was to be reborn mortal, becoming a teacher to those who would study Witchcraft and free them from the wickedness and suffering they had been enduring. She was to be the first of Witches known to this world. She was to teach the art of poisoning the great lords, to ruin crops and destroy all men of evil. They were to study the rituals of the craft naked and free in the moonlight, men and women alike.

Aradia was said to have been born in 1313 in the town of Volterra. As she aged, Aradia began teaching the craft of her mother. Known as the beautiful pilgrim she amassed a following of disciples who studied the art. She dressed as a pilgrim, going from town to town teaching by the moonlight the ways to be free of oppression, to gain what was in need and to follow the teachings of the Goddess Diana. Passing on the knowledge of her mother's wisdom and tales of her great acts of sorcery, Aradia was becoming seen as the Goddess she is, and a formidable opponent to the rich. She was empowering a people to rise up against tyranny and also empowering them to be free. Along with this she also requested that after she had left this world, once a month on the night of the full moon, a supper should be held with meal, salt, honey and water to be consecrated to Diana along with an incantation.

Having finished her mission and her time on this earth Aradia returned to her mother. Never truly leaving her pupils, Diana had given her the power to grant favors to those who had invoked her or conjured her. Aradia could now grant success in love, the power to bless or curse friends or enemies, to converse with spirits, to find hidden treasures, to conjure priests who died leaving hidden treasures, to understand the voice of the wind, to change water into wine, to divine with cards, to know the secrets of the hand, to cure diseases, to make those who are ugly beautiful, to tame wild beasts. Whatever thing that should be asked of Goddess Aradia should be granted to those who deserved her favor.

The teachings of Aradia have crossed many borders and passed into many countries through immigrants leaving Italy and moving across Europe as well as into the United States. Some rituals have been incorporated into solitary practices and Wicca has been integrated into some aspects as well. Modern Witchcraft allows us to pull material from many paths to accomplish worship that works in various situations or that is just deemed a better fit for certain individuals. Some holes have been left in source material, from many years of interpretations. It is possible to fill them with a spiritual sense of what the Goddess is with contact through invocations and conjurings. Stregheria and Goddess Aradia offer a viable practice and an invaluable tool for a higher spirituality. Her mission, given to her by the Goddess Diana, is ongoing.

The legends of Aradia have been passed down through generations of Tuscans, her teachings have become hereditary in nature. The greatly detailed worship and ritual, that was held in much secrecy, became part of folklore and superstition. However, the practice is far from forgotten through teachings written by Charles Leland in *Aradia: The Gospel of the Witches* and *Italian Witchcraft* by Raven Grimassi, which are referenced here. There are also many others who have kept this art alive, including families who have passed the teachings down throughout the generations. Aradia will always be a part of self empowerment, awareness and knowledge. The Witchcraft she has brought to us through her teachings are powerful and forthright – a beautiful nature-based art that should never be left to fall to a specific nationality, gender or status, but should be embraced and seen as exactly what it is, equality, empowerment and strength of courage.

Sindy Leah Coumes Fitz is an occultist, solitary practitioner and advocate for Pagan Rights. She contributes to Pagan-based organizations and workshops and is an ongoing pupil of Aradia.

Arianrhod

Arianrhod is the Goddess of the Silver Wheel, ruler of Caer Sidi, (a magickal realm in the north) and is from the Celtic Pantheon. Her celebratory day is the 2nd of December. She is also a major Welsh Goddess. Her palace was called Caer Arianrhod, also known as the Aurora Borealis, and she is known as the Goddess of time and karma. She is the mother aspect of the Triple Goddess in Wales, the Goddess of beauty, and of the moon, fertility and reincarnation. Arianrhod is the Mother of Dylan and Llew Llau Gyffes by her brother Gwydion, her consort Nwyvre ("sky, space, and firmament") has survived only in name.

"Caer Arianrhod" are the circumpolar stars, to which souls withdraw between incarnations, she is consequently a Goddess of reincarnation and is honored at the full moon.

Daughter of the mother Goddess Don and her consort Beli, she was worshiped as priestess of the moon.

A star and moon Goddess, Arianrhod was also called the Silver Wheel because the dead were carried on her oar wheel to Emania (the moon-land or land of death), which belonged to her as a deity of reincarnation and karma. The moon is the archetypal female symbol, representing the mother Goddess connecting the womb, death, rebirth and creation. The Celts counted time not by days, but by nights, and made their calendars not by the sun, but by the moon.

In Celtic myth the Goddess has three major aspects: the maiden, the mother and the crone. These three represent the three stages in life of a woman. Blodeuwedd is the flower maiden, Arianrhod represents the mother and The Morrigu at last is the crone. These three aspects of the Celtic Goddess may have different names in different localities.

Arianrhod is said to be able to shapeshift into a large owl and, through owl-eyes, sees into the darkness of the human subconscious and soul. The owl symbolizes death and renewal, wisdom, moon magick, and initiations. She is said to move with strength and purpose through the night, her wings of comfort and healing spread to give solace to those who seek her.

Arianrhod is the daughter of the Welsh Goddess Don and the sister of Gwydion. Gwydion was counselor to King Math who could only remain alive if his feet lay in the lap of a virgin at all times except when he led his armies into battle. During one such battle the virgin who had held King Math's feet was raped, and so there was a need for a replacement. Gwydion recommended his sister, Arianrhod. King Math put her virginity to the test by asking her to step over his magic rod. As she stepped over the rod she gave birth to a boy with yellow hair. The child cried loudly, and Arianrhod, humiliated, ran for the door, dropping yet another small object on the ground in the process. Before anyone could catch a glance at the object, Gwydion wrapped it up and hid it inside a chest. King Math then performed rites for the yellow haired boy child, naming him Dylan. Dylan immediately ran into the sea and was swallowed up by the waves and was never seen again.

Later Gwydion presented Arianrhod with the object that he had hidden in the chest – a second child. Arianrhod was outraged at her humiliation at the hands of King Math and rejected the child.

She laid on him three curses:

He shall have no name except one she gives him.
He shall bear no arms except ones she gives him.
He shall have no wife of any race that is now on the earth.

Gwydion, outraged by these curses, worked to break them. He disguised himself and Llew as shoemakers and traveled to Caer Arianrhod. When Arianrhod went to have shoes fitted, the boy threw a stone at a bird and skillfully hit it. Arianrhod commented on the child's adept hand, and at that Gwydion exposed his true identity and that of the boy, and said that she had just named him Llew Llaw Gyffes, he of the Shining Skilful Hand. This made Arianrhod go into a fiery rage. She stormed back to Caer Arianrhod swearing that the boy would never bear arms or have a human wife.

Again Gwydion deceived Arianrhod into breaking her own curse. He disguised himself and Llew as travelers and sought sanctuary in Caer Arianrhod. While they were there Gwydion conjured an illusion showing a powerful armada of ships advancing on Caer Arianrhod. Getting ready for a battle Arianrhod unlocked her weapons store and armed her retainers. Gwydion suggested to Arianrhod that she give arms to him and Llew (still in disguise) and they would fight at the defense of the castle. She agreed and thereby, inadvertently, granted arms to her son, breaking the second curse. Gwydion and Llew then revealed themselves to Arianrhod and told her that she may as well take the arms back from her son, as there was no battle to be fought.

Enraged at being tricked a second time, Arianrhod took comfort in her third curse – that Llew would have no human wife. Gwydion, upset at the cruelty Arianrhod was showing her son, vowed to break this curse also. Gwydion went to King Math and explained Llew's predicament. Combining their magic, they created a woman made of flowers, Blodeuwedd, to be wife to Llew, and broke Arianrhod's third curse.

Humiliated by King Math, thwarted by her son, and forsaken by her brother, Arianrhod retreated to her castle Caer Arianrhod. She later drowned when the sea reclaimed the land.

Although Arianrhod is not a well known Goddess, followers of the Celtic tradition look upon her reverently. I feel that as the world changes we are being drawn to more spiritual pursuits and more people will find Arianrhod, or she will find them, being a moon Goddess she exudes the strength and pull of the moon.

Willow Mooncloud is an Eclectic Witch and Contributor to *Paganism 101.*

Arnemetia

"She changes everything she touches, and everything she touches changes" – as I was about to find out when leaving my homeland, the Highlands of Scotland, to move to the High Peak district in England more than ten years ago. When you hear the call of the Goddess, there is no choice but to leave behind all that you once knew and go. This certainly was the case for me when I journeyed to the Roman town of Aqua Arnemetiae, or Buxton, as it is known today. James, my partner at the time, suggested we move and invited me to choose the place I would most like to live in the United Kingdom. But I was more than happy in my beloved Scotland and couldn't say where else I would prefer. Then in that very moment I was "guided" to open a map, close my eyes and point to a place at random. I opened my eyes and I saw Solomon's Temple in Buxton, a place I was unfamiliar with. Nonetheless, that is where we headed.

The ancient land of Buxton is a sacred backdrop for the groves and Mesolithic monuments, circa 5300BC, that lay nearby, such as Arbor Low and the Bull Ring. Burial cairns and stone age circles, from Neolithic settlements of 3500BC-1800BC and the Iron Age castle sites of Naze and Mam Tor all give testament to it once being a flourishing center of considerable importance in addition to it becoming one of the great bathing centers of Britain, because of its thermal spring. So, unsurprisingly, this land was acquired by the Romans in 70AD and renamed Aquae Arnemetiae, meaning "the waters of the Goddess of the grove". The well was Christianized after the Roman exodus, like many pagan-seated sites and monuments, and is visited by thousands each year. The water is pure and warm, coming out of a tap where the spring waters are piped to a well, a stone feature right in the center of the town.

But, long before the Roman occupation the land, its Goddess

was revered and honored by the indigenous, agricultural tribe known as the Corieltauvi. This Brythonic Goddess appeared to me the day I arrived at my new home, Fern House. I was in such a hurry to explore, and hearing the ancient lands calling to me I walked to the woods from the back of the house and she appeared! I had never visited Buxton before, knew nothing of the history, and here was I facing a Goddess. So began an incredible personal experience of connection with this ancient Goddess of the old ways. She told me that I had been called to her lands to experience the remembering of the sacred Divine Feminine. Later that night she appeared to me in the dreamtime. The image is still clear, of a luminescent green figure, clothed in robes of green, leaves and twigs intertwined in her hair that dripped with water.

Then she spoke, "I am Arnemetia, Goddess of this ancient site. I have been forgotten by the people who once honored and revered this land. My sacred grove cut down, my springs, in which the people came to heal and drink my waters, now covered over. My name changed and dishonored, adulterated by religion. I have now retreated to the ancient site upon which my temple lies. Here I have waited in hope that someone would again honor my name; carry the memories forward so that I am not forgotten. Look, with your eyes and your heart, at the lands I once walked upon." With that I was given a vision of temples, springs and a sacred grove. I saw people coming to this place, drinking the holy waters, visiting the temples to heal. I watched a community with the members helping each other.

What I was seeing struck at a chord with me. I had a memory of once walking upon the land in that time. Now I understood why I had been brought to this town. Arnemetia then spoke, "Discover the hidden truth. Let my name be spoken in this town. Tell people of the true origins of the water, of the sacred temples that were once worshipped in, of the sacred land, and the truth of why I was forgotten."

Then these words for a song were given to me:

In a lost chamber of the world, a serpent flower she unfurls.
A woman rises up divine, revealing herself to the edge of time.
Edge of time, woman divine.
Edge of time, woman divine.
Reawakening the Goddess, reawakening in you.
Reawakening the Goddess, reawakening her in you and me and all
* we see.*
A marble temple, a turquoise lake, a new moon shines on an ancient
* snake.*
The earth's aligning the sun and the seas.
Reawakening setting free.
It's destiny you and me, the sun and the sea.
Setting free.

My life changed. I had been touched by the Goddess. I was living on her sacred lands and nurtured by the water beneath me. I looked for information about this Goddess. Her sacred grove had indeed been cut down, replaced by buildings. The natural springs were covered by Roman baths and her name changed from Arnemetia to St Anne. St Anne's Well was put in place during the Medieval times and became a shrine. In 1583 King Henry VIII destroyed the chapel as part of the dissolution of the monasteries, and the shrine was ravaged. However, people were still able to access the natural spring and many visitors came to "take of the waters" for medicinal purposes. This included Mary Queen of Scots, who suffered from acute rheumatism. The geothermal spring water is still much sought after today and has become part of the ever growing bottled water industry, and sold worldwide.

Through Arnemetia's teachings I have come to know her. She calls to those with innate wisdom and knowledge and invites you to experience a deep connection with this very real deity. If you hear her calling then come walk on the lands and drink of her water from the well. The next time you sup a bottle of water with the name Buxton Water on it, know that Arnemetia's spirit flows through it, the blood of the ancestors, nurturing you, healing you. Take the opportunity to connect with her, as she becomes part of you, and listen to her, as I did. I was guided to open a Pagan shop in a building that sits on Roman foundations. The road leads directly to the market place, where the temples once stood to celebrate and acknowledge Pagan traditions. And, naturally, I named the shop Arnemetia's.

Barbara Meiklejohn-Free is the author of *The Heart of All Knowing* and *The Shaman Within*.

Artemis

Artemis, the chaste lunar Goddess of the wild hunt, lady of the beasts who has seen more than 3,000 years of worship, both ancient and modern. The ancient Greek poet Homer referred to Artemis as, "Artemis Agotera, Potnia Therion – Artemis, mistress of the wild land and animals." Etymologically speaking, Artemis is a derivative of arktos or "bear" and had ties to the bear cult in Attica.

Artemis's birth story starts with her parents: Zeus, the father of all gods, and Leto, Titaness of motherhood. While Leto was pregnant with the twins Apollo and Artemis, she was also hunted by Zeus's wife Hera. Leto eventually received help from Mother Gaia who helped hide her on the island Delos.

Jealous and unable to get to Leto, Hera kept Ilithyia, the midwife, from visiting Leto while in labor. Artemis was birthed first before her brother Apollo, and even gave her mother midwife assistance while Apollo's birth progressed. This earned her the title Locheia, or helper in childbirth.

When Artemis was three years of age it is said that she crawled upon Zeus's lap with six requests for him. Her first wish was to always remain a virgin. Of course it is debated what exactly the word "virgin" meant in pre-Christian times and some sources claim it meant to not be owned by marriage. Her second wish was for her to have many names to separate her from her brother Apollo. For her third wish she wished to always have a bow, arrows, and a short knee-length tunic so that she may hunt. Her fourth wish was to be a lightbringer, because while she is a lunar Goddess she isn't always associated with the night. Her fifth wish was to have 60 "daughters of Okeanos", all nine years of age, to serve as her choir. Her sixth wish was to have 20 amnisides nymphs as handmaidens to watch her dogs and bow as she rested. Even as a small child, Artemis's independent nature was already apparent, thus making her a favorite Goddess amongst feminists.

Artemis was not known to have a consort. However, she did have a best friend in Orion. According to Robert Graves, the story of Artemis and Orion is a tragic one. Artemis and Orion spent days hunting from mountain top to mountain top, laughing and carrying on. One evening they lay about the fire after a particularly hard hunt, laughing and conversing about how much they both meant to each other, and what great friends they were. They ended up snuggling together and falling asleep. The next morning Apollo caught them still sleeping so snugly and worried for his sister's virginity. With a loud whistle Apollo woke them both. Artemis left Orion behind with Apollo to go to tend to her priestesses.

Apollo, who is a sun God, is very beautiful and known for his bisexuality and many lovers. He seduced Orion with his beauty and after their day took its course and both men were satisfied with one another, they lay sunbathing. Orion brought up the subject of Apollo's sister. Apollo became violently angry, questioning Orion about his sister's virginity, but Orion reassured him that Artemis was still a chaste Goddess and that no man had touched her. Apollo was easily insulted and set about plotting Orion's destruction with a large scorpion, in the end tricking Artemis herself into shooting Orion in the head with her bow. In her grief she made Orion a constellation along with Scorpio.

In Asia Minor, near the modern day city of Selcuk, Turkey, there once stood the Temple of Artemis of Ephesus. Artemis of Ephesus was a bit different to Artemis of the mainland. The original people of Ephesus equated Artemis with their own Goddess, Ephesia. It is also said that the matrifocal and matrilineal Anatolian Amazons who worshiped Cybele, built a temple there. In a politically charged move, Alexander of Macedon refurbished the temple to Artemis. Historians generally place the

Temple of Artemis of Ephesus as first being built around 800 BCE and then being destroyed and rebuilt many times, each time becoming more majestic. Antipater of Sidon, who compiled the list of the seven ancient wonders of the world, said upon seeing the temple, "Lo, Apart from Olympus the sun never looked on aught so grand". According to some historians the temple measured 415 feet by 225 feet, with 127 marble columns, each with a 60-foot diameter. The City of Ephesus, along with the temple of Artemis, continued to prosper for hundreds of years until 57 AD when St. Paul came to Ephesus looking for new converts to Christianity. In 391 AD the temple was closed as the city and spirituality started to wane. Emperor Theodosius made Christianity the state religion and the temple was eventually destroyed by mobs. Ephesus never again became the crossroads of trading and prosperity it once was.

Contemporary worship of Artemis by Hellenic Pagans and reconstructionist Pagans owes a lot to one woman by the name of Thista Minai, who founded the temple of Artemis at Cataleos in 2005, in Cambridge, Massachusetts, USA. The temple does share a few cosmetic similarities with Wiccan-related Pagan practices. Temple attendance to the six festivals can range from three to 40 people, all gathering to honor the Goddess of the wilderness. Like most Neopagan temples, children under the age of 18 are not allowed without a guardian. Miss Minai also has many published works focusing on the Goddess Artemis for those of us who live too far away to participate in her temple. *Dancing in Moonlight: Understanding Artemis Through Celebration* is filled with rituals, celebrations, and devotions for those seeking to worship Artemis. Despite being 3,000 years old, Artemis is still a living and fiercely independent Goddess. Women love her, patriarchy misunderstands and fears her.

Amber Tuma is a witch living on a farm in the heart of Texas. More of her writing adventures can be found at WovenMagick.com.

Astarte

First mentioned in ancient Phoenicia and dating back to the Neolithic and Bronze ages, Astarte is one of the oldest Middle Eastern aspects of The Great Goddess.

As a Goddess of the planet Venus, two of her aspects are that of the Goddess of War and the Goddess of Love. As Venus the Morning Star, Astarte is a Goddess of War and Hunting; and as the Evening Star, she is the Goddess of Love, Sex, Fertility, and Vitality, being depicted as a nude woman. In her Warrior aspect, she championed Ba'al, her consort and brother, by vanquishing his enemies and walking in their blood.

Astarte was the most important goddess of the Pagan Semites. She was the Goddess of Love, Fertility, and Maternity for the Phoenicians, Canaanites, Aramaeans, South Arabs, and even the Egyptians. Her name was Ishtar in Babylonia and Assyria, where she was also the Goddess of War. Some Old Testament stories call her Ashtoreth, and describe the construction of her altar by King Solomon and its destruction by King Josiah. Astarte was identified with the planet Venus. The Greeks called her Aphrodite, and the Romans knew her as Venus. [*World Book*, Vol. 1, p. 782.]

Prophets of the Old Testament condemned worship of her because it included sexual rituals, and sacrifices to her of firstborn children and newborn animals. She is called "an abomination" in the Old Testament.

King Solomon, famous for his great wisdom, was said to have had 700 wives, many of whom were from neighboring Pagan tribes. To accommodate their religions, he built temples to their Gods for them, including a sanctuary to Astarte in Jerusalem.

"For Solomon went after Ashtoreth, the Goddess of the Sidonians..." [1 Kings 11:5] and built a temple for her. "And so he did for all his foreign wives, who burned incense and sacrificed to their gods." [1 Kings 11:8] Bread, liquors and perfumes were typical temple offerings for her. She was the primary deity of the cities of Sor (Tyre), Zidon (Sidon), and Gubla (Byblos).

Astarte also had temples in Ascalon in Philistia, about 40 miles southwest of Jerusalem; and Beth-shean (Scythopolis) near the Sea of Galilee. Hebrew temples to Yahweh and Astarte were actually erected side by side at Mizpah. Her image is found on ancient coins from Sidon.

She is the western Semitic equivalent of the eastern Semitic Inanna of the Sumerians and Ishtar of the Babylonians; the Greeks identified her with their Aphrodite, who may have had her origins in Astarte as she was believed to have come from the east. Some scholars contend Astarte was a prototype of the Virgin Mary, their theory being based on the ancient Syrian and Egyptian rituals of celebrating Astarte's rebirth of the solar God on 25th December.

The Scripps Howard News Service states in its 2008 article, *Christmas Celebration Crosses All Faiths*:

Yule is the Chaldean name for "infant" or "little child." In ancient Babylon, the 25th of December was known as Yule day or the birth of the promised child day. This was the day of the birth of the incarnate sun who appeared as a baby child to redeem a world bound in darkness. It was an essential belief of the Babylonian religious system that the sun god, also known as Ba'al, was the chief god in a polytheistic system. Tammuz was also worshipped as the god incarnate, or promised baby son of Ba'al, who was to be the savior of the world.

Sir James Frazer in the *Golden Bough* writes:

No doubt the Virgin who thus conceived and bore a son on the twenty-fifth of December was the great Oriental Goddess whom the Semites called the Heavenly Virgin or simply the Heavenly Goddess, in Semitic lands she was a form of Astarte.

Donald Harden in *The Phoenicians* discusses a statuette of Astarte from Tutugi (Galera) near Granada in Spain dating to the 7th or 6th century BC in which Astarte sits on a throne flanked by sphinxes holding a bowl beneath her pierced breasts. A hollow in the statue would have been filled with milk through the head. The Queen of Heaven is honored on 7th October, the Sumerian New Year, and at the Day of Willows, a Mesopotamian festival on 22nd October.

She is cited in The Charge of the Goddess by Charles Godfrey Leland in *Aradia: Gospel of the Witches* [1899], and is one of the seven Goddesses in the popular energy-raising Goddess chant: "Isis, Astarte, Diana, Hecate, Demeter, Kali, Inanna".

As a virgin-mother warrior, Astarte is a powerful Goddess from whom wisdom, inner strength and courage can be drawn. She teaches us to love and to mother ourselves, quelling the doubt that can cripple us from accessing the creative and spiritual potential waiting to be tapped deep within us. The Great Goddess shows us that with the determination of the bull and the peace of mind and focus afforded by the dove, we can manifest productivity and prosperity.

Sherrie Almes is a priestess, Tradition of the Witches Circle, Virginia USA.

Athena

Greek Goddess, daughter of Zeus born fully grown and in full armor ready for battle. She is a virgin Goddess. There are many different versions of Athena's birth and her conception. Often it is read that Athena did not have a mother but that Zeus laid with Metis, the Goddess of crafty thought and wisdom, and it had been prophesied that Metis would have many children and that they would indeed be more powerful than the sire including Zeus himself. Zeus simply could not accept this so he swallowed Metis whole, but it was too late, Metis had already conceived.

One day Zeus experienced a terrible headache, he got Herpnase to split his head open to ease the pain and with that emerged Athena fully grown and in full armor. It is said the skies darkened, the sea got angry and the waves rose... Athena had arrived.

Athena is a warrior Goddess, a wise woman, and is normally depicted with a shield, a sword and a breastplate. She rides a chariot; she is a protective Goddess and inspires women to empower their inner strength and courage. She is fierce and brave in battle. The animal associated with Athena is an owl, probably due to her wisdom aspect.

Athena, although a battle Goddess, used initiative and wisdom to beat her opponents instead of using violence and anger. She did not like fighting without purpose. Athena is a Goddess that gets things done; nothing is too big for Athena to take on. As well as being a warrior Goddess, Athena was also involved in crafts. She invented the horse's bit, so horses could be tamed, and is a protective guardian of horses – often depicted in a chariot pulled by them.

The olive tree is another symbol related to Athena. She competed with Poseidon to become the patron of Athens, which before that time was unnamed. It is said that Poseidon, God of the Sea, struck the earth with a trident and a spring emerged, giving water and means of trade. However, the water was salty and unfit for drinking. Athena gave the gift of the olive tree as it provided wood, oil and food. King Cecrops accepted the tree and gave Athena the patronage. The Athenians founded the Parthenon, which they dedicated to Athena.

Athena would stand up for and fight for what she believed in, but she would not hold back if someone crossed her path. She protected her chastity fiercely and woe betide anyone who questioned or challenged it. She was a proud Virgin Goddess. One of the stories is that one day Athena went to see Hephaestus for some armor. He became amorous with Athena and tried to violate her, but she protected herself so fiercely that Hephaestus could not have what he wanted. Instead, he scattered his seed onto the earth which shortly gave birth to a son called Erichthonius. The child was found by Athena who brought him up. He grew to maturity and became King of Athens, where he established the solemn cult of Athena.

As mentioned before, Athena, although a battle Goddess, used initiative and wisdom to beat her opponents instead of using violence and anger. She is a very protective Goddess and can be called upon in many situations, she will fight your corner but at the same time bring a gentleness along too.

Athena is a Goddess to call upon if you find yourself being treated unfairly, especially in the workplace. If you feel that your work is not appreciated or that you do not get the recognition you deserve, call upon Athena to help you stand up for yourself and she can support you. She will offer a gentle hand, but will not necessarily accept this situation without upsetting everyone. Athena can also be called upon if you work with animals, especially horses. If you have ever experienced a horse being difficult to handle or settle, then call upon Athena. She was a very skilled horsewoman. She always made sure the horses' needs were looked after first and foremost; she will help you become a better handler or be more understanding of that horse's nature.

As well as her warrior aspect and skill with horses, Athena also is a Goddess of arts and crafts. She can be called upon if you experience artist's block or need inspiration for a piece to paint, create, and make. She can inspire you to think outside the box. Remember that you are a unique individual and what you do will be different from the work of others, but that is never a bad thing. If we all created the same things, it would be pretty dull.

Athena is often depicted with an owl that accompanies her. Many people believe it's due to the wisdom aspect attributed to her. Other attributes of Athena are wisdom, courage, justice, inspiration, strength, arts, strategy, and studies.

A small prayer to invoke Athena could be:

Athena Goddess of purity, fight and will, please come to my aid. I need your help with [insert here what it is you would like her assistance with]. *I thank you from the bottom of my heart for helping me and I know your strength will help me along my chosen path. Thank you and blessings.*

You can of course you can make up your own prayer to Athena, whatever feels right to you. The words above are just guidance. Most of the Goddesses know before you actually realize that their assistance is required. You may often see symbols related to them, they are purely letting you know that their presence is with you and they are ready to help.

I would like to add that all the above is what Athena is to me and what I believe, but I understand that there may be some of you who disagree with my point of view. The important thing to remember is to always follow your own truth, my words are merely a guide.

Debbie Antara is a solitary witch who lives in Norfolk with her black cat Ostara.

Baba Yaga

She is old, really old. She is definitely not beautiful. Conventional beauty slipped away from her long ago. Usually depicted as gnarled and ghastly, she is the quintessential wicked, old witch. Baba Yaga, the Slavic old woman who hides in the woods and eats children who cross her path, was used in Russian fairytales to frighten children into submissive behavior; to obey or face awful consequences. These descriptions of Baba Yaga are still used in modern translations, but she has a longer history, one that is difficult to document other than her physical features.

Along with her archetypal ugly features of a large body, ungainly nose and chin, missing teeth, and crooked fingers, Baba Yaga is also frightening because of her trappings. She travels in a mortar and pushes herself along with the pestle; she sweeps away her tracks with a broom. Her house stands on chicken legs and rotates magically for a variety of purposes, depending on the needs of the story. She commands inanimate objects and animals to do her awful bidding.

Can this monster be seen as anything other than the horrible and stereotypical witch she is made out to be? While her Slavic name means "grandmother", she is not grandmotherly. Instead, when she is compared to other frightful deities, her features and aspects are reminiscent of the Hindu Goddess, Kali. However, she seems even more frightening, more primal, more raw. She is dressed in rags, uses her unusually large nose to smell her prey and orders her toads and enchanted house to trap her prey. The many stories where she surfaces as the main antagonist or merely a side-step in the plot, were passed down through oral traditions and connect possibly to death rituals that have died away, leaving metaphors that are complex and often dual in nature.

That duality is what confuses seekers of this Goddess; sometimes she grants favors; other times she exacts punishment.

Underneath her raw exterior she is a wild woman, a guardian of the deepest of secrets with a keen understanding of death, the darkest of mysteries. However, as a dark Goddess, she helps us to remove the niceties of life, especially when they burden us and keep us from understanding our own shadow.

There are some examinations of Baba Yaga as Goddess found in descriptions throughout the internet that give rise to a 21st century viewpoint of the Goddess, sometimes redefining what the Goddess means rather than just relying on the ancient descriptions. Most of these look at her through the Crone aspect, but definitely the darker aspect of Goddess; her dual powers are her ability to grant wishes when a seeker does something for her in return, and to punish when those tasks are not done to her satisfaction. When she does grant wishes, she does so begrudgingly.

Even with this dark Crone aspect, there are very few actual workings that mention Baba Yaga, save for those dealing with death and transition. One written work named *Goddess Meditations* by Barbara Ardinger gives a guided meditation that allows the Seeker to see her in a frightful, yet inquiringly manner as she asks stern questions that must be answered in order to progress to the next level of our own understanding.

This and other re-imaginings of her as the Crone Goddess are common in modern interpretations and her physical features place her typically in the category of Crone. There are also instances where Baba Yaga is also the mother, if you look beneath the many layers. She is the Goddess of contradictions and, as such, also embodies the side of Goddess qualities that are often associated with mother. We are so accustomed to the mother Goddess being depicted as beautiful and benevolent that we forget the other side of mothering, the harsh realities of life that she teaches us.

Author and researcher Andreas Johns examines the mother aspect of Baba Yaga, particularly in terms of the ambiguous mother. She is the contradiction in her stories and the stories where she emerges, demonstrating this alternative view of motherhood. Johns states that Baba Yaga "represents a reversal or inversion of the cultural expectations of motherhood." [*Baba Yaga: The Ambiguous Mother and Witch of the Russian Folktale*, p. 268.] In addition, she draws from a longer history, one that refers back to the old fertility rituals where death brings new life and seekers must wander in the dark forests in order to emerge once again with a new life and a new purpose.

Baba Yaga is not like the other mothers and Crones that populate pantheons. This is a mother who punishes when her seeker is lazy or unethical. Certainly a mother would not eat her children if they misbehave, but there are many children who know they will be figuratively chewed up and spat out if they cross the boundaries of good behavior. Baba Yaga is not for the faint of heart; she is the mother that you fear if you lie to her and she discovers the truth. However, she is the mother that will keep you on your toes, if you are brave enough to seek her out.

Like other Dark Goddesses, Baba Yaga is the embodiment of death, but she also is bringer of knowledge to those who have the ability to find it. She lives in the forest, deep within, in a place that is difficult to find. In her presence, a potential victim or a seeker is never forced to their fate, but must choose their own destiny. If the seeker is strong, intelligent, and often witty, he or she can overcome the barriers and escape death.

She is, therefore, empowerment with no need of conventional beauty. This is a newer concept. We are so accustomed to our maiden and mother Goddesses possessing conventional beauty and long flowing dresses, that we forget that there are other sides to women and their archetypes. Baba Yaga gives us the ability and the permission to see past the surface beauty and dive into the rawness of our souls.

Margo Wolfe is an educator, Pagan, and member of the Sisterhood of Avalon. She co-ordinates many local events for adults and teenagers, including a Teen CUUPS (Covenant of Unitarian Universalist Pagans) group in PA, working with many amazing young people. Her forthcoming book is entitled, *Turning the Wheel and Mentoring our Pagan Youth: A Curriculum Guide for Instructors of Pagan Teens.*

Badb

Conflict scares us; we naturally shy away from it in our day-to-day lives unless we are assured of victory. It takes a special kind of bravery to step into a situation that we have no guarantee of coming away victorious from. I'm not just talking about fights or walking through a rough neighborhood, but that discussion with your boss; arguing with the shop assistant; pointing out when your loved one is *definitely* wrong this time; telling a friend when they have made a mistake. These are all aspects of our humanity that stem from the way we communicate with each other and the society we have created. Our wars are small and often never occur at all, because we do all we can to live the quiet life; to get on with what we need to do and stay as far away from trouble as we can.

Sometimes, you know you can't stay out of trouble though. Sometimes you have to reach for that promotion, which may look like you are stepping on someone else's toes. Sometimes you have to make that complaint that will have you arguing on the phone for hours. And sometimes, just sometimes, you may have to put yourself in physical danger to aid another. We don't like it, but it does happen.

So, what's the relevance of all this? Well, I tell you these things to give a little background into the times when Badb comes into her own. Badb is a Celtic Goddess, a creature from the time of the Tuatha Dé Danann. Seathrún Céitinn (Geoffrey Keating, 17th century priest and historian) believed she was also Ériu, the Goddess Ireland is named for. She is alternatively a war Goddess in her own right, and one of a trinity along with Macha and Nemain, who make up the Morrígan when Morrígan is seen as a triple Goddess. She is also *sister* to Macha and Morrígan, each holding their own power across the battlefields of the Celts. War is the garden of Badb, each conflict the seed and blood the fertilizer. But she revels not in the death and destruction. Instead, she mocks humanity for its foolishness by working with her sisters to cause confusion and mayhem; sometimes increasing the death toll as she points out the ridiculous futility of bloodshed in the name of an unjust cause. Badb Catha, the battle crow, would be seen crying out a harsh song before the battle commenced. This was seen to be a prophecy of which way the battle would go, and indeed, Badb would move the confusion into the side of fighting she deemed least worthy, to save lives on the side she believed was right.

Of course, in any conflict, the side deemed "right" is decided mainly by the victor, but in your own personal conflict, you, and you alone, decide what is the right and justified cause and course of action. What makes you correct, in your situation? What gives you the right to come away from your tiny battle victorious? If you can justify this to yourself and be in no doubt whatsoever about your actions, then you may indeed be in a position to call upon the Badb Catha to fly alongside you. For she will only bring courage to those who truly believe they need it.

This courage and connection can be found through meditation and a connection to nature. Walk until you find a crow's feather (or rook, jackdaw or raven; rook is for more family based concerns; jackdaw for material concerns, the raven for internal or intellectual problems and the crow for magic or the divine) and when you find it, keep it safe and remember where you found it. Take a note of your surroundings; the smells, sounds and sights. This is the moment you have been given a gift, an opportunity to maybe connect with Badb, the Badb Catha, the ultimate corvid and embodiment of all battles. Use this feather in your next meditation. Focus on it, feel it, try to take it with you into your meditative mental space. Write down all that occurs, and any dreams that may come after. Badb, like the Morrígan, is strongly associated with prophecy, and you may be gifted with the odd glance of the future if you walk this path with her.

The deepest conflict we can have is, unfortunately, within ourselves. Indecision, insecurity and doubt are the enemy soldiers in our internal wars, and though we have love, pride and confidence as the generals of our armies, every good general needs an adviser or, if we hark back to Celtic times, a seer. Badb allows us to focus our intent internally, to turn back the tide of battle with the beat of a bloody wing. And bloody it shall be, as there is nothing so painful as true introspection. Badb, like the Morrígan and her ilk, forces you to really see those darker aspects of yourself, face them head on, and either embrace or discard them accordingly. This process is never, ever, easy, and I would caution anyone attempting such a journey of self-discovery to take advice from another who has been down this path, or at least have a confidant to share the experience with. Badb is associated with madness and the cackling crone; no wonder, when the scariest aspects of the universe reside within our souls and she forces our psychic heads around, like the crow, to stare inward, eyes unblinking, and drink in the true horror of war.

Mabh Savage is the author of *A Modern Celt* exploring the relevance of Celtic culture in modern Paganism and spirituality. A witch following Celtic tradition, she has a close relationship with Badb, The Morrígan and her kin. She is also a member of The Covenant of Hekate and writes regularly for their e-zine, Askei Kataskei. She also keeps a blog covering Paganism, politics and the turn of the seasons. A singer and musician too, she gigs and does spoken word at venues across the UK.

Bast

With her head of felis catus and her decidedly elegant feline form, Bast is one of the most recognizable deities of the Egyptian pantheon. Her mother is thought to be the Goddess Isis, High Priestess and Queen of Magic, Mysteries, and the Moon. Prior to Bast's deification, the cat was a sacred animal to Isis. Her father is the Sun God, Ra. Bast is one of the few Goddesses known collectively as the "Eyes of Ra." These sister-Goddesses act as guardians, steadfastly protecting their ageing father. The consort of Bast is Ptah, the great Creator God of the Earth, the Underworld, and Craftsmen. Her children are Nefertum, God of Perfume, and Mihos, the lion-headed God of Vengeance.

The Cult of Bast flourished throughout ancient Egypt for more than two thousand years. The great temple was located in Bubastis, which was named for the Goddess. Very little regarding the rituals that took place in the temple survived the never-ending march of time but Her annual festival was quite a spectacle. To begin with, in April or May, devotees would board boats that floated to each riverside community. Playing musical instruments and shouting jokes of an explicit nature to draw the attention of those on shore, the women would disrobe and throw their garments to the gathering crowds or they would simply lift their skirts. Then the entire party would make its way to the temple to enjoy food, wine, music, dancing, ecstatic trysts, and to place offerings to Bast.

She was honored and revered in many Egyptian homes, as is evident in the discovery of feline bas relief and statuary found in the ruins of ancient homes. Most families had their own house cat who was viewed as the living embodiment of the Goddess. Harming or killing this sacred animal of Bast was punishable by death as it was considered an affront to the Goddess. Bast's name has been translated as both "perfume" and "Devouring

Lady/Devourer." This seeming contradiction is due to the Greeks emphasizing the ending sound so that Bast was pronounced Bast-et instead. Eventually, they also identified and blended Bast with their Goddess Artemis.

A lack of archaeological and historical evidence coupled with the ancient practice of deity-combining as nations were conquered and thrown into awkward alliances makes it quite difficult to know with any certainty how Bast was truly worshipped.

There has been renewed interest in Egyptian, or Kemetic, spirituality ever since archaeologists first started digging around in the Nile River Valley. Modern devotees tend to come to worship Bast through a sincere adoration of cats. The first thing evident about her is her association with those furry beasts, after all.

Bast was often portrayed with a litter of kittens. In this true feline queen form she portrays a strong and patient mother aspect, ever watchful and protective of her litter, all cats, and their devoted caregivers. As a mother herself, Bast can easily understand the inherent complaints of motherhood. Mothers can call on her for assistance and protection during all phases of motherhood, from pregnancy to child-rearing. Children can also call upon her for assistance and protection. Bast is a fierce and loyal guardian. Women experiencing domestic violence, mothers, children, "certified cat ladies" and loyal feline caretakers can petition Bast for her protection.

Bast is often associated with fertility and sensuality. Couples trying to conceive and women in need of confidence in their sexuality will benefit from Bast's ability to help us embrace and exhibit our sensual, and downright sexy, sides. Although modern-day devotees of Bast will see that she has both lunar and solar qualities, people tend to associate her mostly with the moon. People only marginally familiar with cats recognize that felines have an obvious connection with the sun. When a cat lies outstretched in sunlight it can be difficult to know if the cat worships the sun or if the sun worships the cat! It makes sense that the grandchildren of the Sun God would adore him as much as his daughter does. Bast's lunar aspect is reflected in the cat's nocturnal activities. Middle of the night yowling, playfulness, and journeying show a fondness for the night one can be envious of. Cats commune with the moon. In all honesty, the shortest road to worshipping Bast is through cat husbandry. Those who treat her children well, as the furry deities they are, are most likely to enjoy her beneficial qualities. Sure, cats are sacred to a number of Goddesses, but Bast is the only one to be a cat. Mistreating a cat is the surest way to earn her wrath or, worse yet – and most cat-like – her disregard.

It is unfortunate that time has erased most of the ritual practices associated with the cat Goddess Bast. Her modern-day followers can happily incorporate whatever practices they believe will please Her and know that she is accessible today regardless of what happened in the past.

A.C. Kulcsar has been a practicing solitary witch for more than 20 years and a cat lover her entire life. She currently works with Bast while caring for her children, a grumpy old house cat named The Pauper, and a colony of feral and stray cats.

Branwen

Branwen, whose name means "White Raven", is featured in the eponymous tale Branwen, Daughter of Llyr, the Second Branch of the Welsh mythic cycle *The Mabinogi*. Although Branwen is not directly referred to as a deity in the narrative, scholars believe that most of the major characters who appear in this medieval collection of tales are likely of divine origin. The ancient stories which form the Four Branches of *The Mabinogi* were gathered from oral tradition and written down between the 11th and 12th centuries CE, possibly by clerics or lay scholars interested in preserving Welsh culture in the face of the Anglo-Norman conquest.

As these myths were set in writing in a cultural and temporal context different from their origins in Pagan Celtic Britain, the redactors of these tales may well have been confronted with details from the oral tradition which appeared strange or foreign to them, especially when it came to the rights and privileges of women in pre-Christian Britain. Further, it is natural to expect that with the oral transmission of stories, characters would evolve over time especially as worldviews and cultural mores changed. Thus, Goddesses would be reduced in stature to powerful queens, nature spirits turned into fairy women, priestesses transformed into witches, and sexual initiators rendered as faithless harlots. It is necessary, therefore, to read between the lines when approaching the stories of *The Mabinogi* from a Pagan perspective, in order to peel away the medieval Christian filters which overlay the tales so that the ancient British divinities which lie beneath the surface can be revealed.

With this in mind, Branwen emerges from the narrative of the Second Branch as a Goddess of Sovereignty. She is the sister of Bran Bendigeidfran (Bran the Blessed), who is the king of Britain, and she is called one of Three Chief Maidens of the Isle of the

Mighty. When Branwen consents to wed Matholwch, the king of Ireland who comes to Bran's court seeking her hand, she enters into a sacred marriage to confer sovereignty onto the Irish king, while also taking on the role of the Peace Weaver – one who lays down her body to serve as a bridge that unites two nations. During the wedding feast, Branwen's half-brother Efnysien mutilates the horses of the Irish contingent, angry because he hadn't been consulted about the marriage. This was an enormous insult to Matholwch as the horse is a symbol of sovereignty in Celtic tradition. As part of the compensation for Efnysien's actions, Bran gifts Matholwch with the Cauldron of Regeneration, a magical vessel which could bring back to life any dead warrior placed within it.

Appeased, Matholwch returns to Ireland with Branwen at his side as queen. During the first year of their marriage, Branwen was much beloved by the people of Ireland, and she bore Matholwch an heir. However, in the second year, the insult Matholwch suffered at the hands of Efnysien resurfaces in the minds of the Irish, and Matholwch puts Branwen aside, banishing her to work in the kitchen where she is beaten daily by a butcher. While accepting her unjust punishment with grace, Branwen nevertheless teaches a starling to speak, and after three years sends it with a message to Bran, apprising him of the dishonor she is suffering. When Bran invades Ireland to rescue her, Branwen correctly interprets for Matholwch the vision of the scout who describes the coming of Bran and his armies to Ireland, and it is she who brokers the peace between Britain and Ireland by suggesting that Gwern, her young son, be made king – a proposal accepted by both sides of the conflict in the interest of peace.

Yet in the end, Branwen's story is a tragic one, and Efnysien strikes once more, throwing Gwern into the fire and fanning the flames of war between the two kingdoms once again. It is a destructive battle, and ultimately leads to the shattering of the

Cauldron of Regeneration, the devastation of the Irish population, and only seven of Bran's retinue survive to return to Britain. Bran has been mortally wounded, and Branwen herself dies of a broken heart because of all of the destruction that has occurred in her name. She is buried in a four-sided grave on the banks of the river Alaw on the island of Anglesey, which lies between Ireland and the Welsh mainland. Her bond to Ireland broken, the Lady of Sovereignty returns to the very ground of Britain, from which she draws her power.

Near the river Alaw there is a Bronze Age round barrow called Bedd Branwen – Branwen's Grave. Although it is from an earlier time period, the central stone of the cromlech is split in half, evoking Branwen's broken heart. The possibility that the site is associated with Branwen could perhaps serve as another clue that she was a sovereignty or land divinity in pre-Christian times. Further, her connection to the Cauldron of Regeneration and the raven – a messenger bird associated with death and battle – may indicate that she held a more chthonic function as well.

Branwen's status as a Goddess has been renewed in modern Pagan practice, where she is honored by those whose spiritual paths are inspired by Celtic British or Brythonic traditions. Since her legend was not written down by those who worshiped her as a Goddess, we do not have a traditional depiction of Branwen as a fully-realized deity. Instead, the rawness of her story makes Branwen an emotionally accessible Goddess; because she has experienced suffering, she is an overflowing vessel of compassion for those who have been unjustly punished, have lived through domestic violence, and who have endured enormous loss. Branwen's story teaches us that we have the power to remain sovereign within ourselves no matter what may be going on around us, and by learning to ask for the help that we need, the Universe will answer our call. Rather than a tale of a tragic woman abandoned to the cruelties of fate, Branwen's myth teaches that the path to divinity can be found when we seek harmony between the shadow and sovereign aspects of the self. When we learn to bridge what is with what we desire – even if a part of us must die – we find the path which leads us back to Source.

Jhenah Telyndru is the founder of the Sisterhood of Avalon, Academic Dean of the Avalonian Thealogical Seminary, and author of the book *Avalon Within: A Sacred Journey of Myth, Mystery, and Inner Wisdom*. She is a graduate student in Celtic Studies at the University of Wales, Trinity St. David and welcomes your contact at www.ynysafallon.com.

Brigid

Brigid. Bridgit. Brigantia. Bride. Breo Saighead. Exalted One. Shining Arrow. Goddess. Saint. Midwife to the Virgin Mary. Foster Mother to Jesus Christ. These are just some of the many names for one of the most enduring and well-loved Goddesses of the Emerald Isle. The story of the Celtic Goddess Brigid has been woven among many others throughout the changing culture of the British Isles and beyond, creating a unique tapestry that has expanded over time. From legends of her birth and her impact as Goddess, to her canonization as Saint Brigid and her current influence within the Pagan community, the stories of Brigid are firmly embedded within the culture of the British people.

As Goddess, Brigid is the daughter of the Good God Dagda, known as the Red Man of all Knowledge and the leader of the Tuatha de Danann, the ancient race of earthly Gods that once inhabited Ireland. Brigid was born at sunrise, flames of knowledge, inspiration and healing bursting from her head to connect earth and heaven. This image of her as a Fire or Sun deity remains visible today in many artistic interpretations of her, both as Goddess and Saint. She is also associated with healing waters, and many rivers, springs and sacred wells across the British Isles are named after her. As a triple Goddess, Brigid is a single deity comprising three sisters distinct and separate in aspects and qualities. One sister is the Goddess of Healing, Midwifery and Husbandry; the second a Goddess of Fire, Protection and Smithcraft; the third a Goddess of Inspiration, Prophecy and Poetry. Together, they create the Goddess Brigid as one whole form, a patroness of many skills.

In legends it is told that Brigid bore three sons with her consort Tuireann, called Brian, Iuchar and Iucharba. As a child of Danu, the Mother Goddess of the Tuatha de Danann, she also married King Bres the Beautiful, ruler of the Fomorians, in an effort to unite the two warring factions. With Bres she bore one son, Ruadan, although some myths claim that Brian and Ruadan are the same child, her eldest son. Ruadan's death upon the battlefield led Brigid to such extreme grief that her song of sadness became the first form of keening heard across Ireland. Another myth states her sons by Tuireann killed Cian, father of the Celtic God Lugh. Although skilled in warfare herself and a patroness of the forge fires, Brigid does not often wield weapons of war. Instead, she seeks to heal those who suffer by granting what is needed in order to learn, grow and pass on such wisdom to others. This form of healing manifests upon many levels, not just physical. In those who suffer from pain or pride, grief or greed, disease or despair, ailment or anger, Brigid works tirelessly to show the power of healing oneself and others. Brigid is also the Goddess of Hearth and Home, and she inspires the productivity of a happy, healthy household. From weaving her mantle by the family fire, to tending the animals and blessing each meal, Brigid evokes the sacred divine within every humble home.

The Celtic peoples' love for Brigid was so great that during the time of the conversion to Christianity she could not be eradicated, and was incorporated into the new Christian faith as Midwife to the Virgin Mary, Foster Mother to Christ and eventually as a Saint. Although based upon the physical life of Saint Brighid of Kildare (c451 to 523CE) who was baptized by St. Patrick and consecrated by Bishop Mel of Ardagh with a Bishop's Ordination, the story of the birth and life of St. Brighid resembles that of the Goddess. In many instances the stories are so intertwined that they are almost indistinguishable.

The life of St. Brighid is filled with tales of healing, generosity and wisdom. In approximately 470CE she founded a community at Kildare (from Cill Dara, "Church of the Oak"), now famous for the 19 nuns who kept an eternal fire burning in her honor. The fire shrine may have actually been much older than Christianity implies, a Druid temple tended by 19 virgin priestesses representing the 19-year solar cycle associated with Goddess Brigid, only later transforming into a monastery. On several occasions the eternal flame was extinguished, but just like Brigid herself, it has always been rekindled. In the 1960s St. Brighid was decanonized by the Vatican who denounced her Pagan roots, but in the 1990s her flame was relit and tended by the Brigidine Sisters who continue to blend the teachings of St. Brighid with the rites of the Celtic Goddess, revealing the enduring influence of Brigid within modern culture.

The overlap of Celtic Goddess and Christian Saint can be clearly seen during Brigid's feast day of Imbolc on the 1st of February, a festival that tends to the lighting of sacred fires, the ushering in of spring, the blessing of healing waters and the care of birthing animals. This festival later evolved into the Christian Candlemas, yet the themes of sacred feminine remain visible in the celebration of St. Brighid and the Feast of the Purification of Mary. Modern Pagans celebrate Imbolc as the harbinger of spring, the time when life stirs deep within the belly of the earth, and honor Brigid with creative expressions, poetry, music and the lighting of fires.

Many Pagans believe that all the stories of the ancient Goddess, Foster Mother of Christ, Priestess and Saint, are just different aspects of the same story – in the same way that the three sisters each known as Brigid are all one Goddess. It is very challenging to unravel the various threads without destroying the stunning tapestry this Goddess has woven over time. In her ability to blend within ancient mythology, developing Christianity and modern Paganism, Brigid shows us all that the enduring nature of the sacred feminine connects each one of us through the universal concepts of healing, creativity and inspiration.

Romany Rivers is an artist, author of *Poison Pen Letters to Myself* and *The Woven Word*, and a regular contributor to various magazines and blogs as writer and Pagan poet.

Cailleach

Her face had the black-blue shine of coal.
Her one bony tooth was red like rust.
Her hair was thick and dense and gray
like brush wood in a dying forest....
[From: *The Goddess Path* by Patricia Monaghan]

Primal and ancient, the Cailleach is a Goddess as old as time. She is the Hag Goddess of Scotland and Ireland, dating back to the tribes that migrated from Spain over two thousand years ago. In *Visions of The Cailleach*, Sorita d'Este and David Rankine speak of the Kallaikoi and Callaeci, suggesting the names could mean worshipers of the Cailleach. It is believed that the Celts originated in Spain, thus bringing the tribes of the Callaeci and the worship of the Cailleach to Ireland and Scotland.

The Cailleach has been known by many names. Black Annis in Britain, the Hag of Beare in Ireland, and Cailleach Bheur in Scotland. She has been linked with the Carlin and Nicneven. Both are known to be witches. She is associated with many landscapes in the Celtic lands; Hag's Head and Slievena Calliagh in Ireland, and the Cailleach naCruachan in Scotland. She is also connected to the Corryvren whirlpool, known as the tub of Cailleach.

There are a number of different interpretations of the name Cailleach. Hag, witch, old woman, the veiled one, crone, and nun are the most widely used. She is seen to be old and ugly one moment, then young and beautiful the next. In this way, she can be seen as Sovereignty Herself. She is known as a carling, which means both old woman and witch. The Cailleach is also known as a giant, bringing to mind the giants, or Jotnar, in Norse mythology, the Titans of Greece, and the Formoire of Ireland.

The Cailleach is recognized as the Earth Shaper. A common

motif is of her forming landscapes by dropping boulders and stones from her aprons. She is the shaper of mountains, caves, lochs, and cairns. In Scotland, the Cailleach is responsible for the forming of Loch Eck. It was her duty to remove and replace the capstone on the well on Ben Cruach every day. One night, after a grueling day of work, she fell asleep before replacing the capstone. The well flooded the lands, forming what is now the loch. In Ireland there is a tale of a fight between two Cailleachs. During the fight they threw boulders at each other, forming a hillock and a small cairn.

When the Cailleach is in her witch form she is said to be able to control the weather. In the *Lament of the Old Woman of Beara,* she is linked to a great flood, and in many tales she is known to cause the formation of lochs. In this light she can be seen as a water witch. As the Hag of Winter, she takes over the lands from Samhain to Beltane, blanketing the Earth in her frosty breath. The Cailleach rides through the night skies on the back of her black wolf, sending the snows and arctic winds across the barren lands. She is the Old Witch of Winter and is seen to be a sister witch of the Germanic Goddess Holda. Both are equated with winter, wells and magic. The Cailleach is also a Spinner Goddess, connecting her with Old Fate. As a witch, she is able to predict the future and often foretells doom.

There are a few animals equated with the Cailleach through her stories. The most prevalent is the deer. She is known as a Deer Goddess and is linked to the Deer Cult and their priestesses. A discussion of this can be found in *Visions of The Cailleach* by Sorita d'Este and David Rankine. Other animals that she is connected to are the wolf, owl, heron, and goose.

In modern times, the Cailleach and Brighde are said to rule opposite sides of the year. Cailleach rules the dark half, and Brighde, the light half. In *Priestess of Avalon* by Kathy Jones, the maiden Brighde receives the White Rod of Winter from the crone Cailleach, transforming it into the Green Rod of Spring. Cailleach rules over winter as Bone Woman, Stone Woman and Nolava of Air.

Many see the Cailleach as the Great Grandmother of Time. Ever ancient and primal, she knows and sees all. She is honored in the rites of croning and is called upon when grandmotherly wisdom is needed. Today she is revered for her great knowledge and feared for her ability to create change that most are not ready for.

It is not known how the Cailleach was worshiped in the past, so it is necessary in these modern times to create ways in which to honor her. In *The Goddess Path*, Patricia Monaghan highlights a few ways to hold rituals in her honor. In my research, I have found a few methods to pay homage to this prodigious and primeval grandmother.

Her feast days can be held at Samhain and Yule, both times of darkness and reflection, and again at Imbolc or Beltane, when she passes the rod to Brighde. The modern symbols for the Cailleach are stones, bones, shells and fossils and anything of great antiquity. When caring for our elderly, we can call upon the Cailleach to guide us. Whether we are creating art or a delicious dinner, she can be called to lend a hand. As the creator of countless wonders, the Cailleach and her strength and cunning are sure to help.

In this day and age when the elderly are looked down upon, the Cailleach and her infinite wisdom are needed. Many fear old age and death. The Cailleach can transform that fear and turn it into something of beauty. She teaches us not to scorn the elderly, but to honor and cherish the wisdom and beauty they hold within.

Vivienne Moss spends her days brewing up trouble with her two daughters, and her nights casting spells. When she's not writing, you'll find her meandering through the enchanted forest with her witch sisters, her cat Marcee, and her dog Paco standing guard. A lover of all things occult, Vivienne dedicates her time to the study of esoteric knowledge. Vivienne's hope is to share the magic of the Other-Worlds with fellow seekers of Witchdom.

Cardea

Cardea is not well known today, yet in Roman times she was vitally important. The Roman writer Ovid (43BC-17AD) both preserved and obscured her story, seeming either to confuse or intentionally blend her with other Goddesses (Carna and Cranaë). Alternatively, he may have been suggesting that these three were actually facets of the same deity. It seems likely that she predates classical Rome, possibly originating with Etruscan or early Latin culture.

Ovid introduces us to her as *Carna*, "Goddess of the hinge: She opens the closed, by her power, closes the open." He then describes her as the nymph *Cranaë*, a huntress similar to Diana, who evades her male pursuers by suggesting that they go ahead of her to a secluded cave, where they might make love to her. However, she melts into the bushes behind them, and they lose her. The God Janus then pursues her, but since he has two faces, one looking forward and one looking back, her ruse fails and he forces himself on her. Being the God of gates and doorways, Janus rewards her with power over hinges – which is *Cardea's* best known attribute in Roman culture – giving her a hawthorn branch as a token of this, "with which to drive away evil from the threshold."

Ovid then moves to another tale of Cranaë, in which she is called upon to rescue a child called *Proca* from night-time attacks by striges, which are hags or witches transformed into owl-like creatures. She achieves this by first touching the doorposts and threshold of the house with arbutus and with "medicinal" water, then by offering the entrails of a young pig as a substitute for the child's, and finally by planting a rod of hawthorn outside the child's window. Other writers suggest that Proca was the son of the union between Janus and Cardea.

Ovid concludes by discussing Carna in connection with the

June calends (1st June) when a rustic meal of beans and pork was eaten, which was believed to protect the inner organs and digestion.

Many references exist to the rites of lustration of household doorways connected with Cardea, particularly the custom of a bride anointing the doorposts with fat and wrapping them in wool fillets on her arrival at her new home on her wedding day. These customs, as well as her connection with Janus, have established Cardea as a Goddess of liminal space and a guardian of such openings. Her specific relationship to *hinges*, however, moves her from the sphere of household magic into something altogether grander. As well as meaning a door hinge, *cardo* refers to all that is important, or *pivotal*: the cardinal directions, the four winds, the *axis mundi* and so on. Acts representing this pivotal aspect of the Goddess probably included singing games played by young girls which involved swinging the arms, and also the hanging of *oscilla*, which were baubles, dolls and other objects suspended in trees to swing in the wind.

Various authors have attempted to explain Ovid's combining of Carna, Cranaë and Cardea by asking what their differing aspects and associations have in common. This is worth look at, if we are to understand how she might fit into our lives today.

In 1892, folklorist C. G. Leland wrote *Etruscan Roman Remains in Popular Tradition*. In it, he relates a folktale of a witch called Carradora, "a witch who did good as well as harm." She was approached by a mother whose babe was wasting away. "Then the witch took *corbezzole* (arbutus), and thorns, and put them in red bags and bound them to the door-posts and windows, and then took the entrails of a very small pig..." and so, we have essentially the same story as that of Cranaë and Procus, plus a mention of binding the doorposts. Whether Cardea passed into folklore as Carradora, or whether Carradora became Cardea as Etruria morphed into the Roman Empire, we may never know, but the story seems to record a genuine magical practice.

Robert Graves in *The White Goddess* (1948) suggests that Cardea, the protectress of children and the home, had previously been their attacker.

Cardea was Alphito, the White Goddess who destroyed children after disguising herself in bird or beast form. Thus as Janus's mistress, Cardea was given the task of keeping from the door the nursery bogey who in matriarchal times was her own august self.

While Graves has been discredited on many things, this is interesting in the light of the quote concerning Carradora as "a witch who did good as well as harm."

More recently, C. M. McDonough, in his paper *Carna, Proca and the Strix on the Kalends of June* (1997) suggests that, having raped Cardea, Janus belatedly gives her power over thresholds in the sense of power over the thresholds of the body. This has significance beyond the sexual. After all, the striges are vampire-like in their attacks, seeming to devour the body from within, perhaps, leaving only a shell. Part of Cranaë's incantation concerning the piglet sacrificed for Procus runs, "Heart for heart! Bowels for bowels, Soul for soul!" In this way, we find a connection between Cardea's association with the openings in houses and Carna's with the protection of the openings and organs of the body.

Today, Cardea is honored in ritual and prayer by followers of Roman polytheism and other neopagans. She is invoked by witches working in Stregheria, in other traditions, and in no tradition. She has a great deal to offer us in her best known roles as protectress of the home, of children and our bodies, and there is more to explore with her in the realms of liminal time and space, in her potential as an ally for weather working, healing and the setting of boundaries.

Kris Hughes is a writer, oracle reader, poet, musician and horsewoman. She spent most of her adult life in and around Edinburgh, Scotland, and currently resides in southeast

Colorado. She has diverse interests including plants and animals, meditation, mythology and folklore.

Ceres

Ceres is an Earth Mother Goddess. She was the Goddess of fruit, grain and flowers in the pre-Christian Roman Pantheon, but is still worshipped today by modern Pagans. In the Greek Pantheon she is known as Demeter. Her consort was Jupiter. Ceres was the daughter of Saturn and Rhea, wife-sister of Jupiter, mother of Proserpina by Jupiter, sister of Juno, Vesta, Neptune and Pluto, and patron Goddess of Sicily.

Adrian Room, in his book *Who's Who in Classical Mythology*, writes that Ceres was the only Roman agricultural deity who was considered part of the *Dii Consentes*. The *Dii Consentes* is the Roman equivalent of the Twelve Olympians in Greek Mythology. The Roman historian Livy arranges the *Dii Consentes* into six male-female pairs: Jupiter-Juno, Neptune-Minerva, Mars-Venus, Apollo-Diana, Vulcan-Vesta and Mercury-Ceres.

Ceres is said to have been adopted by the Greeks in 496 BC in the midst of a horrendous famine. In order to free themselves from this famine, the Sybilline books directed the Romans to worship Demeter, Kore (Persephone) and Iacchus (Dionysus). The worship of this new triad is said to have delivered the Romans from their famine as Ceres taught them how to sow, tend and harvest grains at this time.

There are twelve deities who assisted Ceres in her work. Each of them is associated with a different aspect of agriculture. Wilhelm Heinrich Roscher lists these deities as follows:

1. Vervactor turns fallow land,
2. Reparator prepares fallow land,
3. Imporcitor plows with wide furrows,
4. Insitor sows,
5. Obarator plows the surface,
6. Occator harrows (hoes),

7. Sarritor weeds,
8. Subruncinator thins the seedlings,
9. Messor harvests,
10. Conuector carts the harvest,
11. Conditor stores the harvest,
12. Promitor distributes it.

In a modern twist on an ancient prayer to Ceres, M Moravius Piscinus illustrates the importance of these twelve deities:

> O most holy Ceres, nurturing Mother, whose sacred womb gave birth to both Gods and men; You, Vervactor, who first yoked the oxen and placed the ploughshare to virgin soil; You, Reparator, who first prepared furrows in fallow land; You, Imporcitor, who first made wide our furrows; You, Insitor, who first cast Your bounty on the earth and taught the seed to grow; Obarator, Sarritor, Subruncinator, and You, Sterculinia, who first cared for crops; You, Flora, who make the grain to bear fruit; You, Messitor, who first set scythe to grain stalks; You, Convector, who first spread grain on the sacred harvest floor; You, Noduterentor, who first showed us how to thresh, and You, most holy Ceres, whose very breath separates the white chaff from the golden grain; You, Conditor and Tutilina, who guard the grain in storage; You, Promitor, who first milled the grain and distributed its flour for our daily bread; You, eternal savior, Ceres, lavishing Your bounty upon me and mine, to You, flaxen-haired Ceres, gladly I give thanks and praise, and, from the little I have, to You I willingly make an offering. Accept these, the first fruits of my fields. May my offering incline You more towards me. May You ever nourish me and mine with Your bounty, O most holy and nurturing Mother, gentle Ceres.

Unlike other Gods and Goddesses who only made an appearance to people when it suited them, Ceres was part of the everyday lives of the Roman people. Without her, there was no agriculture, no food. So her presence was felt daily. She was worshiped in her temple on Aventine Hill in ancient Rome and her festival of Cerealia was celebrated on 19th April.

Ceres has many favored offerings including: grains, specifically Spelt wheat which she is said to have developed; a pregnant sow; bread; pomegranates; and first harvest foods. The poet Ovid wrote that Ceres is happy with little in the way of offerings so long as those offerings are pure. Many of us are familiar with the story of the Greek Goddess Demeter and the story of Ceres is nearly exact. Ceres and Jupiter had a daughter, Proserpine. She was kidnapped by Pluto and taken to the underworld to be his bride. Ceres was heartsick and did everything she could to get Proserpine back. Ceres was furious when she learned that Jupiter had agreed to wed their daughter to Pluto. She left him to live in the world of men where she disguised herself as an old woman and made all the crops die and the soil infertile.

Jupiter realized he had to get Proserpine back, but Pluto had given her food to eat which tied her to the underworld forever. Proserpine was forced to return to the underworld for four months every year. These are the fall and winter months and her departure to the underworld causes the leaves to fall from the trees and fields to lie fallow. Nothing grows until spring when she returns to her mother.

As the word cereal is derived from her name, she continues to hold great significance in the production of grains and the harvest. In fact, a statue of Ceres graces the top of the dome of both the Missouri State Capitol and the Vermont State House showing the great importance of agriculture in those states' histories and economies. Ceres is even pictured on the official seal of the state of New Jersey representing prosperity.

In her 1995 book *The Roman Goddess Ceres*, Barbette Stanley Spaeth examines the concepts of fertility and liminality as they relate to the plebs and women of Roman society. There is even an entire manga series written by Yuu Watase called *Ceres, Celestial Legend*, which borrows aspects of the original Roman myths. In the series, the protagonist Aya Mikage, learns on her 16th birthday that she is the reincarnation of a celestial maiden named Ceres, and her twin brother Aki is the reincarnation of Ceres' former husband, Mikagi.

Ceres is still worshiped multiple times a year by modern Pagans in the Mother aspect as the bringer of the harvest and agricultural success. She is also seen as the Wise Crone whom people come to as a sort of oracle. She is best called upon to aid in issues of family, fertility, growth, nurture, rebirth and wisdom. She represents abundance, acceptance and affection as well as gratitude. Ceres is associated with the Cancer sign of the Zodiac, so she also represents harmony at home. While she does not enjoy the same celebrity she did in ancient Rome, Ceres can still be considered a Goddess connected to modern Paganism.

Heather Lea Marano

Cerridwen

"I'm having trouble relating to her – she just seems so angry and vengeful." The student had been studying the Tale of Taliesin and was meditating on the Goddess Cerridwen, who plays a leading role. This legend, set in Wales on the banks of Llyn Tegid (Lake Bala) can be found in the late medieval text *The Mabinogion*, but has been translated and retold countless times since and may indeed be based on folklore older still.

In the tale, Cerridwen is married to a local lord, Tegid Foel, and together they have two children, a girl called Creirwy and a boy called Morfran (also known as Afagddu). Creirwy is beautiful and pleasant natured – a shining child – but Morfran is terrible to look upon and tortured by dark thoughts so Cerridwen resolves to help him. She searches for a solution and travels to consult the Fferyllt – alchemists who live high in the mountains. Deciding that the best option for Morfran is to give him the gift of brilliance and knowledge to balance his outward appearance Cerridwen settles on brewing a potion of Awen in her cauldron. Otherwise known as inspiration, Awen is able to provide great knowledge but the brew would take a year and a day to complete so she employs two assistants: Morda and Gwion.

The story continues with Gwion receiving the inspiration from the cauldron instead of Morfran, and Cerridwen pursuing him through many changing forms. Ultimately he becomes a grain of wheat and she a hen who unerringly ingests him. Cerridwen becomes pregnant with his essence and after nine months she births him. Unable to further harm him she places him in a leather bag that she throws into the sea. This discarded baby Gwion is later found in a salmon weir by the King Elffin and, still having the gift of Awen, grew to become the renowned poet Taliesin.

It is easy to see why Cerridwen may not initially appear the hero of this tale, but many modern Pagans see her as a benevolent Goddess of inspiration, knowledge, transformation and rebirth who represents feminine strength leading to the dilemma faced by the student.

But, by reviewing her myth from the perspective of her primary situation – that of a troubled mother trying to aid her child – it becomes easier to see how she would be rightfully unhappy that her employed servant had taken that which she had prepared for her son. Parents the world over can relate to the desire to aid their children as they grow, to give them whatever advantages they can, and can empathize with the long search and hard work that might come with such desires. In this, Cerridwen offers us the knowledge that wisdom comes from dedicated inquiry and the necessary toil to achieve your goals.

Cerridwen becomes the Goddess of inspiration as she prepares the physical representation of the Awen in her cauldron. She adds levels of female intuition and the maternal creativity by brewing this potion in the inherently feminine vessel that has become associated with her. As a busy mother, Cerridwen does not have time to personally tend the cauldron constantly for a year and a day so she acquires aid. Here she shows us that accepting our limits will help us achieve our goals, but we are reminded that bringing others into our plans always holds a risk.

In this case the unprepared Gwion is the recipient of the gift of Awen instead of Morfran who Cerridwen would have been preparing for this event. Many simply see the ensuing drama as solely merciless punishment. However, the ease with which Cerridwen finally consumes the grain of wheat suggests something else: that these transformations are necessary for Gwion to be able to process the knowledge he has suddenly gained. In this way Cerridwen offers us the lesson that knowledge will always be transformative. It cannot be denied that there is an element of reprimand in the chase – Cerridwen is always the aggressor, always pushing Gwion onwards and here she reminds us that our actions come with consequences and evolutions are never straightforward.

In her final pregnancy Cerridwen shows us her metamorphic powers in relation to her own psyche. When the seed that is Gwion first takes root in her womb she is certain she will continue her campaign to destroy him for his actions. However, by the time he is reborn she has been changed by her pregnancy and shows compassion. She encourages us to similarly transform our attitudes and lives and reminds us that even in the darkest moment there is a grain of hope and the possibility of something beautiful.

Even her final act with the boy who is now Taliesin is not as uncaring as it first seems. In Lady Guests' 1877 translation of *The Mabinogion* it states that she "cast him... to the mercy of God". This becomes more comprehensible when you consider that Celtic animists would have considered the sea to be a God in its own right and an additional incubation period with a masculine deity could be most helpful to a soul who had vast knowledge thrust upon it without preparation. In this Cerridwen reminds us that letting go is an important part of any evolution, and that knowing when to give something up is just as important as knowing when to fight for it.

Looking at Cerridwen's mythology from this perspective it is easy to see her as a Goddess who balances vengeful death and inspired rebirth just as her children balance dark and light. Through this interpretation of her myth we realize her story holds many more secrets for the contemporary spiritual explorer.

Ngatina C Sylvanius is a member of OBOD who looks to Cerridwen and The Morrigan in her daily practice. She has previously written about nature in *Paganism 101*.

Cordelia

This gorgeous Goddess of British descent is known for her work with Nature. She is so lovely and such a part of the spring and summer season that May 1st, known as Beltane or May Day, is a day in celebration of all she represents. She is also part of every spring and summer flower that blossoms. Due to her having such glory and power, she is forced to wait until this time of year because then the earth will be ready to handle her because it will be fertile enough to sustain her.

Cordelia is an incredibly graceful fairy spirit, but do not let her delicate appearance fool you as she also teaches that you must always stand your ground so that good things will come your way. Her themes include blessings, prayers, flowers, beauty and wishes. Cordelia brings beauty into all of our lives along with all of the positive energies of spring. A suggested mantra for this Queen of May is self-respect. She is also a symbol of celebration, courage, joy, life changes and stress management.

In crystals, Cordelia is represented by garnet and bloodstone, which are the perfect stones due to her representing the root chakra. This makes sense, due to her helping people to keep moving forward and to accept where they are.

It is said that Cordelia defied the wishes of her sea-God father and married the man of her choosing. She always had many suitors falling in line for her, but she did eventually settle down. In doing this and standing for what she wanted, she exemplifies the fact that respect is deserved and is associated with free will.

To honor Cordelia and invite her to be in your life more, place red flowers in your main living area and her spirited persona will always be welcome. Another idea is to have "fairy doors" placed along the baseboards near entrances of your home and bless them. Cordelia will be very interested in the variety of fairies that are welcomed in your home.

Also, due to her association with wishes, make sure you always, always make a wish with a coin when you see a fountain and with a flower of your choice when you see a natural body of water.

When working with Cordelia, here are some affirmations you can say that are directly related to her and her amazing demeanor.

1. I deserve respect – I am important
2. I know the best things I can do for me, which do not require anyone else
3. I can stand up for me and it is easier than I once thought
4. I will always stand up for my beliefs
5. I might be stubborn, but I am gracious about it
6. Not only do I respect my decisions, but others do as well.

Cordelia is the personification of grace without compromising who she is – which is a very good example to follow.

Renee Avard writes at www.worthcatching.blogspot.com and www.reneeavard.com.

Corn Mother

For the indigenous peoples of Northern and Latin America, Corn Mother is a central figure of their Creation cosmology. Known as Selu (Cherokees), Ut Set (Pueblo), Tonantzin (Mexico), and Saramama (Peru), she is a living Divine Female presence, a historic Mother Creatrix as well as a yearly provider and protector.

Celebrating her motherhood honors her gift of producing from, and providing through, her own body in order to feed and nurture her children. Annual ceremonies to her give thanks for a continued abundance of food, a wealth of the crops that her people need. Her sacred symbols include stalks filled with ears of corn (maize), a basic food for the indigenous people and a plant native to the Americas, most familiarly known in the U.S. as corn on the cob.

However, there is significant debate between the indigenous community and followers of the Goddess path, regarding whether Corn Mother or any other indigenous female divinity is a Goddess. As presented by Yo'sah in a posting to the list-serve, Native-L, the argument against naming Corn Mother a Goddess is that "the concept [Goddess] is suspect because the use of such a term is frequently regarded as yet another form of appropriating indigenous religious ideas into non-indigenous categories."

Additional questions are raised by references to Corn Mother as a Goddess or Divine Female representation in documents from the British Isles and Old Europe, given that corn was not a grain crop on other continents prior to the conquest of the Americas. Research clarified this confusion by explaining that "corn" was used as the translation of the word "grain" in various British and European documents.

Thus Corn Mother in the British Isles as well as Old Europe was a representation of wheat, barley, oats and other cereal grains

– the Goddess of Agriculture, the Creatrix of Abundance, the Mother of Nourishment.

As a result, she was linked to many other Mother Creation Goddesses from other traditions, including Demeter (Greece), Ceres (Roman), Cerridwen (Celtic) and Isis (Egypt). And through the life cycle of the corn and other grains she was a Triple Goddess made manifest: the kernels (seed/spring/Maiden/ waxing moon), the full ear (fully ripened food/summer/ Mother/full moon), and the cut stalk (sheaf/fall/Crone/waning moon.

Given Corn Mother's symbolic significance as the provider of abundance, her ceremonial times are during the summer and particularly at Lammas, 2nd August, the Sabbat dedicated to celebrating the start of the harvest.

One prayer to the Corn Mother that has passed down through the ages as part of the Lammas ceremony is the following:

> *Blessed be the harvest, manifestation of the sacred marriage of the deities.*
> *Blessed be the fruitful Corn Mother. Blessed be the God of the Harvest.*
> *I partake of the First Harvest, mixing its energies with mine, that I may continue on my quest for the Starry Wisdom of the Mysteries.*
> *Many blessings I have been given. I count them now by this bread of the grain of Mother Earth.*

And the celebration of Corn Mother would not be complete without some Kitchen Witch magic. The baking of bread is a very common part of the Lammas traditions, but Corn Mother magic can also be called forth in many other dishes. This magick actually started in the field where traditional indigenous wisdom was to plant "The Three Sisters" together – corn, beans and squash – as they complement and nurture each other's growth. And then this magic was internalized by eating the three sisters together – the source of the traditional "succatosh".

Celebrating the blessings of abundance of Corn Mother emerged several years ago during my initial meditations on the four directions. In my vision of the South (the direction of Earth in the indigenous Medicine Wheel), I saw deeply furrowed fields of rich brown earth in which rows and rows of sunflowers and corn stalks grew, full of ripe fruit, under a bright golden sun, high in the sky. And then working with the 365 Goddesses, I found a name for my vision: "Corn Mother". As I researched her further, I realized that she also is one of the indigenous representations of Divine Female, who became, after the conquest of Mexico by the Spanish and Catholic Church, the Virgin de Guadalupe – my initial guide along with Mary Magdalene to the path of studying, living, and honoring the Divine Female.

More recently, during energetics work to address metabolic imbalances, Corn Mother came to me as the representation of the health and balance of my solar plexus and the organs linked to lipid and sugars – liver, spleen, kidneys and gut. And through her, I was reminded to nurture my "middle fire" (the solar plexus region in Chinese medicine), in order to sustain a healthy "eco system" within both my physical and spiritual realms.

Thus, Corn Mother guides us to give mindful thanks for all manners of abundance in our lives and to be wise stewards for bountiful future harvests – calling us to manifest our spiritual and physical gifts sustainably and responsibly, through a healthy balanced annual cycle of birth, growth, harvest, death, and rebirth. She also serves as the divine mother of the blossoming sustainable agriculture, healthy whole food nutrition, and farm-to-table movements. Through her we are called to live and nourish ourselves in harmony with all our relations within our local and global environments.

Cindy Arnold Humiston/Dreamweaver is a witch descendent of three interwoven ancient feminine energetic lineages and their gifts: the "knowing" of wise womyn of the Celtic/Druid British Isles, the sacred ceremonies of the Mediterranean region's Goddess Priestesses and the shapeshifting of the North American indigenous. With emphasis in kitchen magick and tarot, she is also a High Priestess/Ordained Minister graduate of the Mesa Moon School of the Divine Feminine and the University of Esoterica.

Coventina

The Romano-Celtic Goddess Coventina presided over an open-air well that gained attention in 1731 and was excavated in 1876. Located west of the fort of Carrawburgh at Hadrian's Wall, the well's contents contributed to its own renown and, as Allason-Jones points out in her essay on the site, also the enigmatic nature of Coventina herself. [Coventina's Well in *The Concept of the Goddess*. Ed. Sandra Billington and Miranda Green. New York: Routledge, 1996. 107-119.] Who was she? Who were the deities worshippers and where did they come from? What do their offerings tell us about her? The ensuing theories that posit answers to these and other questions draw from an understanding of the time in which Coventina's cult was at its height in addition to researchers' own modern perspectives.

The healing, nurturing and life-giving properties of water are known today, and this also held true for ancients Celts. Reasonably, water was regarded as the source of life and associated with wisdom and healing. Bodies of water generally had their own attendant deities to whom pilgrims deposited sacrificial offerings of thanks or in exchange for special requests.

As a spring-Goddess, it seems a matter of course that Coventina would have been a healer. Curiously, however, very few if any of the votives deposited there offer any clues for such a connection. Very few (e.g. pins and bracelets) are specific to a healing cult and some that are bear evidence of linkage to another. [Green, Miranda. *Celtic Goddessess: Warriors, Virgins and Mothers,* New York: George Braziller, Inc., 1996.] Allason-Jones references a suggestion that Coventina was a Goddess of war, but this does not bear out given the absence of related ironworks in the well, even though the excavation antiquaries had documented ironworks amongst the well's many contents. A bronze dog statuette cited as evidence for Coventina's healing duties is a latecomer to contemporary documentation and even a human head is discounted given a missing portion, thus ruling out any ritual significance. The water itself, given the lack of evidentiary nature amongst the votives found in the well, is perhaps the greatest indicator of Coventina's healing nature. Barring this, Allason-Jones suggests she may have been an "all-rounder", a deity who concerned herself with all elements of her constituents' lives.

Names are often telling, but Coventina's provides very little clue as to who she was or where she originated. Green asserts the Goddess's name is Celtic and acknowledges a devotee base that spread as far away as northwest Spain and southern Gaul. Allason-Jones, however, in citing the additional shrines, references the debate about whether veterans of a Roman legion stationed in the north of England took the cult of Coventina home with them or it traveled in the opposite direction. Examination of the deity's name on the two continental shrines reveals little except contradictory interpretations. Even a "simple" investigation of her name with the various spellings found on stones in the well comes up with a Celtic preposition, German soldiers, etymology based on Ptolemy's name for the River Tyne and vernacular French! Even altars where worshipers left their names – a sort of guest book of the era – contain entries of those from the Low Countries. The difficulties in pinpointing Coventina as a specifically local deity transfer to her devotees in that their travel – thus their likely origins – is not easily traced.

At this point one might ask if the 19th century discovery contained a lot of valuable negatives, since so many theories seem to be negated based on other information available as discussed. It can be said that Coventina's cult season ran for approximately two centuries. Beginning in about 130 AD, engineers walled in the spring and by 391 the cult had significantly dwindled, albeit much of that slowdown attributable to the Theodosian Edict of that year, which outlawed Pagan rites and forced the concealment of a great many shrines, including Coventina's.

Religious intolerance had been bearing down for some time, however, and Allason-Jones targets the period of 378-388 as the end of the offerings, based on coin evidence. At discovery, the well had been filled with a variety of objects including "bronze, bone, pottery, glass, leather, jet and shale [and] deerhorn." It all may have been devotional or some part of a larger attempt to hide the well and its contents from those who would see it destroyed. Given the lack of breakage and positioning of the items, this would have been a planned retreat as opposed to panicked flight.

It is not difficult to wonder what became of those who had worshiped there as the well's time drew to a close. Even if many never returned to the site, whether from the experience of loss or because they left the area, surely they were unable to pack away the intangible they had carried for Coventina. For a good many, worship of this Goddess would have indelibly marked their life, influenced their perspectives, and it seems likely they would have passed it on to succeeding generations. If not for the bubbling spring discovered to house the shrine of a Goddess, would everything they carried within them and for Coventina have been lost forever?

There has, of course, been resurgence in the worship of various Goddesses and many have been rehabilitated within the context of modern devotional gathering, some of which is clearly linked to the absorption of Goddesses and various symbolism into Christianity. Certain Goddesses still have their own spotlight, though Coventina does not seem to be one of them, except perhaps within very localized settings. It is possible to visit Coventina's Well today, and certainly this has some influence. Nevertheless, Lawson and Rufus seem to believe Coventina has had her time:

You can still visit the stone basin with its energetic little spring. But poor Coventina! She's not enviable after all. She

came *that* close to disappearing altogether, and her once-pampered shrine just another hole in the ground, in a land where few remember that water is a gift, and divine.
[Lawson, Kristin and Anneli S. Rufus. Story of Coventina. *Coventina*. Tehomet, 2005. Web. 24 Nov. 2013.]

While people today still widely recognize the magical properties of water – if in a more secular manner – few in Coventina's territory (and that where descendants expanded to) seem to associate it and its attendant benefits with her or any other name. In fairness, plentiful water and superior medical technologies have become so commonplace as to alter the collective perception of it. Even religious rituals linked to water often maintain a separation between the times in which they are carried out and the ordinary course of human lives.

By circumstance or design, has Coventina really been *that* forgotten? Or have we in the modern world been beneficiary of an understanding we do not realize we have? After all, there is that connection to water we do acknowledge, and we take part in an ancient ritual when we toss coins into a water fountain, an act that seems so instinctive as to be presumed built in.

The practice of water birthing is reminiscent of speculation on the Goddess's status as one who was especially concerned with women in childbirth. Perhaps we have retained something in our psyches of her, courtesy of those who'd been forced away from her so long ago. In our ongoing quest for knowledge and rediscovery of much that we once knew, perhaps it is true that her legacy indeed lives on, though not necessarily in the same name. Or perhaps Coventina is as enigmatic as she ever was.

Lisl Zlitni likes to read about Merlin, Richard III and brain studies. She is currently working on a book of short stories and another of historical non-fiction. Her poetry has appeared in *Alaska Women Speak*; she writes and edits for The Review Group and manages her own literary blog, Before the Second Sleep.

Danu

Danu is one of the most ancient of all Celtic deities, mother of the Irish Gods as well as the mother of the Tuatha Dé Danann (too-ah day Dan-ahn), or the Children of Danu. She is shrouded in mystery, for while the tales of the Tuatha are many, little is written specifically about Danu, Herself. Nevertheless, there is much to gleaned from the study of Her children as well as the study of the myths and legends of Ireland.

The name Danu means "the Flowing One", and indeed, Danu's name and presence can be found in the Danube River, which flows throughout Europe. However, Danu is not only referenced as a river Goddess. Interestingly, author Michelle Skye notes in her book, *Goddess Alive!* that Danu is named in the Rig Veda, the earliest of the four Hindu Scriptures, where she is named as Goddess of the seas.

As mother of the Tuatha Dé Danann, we find a veritable treasure trove of information about Danu, for by looking at the wonders of Her children, we then see the magnificence of the mother. The Tuatha Dé arrived in Ireland at a time when giants ruled that world. The Tuatha Dé burned their boats upon landing on the coast of Ireland, never to return to their former lands. It was after this that they defeated the ruling Fir Bolg and Fomorian races to assume rule of this beautiful Isle. The magic and skill in craftsmanship, healing, artistry and warfare of the children of Danu were unsurpassed. Where Danu is associated with wisdom, knowledge, teaching and abundance, we see that She and Her people possessed all of these. It is here we also see Danu becoming more than a river and sea Goddess, for here She becomes an Earth Goddess, as well.

As an Earth Goddess, Danu is associated with both Faery Hills and Dolmens also known as portal tombs or portal graves. Indeed, Danu's children were eventually overcome by the invasion of the Milesian race who drove them underground. Thus, Danu's children were demoted in the eyes of the people. As legend became myth and centuries became millennia, Danu's children became known as the Faery Folk where they were reduced, oft-times to little more than tiny, mischievous winged beings rather than the brilliant and skilled folk of their time.

Yet not all of Danu and her people were diminished, for we find Her skillfully shapeshifting into differing guises. Authors David Rankine and Sorita D'Este note references to Danu being linked in several Celtic myths and legends to the venerable Goddess The Morrígan. They note in *The Book of Lecan* the two are equated, both directly and indirectly. Additional implications of a direct link between Danu and the Morrígan are found within *The Book of Leinster* and *Cath Muighe Tuireadh.* [Rankine, David & D'Este, Sorita *The Guises of The Morrigan: Irish Goddess of Sex and Battle: Her Myths, Powers & Mysteries* England, UK, Avalonia Books, 2005 p. 138.] Indeed, with her consort, the Death God Bilé, she is in nowise reduced in power, for it was Danu, Herself, who birthed the Dagda – the All-Father God of Ireland.

Today, Danu brings both inspiration and wisdom to those who seek Her out. Any adherents to Faery Shamanism or Faery Craft look to Danu for guidance and awen – the "fire in the head" that sparks creativity, inspires and delights. She is the great, blessed mother who offers the steadfast love and support as only a Mother Goddess can. Like any good mother, she allows us the opportunity to make our own mistakes and glean from them the lessons we need learn.

And yet, she sees and honors potential. She reminds us of our own royal roots – that we are Children of the Universe, full of infinite possibility and limitless potential. As Danu is a skilled shapeshifter, She reminds us of our ability to transform and transcend. She is a skilled craftswoman and creative endeavors are pleasing to Her. We have only to look at the craftsmanship of Her people to know the importance placed upon using one's skills, knowledge and wisdom through inspired works brought to fruition. Thus, she is a Divine Motivator for all works of art, music, and magick.

Below is a list of correspondences for Danu. May Her inspiration be yours today.

Names in Various Cultures
Danu (Hindu, Ireland)
Danu, Danand, Dana, Ana, Anu (Irish)
Don (Wales)
Danuvius (Roman)
Duna (Hungarian)
Donau (German)

Correspondences
Wisdom, Inspiration, Creating, Blessings, Earth Goddess, Great Mother, Foretelling, Health, Magic, Moon Goddess, River Goddess, Sea Goddess, Success

Associations
Colors: Blue, White, Silver, Green
Elements: Water and Earth
Seasons: Imbolc and Lughnasadh.
Tarot: The Empress
Aspects: Mother
Animal: Horses (particularly mares), Fish
Divination: Water Scrying
Essences: Amber, any other "water" scents as the river and sea are her domain
Trees: Rowan, Apple, Hawthorne
Stones: River stones, any stone that has a natural hole in it – aka "Holey stones", Amber, Gold
Symbols: Rivers, Sea, Flowing Water, Earth, Moon, Keys, Crowns
Regions: Ireland, India, most of Europe

Attributes: New Beginnings, Chaos, Cosmos, Creation, Creativity, Fertility,
Manifestations, Oceans (and all other bodies of water), Transformation.

Rowan Galahadria MistWalker (Madison, Wisconsin, USA) is an artist, musician, priestess, and a third generation, professional Tarot reader. She has been published in a number of Pagan and Tarot works, including Circle Magazine and Tarosophy Magazine, International. Since childhood, she has followed the Bealaí Geal Airgead Tradition of her grandmother, steeped in her Irish roots.

Demeter

Demeter is a well-known Greek Goddess of grain and agriculture. Though she was worshiped throughout the ancient world, her rites were centered in Eleusis, a town just north of Athens. She is described as having relationships with Zeus and Poseidon, and with a mortal named Iasion, but Demeter has no true consort. Instead, her most important relationship is with her daughter, Persephone.

The central myth surrounding Demeter connects her to the grain cycle and tells the story of her search for her daughter, Persephone. When Persephone is abducted – or elopes with – the God Hades into the Underworld, Demeter is inconsolable. She stops making the grain grow and wanders the earth carrying a torch – sometimes two torches – trying to find information about what has happened to her daughter. She stops to rest by a well or lake, usually located in Eleusis, but also at Nysa, or in Sicily. Here, disguised as an old woman, she is taken in by a family to serve as a nurse. She tries to make the infant in her care immortal by placing him in a fire, but the mother of the child intervenes. This angers Demeter. The Goddess reveals her identity and the family builds a shrine to her. There she hides, weeping for her lost daughter, while the land remains barren. As the people suffer with famine, various Gods try to intervene. Depending on the version, either Hecate, who heard Persephone scream, or Apollo, who saw what happened, helps Demeter discover the location of her daughter. Then, either Demeter herself, or Hermes, goes into the Underworld to bring Persephone back. Negotiations are held, and Hades agrees to let Persephone go. However, either willfully or because Hades tricks her, Persephone eats some pomegranate seeds. Therefore, she must return to the Underworld for either four or six months each year. During these months, Demeter grieves and crops do not grow. This myth formed the foundation for the two cycles of celebrations dedicated to this powerful Goddess.

The first cycle is referred to as the Eleusinian Mysteries. These initiation rites were open to men and women of all ranks. The Lesser Mysteries were celebrated near Athens, in late February or early March on our calendar. We know little about the rites, except that it cost a piglet and there may have been some element of purification by water involved. Participation in the Lesser Mysteries was a prerequisite to attending The Greater Mysteries. These were celebrated in the temple complex of Eleusis, during the month we think of as September. Strict laws forbade anyone from disclosing what happened during this initiation. To this day, despite extensive research, we still are unsure exactly what went on there. We do know that the dedicants began in Athens and processed to Eleusis. Once there, we know they were given a drink called the kykeon, which may have contained a hallucinogen – possibly ergot – that contributed to the experience. We know that whatever the participants saw, it made them less afraid of death. However, they were still afraid of breaking their vow of silence, so no more is known for sure.

Women conducted the second cycle of celebrations honoring Demeter, although men were allowed at some of the rites. These occurred at various times around the year and commemorated each stage of the grain cycle. They were not initiatory, like the Mysteries, but were seasonal festivals and observances.

In addition to the Eleusinian myth, Demeter is sometimes said to have been raped by Poseidon in the form of a horse while she was looking for Persephone. This union produced Areion, a horse with the ability to speak, and a daughter called Despoina. In this version, Demeter, enraged by the rape, becomes a vengeful Goddess portrayed with images of snakes and horses. There is a temple on the Ladon River dedicated to her in this aspect.

Demeter remains very popular in modern Neopagan

worship, and even in general Western culture. Her themes of the cycles of life, death, love and sorrow, are universal human struggles. Thus, she is still relevant and accessible to our modern minds.

Her seasonal rites have been recreated, allowing devotees to celebrate her festivals throughout the year, without having to develop new rituals. Although we do not know precisely what happened in the Lesser and Greater Mysteries, enough has been discovered that those initiations have been reimagined and are widely available. This has made Demeter relatively easy to worship, and has aided in maintaining her popularity.

She fits in well with other devotion cycles as well, including the Neopagan eight-fold wheel of the year. In Western Europe and America, she is typically honored during the Autumn (Fall) Equinox, because that is the time of the grain harvest in those areas. Offerings of grain or bread are made, and participants are given a drink made of barley water and mint that recaptures the idea of the kykeon.

At other times, she assists women with particular needs. She comforts mothers grieving over the loss of a child or difficulties related to pregnancy or adoption. Parents of children on the autism spectrum may find Demeter helpful in the search for ways to communicate with their sons and daughters. Increasingly, Demeter and Persephone are a part of puberty rites, or at the celebration of a young woman's engagement, when a mother must let go of her daughter in some way. In addition, those who are dealing with sexual assault may invoke Demeter and Persephone's support as they heal. Demeter understands life's tragedies, and provides solace to all those who grieve.

Demeter's themes of lost children, mother-daughter issues, rape, fertility, and sorrow are timeless. She offers a feminine perspective on these issues that particularly affect women, but are not thoroughly addressed by many mainstream religions. Her approach honors strong emotion, but also wise negotiations.

Demeter is the great mother, who has made peace with life and loss.

Ellie V. McDonald is a writer, teacher and mother living in central Ohio. She is a member of Ár nDraíocht Féin and a follower of the Western mystery tradition. She cares about ancient stories, how they develop and change over time, and how shape our future. Find her at ellivmcdonald.com.

Elen of the Trackways

Elen can be quite the elusive Lady, often first appearing to you in a dream, whilst in deep meditation or as a feeling of being watched in the woods. She is one of our most ancient deities, with Her roots deeply embedded within our land. She is in the form of the seen and unseen trackways; sacred wells and springs, and in the womb-like caves carved into our landscape.

Her name appears in the Welsh book of tales *The Mabinogion* in "The Dream of Macsen Wledig". Elen is discovered by Macsen in a dream, Her beauty is compared with that of the Sun: She is radiant and Queenly. The Romans claimed Her as a patron and named many roads and trackways after her, the most well-known being Sarn H/Elen, which forms the backbone of Wales. She was Christianized into St Helen and many wells, springs and trackways still carry this name. In recent times, Elen has been associated with Nehallenia, a Celtic-Norse Goddess whose attributes mingle very closely with her own.

Elen first appeared to me in meditations whilst I journeyed with the Green Man. I would take myself off to my Sacred Grove and call in the Green Man and His Lady. Standing confidently by his side was a beautiful red headed woman with antlers upon Her brow, and the more I worked with this energy the more prominent She became. Each is consort to the other, neither more important, a perfect balance. More recently, Elen has also shown me a deep relationship with The Smith, the alchemist of the land, transformer of the Earth's gifts.

Elen is often, but not always, depicted with antlers. Reindeer (or caribou) are the only deer species in which the females have antlers, and there are many links between Elen and ancient reindeer myths. The Sami and reindeer people of the distant Northern Lands have creation stories that center around female reindeer and deities associated with them. Our island of Britain was once part of those lands, criss crossed with ancient reindeer migration routes, carrying the dreams of those ancestors and the reverence they held for the reindeer. There are an immense number of tales, traditions and references to a pre-Celtic deer-and-deer-priestess cult in the Highlands of Scotland too. When you consider the timeline of ancient Scotland, the first beasts to walk the land were reindeer, so it's not hard to understand why. Ancient bones of reindeer have also being found deep in caves, both in the Highlands of Scotland and the ragged edges of Dartmoor.

Over the last few years the number of our deer herds in the UK has grown and grown. The absence of natural predators, such as wolves, has resulted in deer numbers reaching record levels. I feel the link with this and the rise in awareness of Elen's Call cannot be ignored! The hoof beats of deer upon the land are not unlike the beating of a drum, the heartbeat of the Earth. As the number of deer has risen, the hoof beat, drumbeat, heartbeat of the land has grown louder and the energy of our antlered deity, of Elen, has risen and more and more folk are being drawn to Her.

Elen is the Sovereignty of Albion, the oldest known name for Great Britain. Her name means nymph, light or bright, She is a deity of the "between times", of dawn and dusk, so these are great times to do ritual or journey in Her honor. She has the female association with water and holds the knowledge of ley lines, the energies of the land and the matrix of the power within the Earth. Because of the mentions of gold and seeing her being like "gazing upon the sun" in *The Mabinogion*, Elen is often associated with solar deities. I also find Her wild and shamanic roots much darker and associated with the Moon, but also reflecting those in-between times, the Sun and Moon aspects are all part of the balance.

Elen, as well as being elusive, is a complex Deity and very much about talking the talk and walking the walk, to walk Her trackway is a very practical dedication and spirituality. It's about walking the land and protecting the land; it's about all weathers and seasons; it's about our land and our ancestors' traditions, about ALL our land's beasts, not just the deer. It's about all Her facets: ancestor, priestess, maiden, mother and crone. Her attributes are many, Earth mother, ruler of the web of the wyrd, keeper of fate and destinies, She is the knowledge of the land. She's as wild as the mountains and as rooted as the trees; She is its hoof, antler, blood, bone and spirit.

Over time our land has held and hidden so many secrets of Elen. Ancient reindeer trackways of ancestors and memory. Sacred wells and waterways carry the stories waiting to be told. Ancient stones and wild woodlands are her blood, her bones and her spirit.

Samantha Marks is an artist, mother, retreat and workshop facilitator, aspiring author and a Priestess of Elen. She is co-founder of the Temple of Elen, co-creator of *The Oracle of the Antlered Road* and administrator of the Facebook group Elen of the Ways.

Eostre

Little is known from historical records about the Anglo-Saxon Goddess Eostre. Her name comes down to us in the English title for the Christian holy day of Easter as well as the German name for the same day, Ostern. The name Eostre ultimately derives from an Indo-European root that refers to sunrise, the direction of east and the concept of shining; we can see a cognate in the name of the Greek Goddess of dawn Eos.

The most accessible source of historical information about Eostre is a medieval treatise called *De temporum ratione* (*The Reckoning of Time*), all about calendars and related methods of measuring time penned by the 8th century English monk Bede. In this work he explains that during the month named after Eostre, Ēosturmōnaþ (presumably corresponding to April since he lists it as the fourth month of the year), the Pagan Anglo-Saxons used to hold feasts in her honor. He also states that the practice had died out by his lifetime. In addition to this written reference, a fair amount of archaeological evidence exists to show devotion to Eostre across much of pre-Christian Britain and Germany. Dr. Phillip A. Shaw of the University of Leicester details this evidence in his book *Pagan Goddesses in the Early Germanic World: Eostre, Hreda and the Cult of Matrons* (Studies in Early Medieval History Series, Duckworth Publishers, 2011). His examination of more than 150 votive inscriptions from the second century BCE, all found in the region of the Rhine River, shows that Eostre had an extensive following in Germany before the introduction of Christianity. Dr. Shaw also points to a number of place names in England as well as personal names in Germanic-speaking areas that derive from Eostre, suggesting that she was an integral part of the early culture of those regions.

Our largest source of folkloric information about Eostre comes from the 19th century German folklorist Jacob Grimm. He collected oral folk traditions from throughout Germany and compiled them into a written collection titled *Deutsche Mythologie*, usually translated as *Teutonic Mythology*. Based on the German term for the month of April ("ostermonat," earlier "ôstarmânoth") and the Old High German word for Easter (Ôstarâ), Grimm reconstructed the German form of the Goddess' name as Ostara. He connected her with the concepts of dawn and light through both the root meanings of her name and the time of year with which she is associated. Rightly or wrongly, he also connected many Germanic Easter traditions – bonfires, sunrise dances, drawing holy or blessed water on Easter morning, Easter eggs and the Easter feast – with Ostara and pre-Christian practices.

The hunting of hares, called "hare coursing," was a popular springtime or Eastertide sport in Britain for a number of centuries. It finally died out in the 20th century, but was long considered to be related to pre-Christian springtime practices involving Eostre. This connection may have little basis in fact but it developed a strong underpinning in folklore, possibly due to the influence of such works as Frazer's *Golden Bough,* and gives Eostre a firm association with the hare in popular culture. *The Aquarian Dictionary of Festivals* (Thorsons, 1990) states that the hare, not the rabbit, was Eostre's animal emblem as well as being sacrificed to her. There is debate as to whether the hare was historically associated with Eostre, but it has definitely become a part of her symbol set in modern Pagan practice.

Thus we see that Eostre is associated with springtime and its attendant symbolism: fertility, new beginnings, dawn, the increase of light. She is connected with hares or rabbits, possibly related to the origin of the Easter bunny, though that tradition is shrouded in the mists of folklore. She is also associated with eggs, another symbol of fertility and fecundity, and with the beginning of day (sunrise) and the growing season (spring equinox).

Reconstructionist Anglo-Saxon Paganism, also known as

Anglo-Saxon Heathenry, honors Eostre as a Goddess of spring. Some groups celebrate her at the spring equinox, others at various times during the month of April, in keeping with the evidence in the historical record. In northern Paganism, which may combine the deities of the various lands where the Norse traveled and settled, Eostre is sometimes equated with the Nordic spring Goddess Iduna who bears the magic apples of life.

Many Neopagans use Grimm's name for her, Ostara, to refer to the spring equinox itself. In this context Eostre/Ostara combines both pre-Christian and Christian-era spring symbology into a coherent and meaningful whole. Modern Pagan spring equinox celebrations often include the hare or rabbit and eggs as well as a focus on birth, renewal, dawn/sunrise, and the triumph of the warm half of the year over the retreating winter. Some practitioners bake hot cross buns in Eostre's honor, relating the cross not to the Christian symbol but to the four directions and the four solar points of the calendar year (equinoxes and solstices). Traditional Easter activities such as rolling eggs down a hill or "battling eggs" (knocking boiled eggs against each other to see which one cracks first) have also been incorporated into the set of customs associated with Eostre. At present there is no way of knowing whether any of these practices took place in pre-Christian times or whether they are more recent introductions; the important point is that they have meaning for the modern Pagans who take part in them.

One final note: Eostre has recently appeared as a character in Neil Gaiman's novel *American Gods*, displaying the extent to which she has been revived and accepted not just in Pagan worship but also in popular culture.

Laura Perry is the author of *Ariadne's Thread: Awakening the Wonders of the Ancient Minoans in Our Modern Lives* and the mystical adventure novel *Jaguar Sky*.

Epona

Epona is a Goddess of Horses. She is thought to have been originally worshiped in ancient Gaul and she was then later adopted by members of the Roman Cavalry. As a result of this adoption, her image can be found throughout the Roman Empire. My first experience of the Goddess Epona came whilst attending a Pagan camp in the New Forest, England. The New Forest itself is famous for its wild ponies and is a beautiful setting with a slightly wild untamed energy to it. Therefore, it was hardly surprising to find that a group of Pagans who had chosen the New Forest as a location for their seasonal gatherings had been drawn to Epona as the patron of their camp.

As a Goddess she is the protector of horses, donkeys and mules, she has also been linked to fertility and the harvest and this can be evidenced by the cornucopia or sometimes large ears of corn often depicted with her in statues and artwork. Her origins may be mixed, although she is certainly pre-Christian and in books she is sometimes described as a Celtic deity and at other times she is included as part of the Roman pantheon. Perhaps this is not so surprising, though, when you look at how many local regional deities were absorbed into the Roman culture as the empire expanded. Epona in particular seems to have been a favorite of the Roman Cavalry and her feast day in the Roman calendar was celebrated on 18th December.

During my time at that first camp and subsequent camps in the New Forest I had begun to feel my own connection to Epona deepening and this inspired my desire to find out more about her.

When I began researching her, the first thing which I found interesting was that she was worshiped in so many different countries, her image being found throughout the Mediterranean as well as in German, French and British culture. This could be in large part because of her associations with the Roman Cavalry, who were known to have been a multi-cultural bunch. It makes sense to assume that they kept up their allegiances with this protector of horses and riders who had served them so well, even after they returned home.

The surviving statuary depicting her does not give us much to go on, but does at least give us two consistent images of her as she is generally depicted in one of two poses. She is sometimes shown seated upon a throne wearing simple robes and with bare feet. In this position she has foals on either side of her and the fruits of the harvest, apples, corn and sometimes vegetables, upon a patera in her lap, perhaps ready to feed the waiting horses. The other common version of the Epona statue has her sitting side saddle upon a horse, normally with the horse facing to her left. In these instances she is still robed and barefoot and she is also carrying a patera or similar.

So how does Epona, a Goddess linked mainly with agriculture and animals, relate to a modern day Pagan? Well for anyone who has ever had the opportunity to ride a horse the connection is an easy one to make. To feel the powerful strength of the horse, the strong desire to mother and protect it and to feel those emotions reciprocated back on us from our mount.

For the city Pagan, Epona may seem at first like a very distant Goddess indeed. When one is surrounded by tower blocks, traffic and pollution why should one bother with a Goddess who seems so completely tied to rural living? The answer here is twofold, one because for some people their connection to their car, giving it a name, feeling a sense of bond closer to a pet than a possession, makes our modern bond with our vehicle just as strong as the farmer's connection to his horse from years past. Secondly, Epona represents family, she stands for the tribe and the clan and having the Goddess Epona in your life is to promise to look out for those around us.

Her association with the harvest is as much to do with her

providing for her tribe as it is to do with her ability to farm. Unlike many other deities, Epona has no obvious consort. In Roman times inscriptions to her sometimes included the names of other Gods and Goddesses, but no one name more than any other. This lack of a single consort may be another factor which helps Epona to remain relevant in a modern world where there is less emphasis on the need to pair up with another person and more often the desire for people to carve their own way in the world. Perhaps she might particularly appeal to those with strong feminist views.

Although she is without a confirmed male counterpart, Epona does have connections to other characters and deities. Most commonly she is associated with Rhiannon. Rhiannon is one of the female characters found in the stories of the Mabinogion and there are certainly similarities between the two of them, from the way in which both Rhiannon and Epona both reportedly sat side-saddle upon their steeds, to the fact that Rhiannon's punishment, when she was falsely accused of killing her son, was to act in the role of a horse and to take people to and from the castle upon her back.

So it seems that Epona is a Goddess for all times and all people. She can connect us to our inner animal, help us feel the maternal pull of the mother and she can show us the seasons of the Earth and the harvest.

Arietta Bryant

Ereshkigal

When the Sumerian Queen of Heaven and Earth, Inanna, decided to descend into the "Great Below", Ereshkigal, its ruler, was far from impressed. According to *The Descent of Inanna*, Ereshkigal fixed her eye of death upon this intruder, pronounced the word of wrath and hung Inanna's corpse upon a hook where it stayed for three days before being rescued. Because of this, Ereshkigal gained the reputation of being vindictive and spiteful towards her beautiful younger sister, and today this mighty Goddess of the Sumerian Underworld is associated with anger and rage, unwanted waste, as well as the neglected aspects of one's psycho-spiritual self, the "shadow". However, as the last two lines of *The Descent of Inanna* record Ereshkigal being praised instead of Inanna, is there something amiss with how we perceive the Sumerian Queen of the Great Below?

The earliest recording of Ereshkigal is found on an offering list from the 21st century BCE, predating many of the later occupations of Mesopotamia, and it is within the "Eridu" model of the Sumerian creation myth that Ereshkigal (the "knowing within") first appears, along with her twin brother, Enki (Lord of Magic and the "knowing without"), as being created from the tears when An (Sky Father) wept for Ki (Earth Mother). When Ereshkigal was kidnapped by the primeval dragon, Kur, and taken to the Underworld, Enki built a boat and descended from the "Heights Above" (heaven, the realm of the Gods) to bring Ereshkigal back. The remaining fragments of this myth prevent us from discovering what happened except that Enki only brought back seeds of the future Tree of Knowledge, the Huluppu tree (which he planted along the banks of the Euphrates River), and Ereshkigal retained the Underworld for her own domain, destined never to return to the Heights Above.

In the *Epic of Gilgamesh* we learn of the demise of Gugalana (the "Bull of Heaven" and Ereshkigal's husband) after being sent to earth to battle against the hero Gilgamesh who had refused Inanna's advances. Upon hearing about the death of her husband, Ereshkigal fell into the pit of despair. So when Inanna arrived unannounced at the first of seven gates to the Great Below to witness these funeral rites (as recorded in *The Descent of Inanna*), this intrusion was not received warmly by the mourning Ereshkigal. As a reminder that only the Queen of the Great Below could pass judgment in this realm, Inanna was made to relinquish an item of status and association to the land of the living until she stood naked, bearing her "true self", before her counterpart. Here, she stayed for a period for three days before being brought back to life only to discover that her own consort, Dumuzi, had not mourned for her.

A less popular myth concerning Ereshkigal is that of *The Marriage of Nergal and Ereshkigal* (of which there are two versions, the Tell-el-Amarna version of only 90 lines dating back to the 15th century BCE, and the longer Assyrian version from the 7th century BCE). Both versions indicate that when An (the Sky Father) decided to hold a feast, he sent an invitation for Ereshkigal to attend to receive her "food portion". However, due to the rules governing the Great Below that prevented her from leaving this realm, Ereshkigal sent Namtar, her trusted vizier, to attend in her place. All the Gods acknowledged Namtar's status except for the young God of pestilence and warfare, Nergal, who declared that as he had never met Ereshkigal, he would not show respect to her or anyone attending as her representative. Ereshkigal took offence at such actions and demanded the young God descend into the Great Below to be punished by her.

In the Tell-el-Amarna version, Enki provides Nergal with seven demons which helped him overpower Ereshkigal and forced her to relinquish her realm to him. The Assyrian version differs greatly in that prior to Nergal's initial departure, Enki made him fashion a special chair upon which only he should sit, and warned the young God not to eat or drink anything, not to wash his feet and, most importantly, not to "do that which men and woman do".

Having passed through the seven gates and arriving at the courtyard of the Great Below, Namtar warned Nergal to leave all prejudices and misconceptions behind for this realm revealed the "true essence of all there is". As such, when the young God caught sight of Ereshkigal, he did not see the expected old hag; instead he saw a beautiful woman. Indicating a desire to bathe before eating, Ereshkigal retired to her bathhouse, knowing that Nergal would follow. The God of war admitted defeat, washed and feasted, and stayed in bed with Ereshkigal until the seventh morning when he eventually returned to the Heights Above, without her knowledge, and was only seen by Namtar. It was only when the heartbroken Ereshkigal threatened to raise the dead until they outnumbered the living should Nergal not return to her, that the young God admitted his feelings and descended into the Great Below where he subsequently ruled jointly with Ereshkigal.

Within modern Paganism Ereshkigal is commonly considered a "dark Goddess" associated with unappropriated emotions such as deep-seated anger and rage. What tends to be overlooked is that her anger was the result of her boundaries being violated or people transgressing against her. As such, Ereshkigal is the Goddess who reminds us of our own boundaries, and gives us the strength to say "no" when people want more of us than we are prepared to or able to give.

Ereshkigal challenges us to overcome our pride and ego, to search for the inner and deeper truths, or the true essence of things. She reminds us that what glitters can often be based on ego and illusion, that the truth may not always be pleasant, yet it reflects the underpinning laws of nature that even we cannot escape from. Once we accept this deep truth, we allow ourselves to experience a deeper and more profound beauty, as Nergal discovered.

Frances Billinghurst is a priestess of As't (Isis) and Priestess in Residence of The Goddess House, based in Adelaide, South Australia. She regularly runs Goddess orientated workshops and devotional services, as well as writing about the Goddess for various anthologies including *Unto Herself: A Devotional Anthology to Independent Goddesses, The Faerie Queens, Queen of Olympos: A Devotional Anthology to Hera and Iuno* and *A Mantle of Stars: A Devotional Anthology to the Queen of Heaven*. For more information, visit thegoddesshouse.blogspot.com.au.

Eris

...in Greek mythology, the goddess of discord, the sister of Ares, and, according to Hesiod, daughter of Nyx (night). Not being invited to the marriage of Peleus, she revenged herself by means of the Golden Apple of discord.

[*Brockhampton Reference Dictionary of Classical Mythology*]

In her mythological and historical context, that short description sums up Eris's main claim to fame. According to the much-told heroic epic of the ancient world, Eris was the Goddess who started the whole Trojan War. In a fit of pique at not being invited to a party all the other Gods were going to, she decided to get her own back. She threw into the room a golden apple inscribed "kallisti", which means "To the fairest one", knowing the deities would row over who should have it.

Hera, Athena and Aphrodite all wanted the glittering trophy. To solve the argument, Zeus asked Paris, the King of Troy's son, to judge the contest. The three Goddesses tried to bribe him. More lad-about-the-walled-city than good leadership material, Paris declined Hera's offer of political power and Athena's offer of battle skills in favor of Aphrodite's proffered chance to have the most beautiful woman in the world. That was Helen, Menelaus of Sparta's trouble and strife. The rhyming slang for wife might not have been coined in Ancient Greece, but Strife was Eris's other name and trouble was what she was all about causing. The Trojan War ensued.

Roll on several thousand years to the 1950s and an all-night bowling alley in America where two young Californians were drinking coffee and discussing how to put the world to rights.

"Solve the problem of discord," said one, "and all other problems will vanish." "Indeed," said the other, "chaos and strife are the roots of all confusion."

So they later wrote in the *Principia Discordia*, the sacred text of the Discordian Society. The book has the subtitle "How I found the Goddess, and what I did to her when I found her..." The Goddess they found was Eris, who appeared to them in a dreamlike vision as "a splendid woman whose eyes were as soft as feather and as deep as eternity itself, and whose body was the spectacular dance of atoms and universes." And here is the charge of that Goddess:

> *I have come to tell you that you are free. Many ages ago, My consciousness left man, that he might develop himself. I return to find this development approaching completion, but hindered by fear and by misunderstanding.*
>
> *You have built for yourselves psychic suits of armor, and clad in them, your vision is restricted, your movements are clumsy and painful, your skin is bruised, and your spirit is broiled in the sun.*
>
> *I am chaos. I am the substance from which your artists and scientists build rhythms. I am the spirit with which your children and clowns laugh in happy anarchy. I am chaos. I am alive, and I tell you that you are free.*

The *Principia* offers a very different view of Eris to that held by the Ancient Greeks. The modern-day Goddess honored by Erisians is a trickster deity of freedom and subversive humor rather than the cruel Goddess who loved warfare and battles. Whether she is the same Goddess or whether there are actually two with the same name might bother theologians, but for Erisians inconsistencies like that are just part of the fun of working with Eris.

Another famous quote from the *Principia* covers potential flame war material of whether two incompatible things can both be true:

GP: Is Eris true?

M2: Everything is true.

GP: Even false things?

M2: Even false things are true.

GP: How can that be?

M2: I don't know man, I didn't do it.

There are many ways of interpreting the seeming impossibility of the idea that "Everything is true... Even the false things." You can take it to mean that everyone has their own truth and we should respect each other's ideas on religion or spirituality even if we don't think their point of view makes sense. You can also take it as a koan – a paradox to be meditated on in an effort to escape intellectual reasoning and gain intuitive enlightenment. Or you can just take it as humor. The *Principia Discordia* is full of humor. It is quite likely the most humorous religious text ever written. Read it and have a good laugh. Eris gets the joke too.

The way I encountered Eris was through reading the *Illuminatus! Trilogy*, a series of science fiction books by Robert Shea and Robert Anton Wilson, published in 1975 and inspired by the *Principia* and Discordianism. I read the novels avidly, one after the other, while lying on my sofa suffering from a nasty bout of flu one winter. I was captivated.

I was no doubt feverish and possibly delirious, but the Goddess Eris seemed to speak to me through the books, and later in my thoughts and dreams. I had been feeling trapped in a lifestyle I found dull, and the message she gave me was that I could change all that if I wanted. Anything is possible. She set me on the way to becoming a Pagan, and a writer, and having lots of fun.

Once, many years later, after I had consumed some then-legal magic mushrooms while on holiday in Amsterdam, she even stepped out of the telly in my hotel bedroom and initiated me as her priestess. Perhaps I should add she was dressed as Barbie at the time and also told me to wear more pink... Well, maybe.

Everything is true...

Lucya Starza is an Eclectic Gardnerian Wiccan and a Priestess of Eris. She writes A Bad Witch's Blog at www.badwitch.co.uk and contributed to *Essays in Contemporary Paganism* and *Paganism 101*. Writing as Lucya Szachnowski, she co-wrote Call of Cthulhu roleplaying game supplements and scenarios published by Chaosium including *The London Guidebook, Day of the Beast, Strange Aeons* and *Before the Fall*.

Faery Queen

In your names, my Queen, I am enchanted, Enchantress.
[From a private prayer to the Faery Queen]

The Faery Queen could be a controversial Goddess, if folk stopped to think about her for too long. As the wilderness personified, however, she doesn't allow too much thought, which is amusing for a Lady who wraps words around her like we would a cloak against the wind. The Fae are the powers of the Untamed Wild, and their Queen is just as untameable, and yet she appears in stories throughout history.

In *The Faerie Queens* Sorita D'Este and David Rankine collect together stories of many Goddesses who bear the title Faerie Queen, and in *Fairies and Fairy Stories: A History*, Diane Purkiss charts the life of faeries throughout written history, beginning with their roots as the desert wildness-that-destroys. Here their Queen appears as Lilith, Queen of the Lilim who steal children. She is the danger of the desert as nature is the source of life and that which can take without warning. A little later, in the forests of the North, Holda stands as our Queen. Her lake in which the souls of unborn children live and her connection to snow show us the Queen's continued role as wilderness personified, and her kinder side teaches us how to live well.

More recently we find the unnamed Queen of Elphame in the ballads of Thomas the Rhymer and Tam Lin, yet again stealing away human beings and whisking them off to another world, just as the appearance of Shakespeare's Titania transports the audience of *A Midsummer Night's Dream* whilst Morgan le Fey guides the boat that carries Arthur's soul across the lake to Avalon and has great healing powers. Through each of these tales we find the power behind the throne in the magic of nature. Historically we can see that Faeryland has often been equated with the land of the dead and its Queen always moves between worlds. Most importantly, however, She is the director of forces beyond human control, the Weaver of the Wild.

I began by telling you she would be controversial, and she does not have an overt following because, unlike Isis, Rhiannon, Brigid, Freya, or other Goddesses who have clear, relatable personalities, The Faery Queen appears almost as an archetypal figure rather than the distinct deity that she is. Which raises the first question: what makes someone a Goddess? In her case, despite the fact that her "name" is a title, she has her own personality that carries through all incarnations. Just as Wiccans may worship The Lord and The Lady, The Queen of Faery is a being in her own right as well as the force of wilderness that is sometimes worn as a crown by other Goddesses.

The Queen takes her shape through stories, which are often considered to be our strongest force to create order. Which raises a second question: how can an untamed power be so wrapped up in words? If you know the tale of True Thomas, you'll know he was forbidden from speaking while in Faeryland and, when he returned, he was given the gift of the tongue that cannot lie. When the true name of something is known it can be summoned. True words have power to invoke truth. Naming the magic of the wildness invokes it in our spirits and bring us to connection, to ecstasy AND we are animals and our power of language arises from us, so words are an expression of nature, and thus, when spoken honestly and with feeling, they come from the untamed heart of us. A prayer spoken with passion, a poem written from deep emotions, a speech given from the heart moves the part of us which belongs to The Faery Queen. Because of this, she often comes to us through stories.

When we give honor to the Spirits of the land, we honor her. When we invite Freya as her sensual, untamed warrior self, we honor The Faery Queen incarnated as a Nordic beauty. When we speak of Rhiannon as mother and compassionate queen, we acknowledge the Queen as the magic in the land which can guide us even within civilization.

Interestingly, the Faery King is rarely found in the throne room. Her consort is the Lord of the Wildwood; Oberon stalks the land and lives within it whilst Titania interacts with humanity. The unnamed Queen stands alone, taking mortals as her lovers because her King is the life within the land. She directs the shape of nature, he enlivens it. I know Him simply as Himself. Throughout R J Stewart's writings, and those of his students, we are encouraged to approach the world of Faery ourselves, learn through experience. The Queen is quietly and powerfully present in these experiences. Having no one name (but the one you discover through relationship with Her) she is rarely spoken of as a Goddess in her own right but she is known by those who speak of Nature as their Muse, by those who dance in the forest and compose poems of love for the magic in the land. There is no one way of approaching her but the tales all agree, she is powerful and must be respected as she is a Lady in her own right. She loves beauty, honesty and commitment, and despises lies. She is not human and never tamed, but crosses the boundaries between the worlds as we would wade across a river and, if she so chooses, she can carry you across too.

The Faery Queen has never left us, through stories which move our heart she dances and in the landscape we see her power shining through. If you want to meet her, take an offering of your favorite drink outside, sing her the most passionate song of love you can find and listen to her laughter on the wind. Read her tales and feel the magic which is hers, regardless of who wears the crown.

Halo Quin is a philosopher and artist who has been enchanted by faery all her life. She recently wrote about the Faery Queen, Rhiannon, in *The Faerie Queens*. She is a teacher in Reclaiming, a storyteller and an Enchantress in her own Fae-kissed path. Find her at www.aworldenchanted.com.

Flidais

Flidais is the Celtic Irish Goddess of Animals, both wild and tame and a protector of the deep and dark forest; an Earth Mother Goddess of Balance; a shape shifter; a Goddess of the Harvest and of Abundance, Sexuality and our Wild Nature. She can be invoked any time but because of Her balanced nature, it is most appropriate to call on Her during Mabon celebrations.

As a Goddess of Harvest and Abundance, we celebrate Her gift of the knowledge of cultivation and for Her herd of magickal cattle, which are said to include the wild beasts of the forest. She is also the comforting Mother of all things domestic, especially cultivated fields and farm animals. She would appear at harvest time and at milking. She taught Her children, Arden and Be Teite, as well as Be Chuille and Dinard, the secrets of cultivation and husbandry. They in turn passed this knowledge to their communities. Thus, they are remembered as heroes and the people were fed.

In balance, in Her aspect as the Wild Woman, She can be seen riding through the forest and field in a chariot pulled by a stag with majestic antlers. As She passes by, She stops for wounded warriors and heals their wounds and nourishes them with the milk of her prized magickal hornless cow, Maol. In one story, She feeds an entire army of 300 warriors with the milk of Her herd of cattle. Some people associate Her with the Green Man, She being the Wild Woman who not only protects and nurtures the wild lands but also gives us license to express the wild sexuality of our base nature. Her sexuality is legend. It is said Her sexual appetite would outlast any seven women and her many daughters inherited the power from their mother.

Flidais is of the Tuatha De Danann who, in defeat, descended into the Underworld to become the rulers of the Faerie Lands. Her tales include several husbands and lovers and her many children have disputed fathers. Her lovers and husbands include Ailill, Adammair and Fergus. Her children include Fand, Li Ban, Dianann, Be Chuille, Dinard, Be Teite, Iaran, Caevog, Arden and Nia Segamain. Little is known about Flidais and even less is known about Her children except as a casual mention in the stories. Fand is the exception; She became a powerful Faerie Queen. Her story is Her own. The rest of Flidais's children are believed to have been powerful witches and sorcerers who aided the Tuatha in their battles for control of Ireland.

I envision Flidais as a hooded Goddess with the long red hair of Celtic royalty. She is naked beneath Her brown and forest green robe. She is tall with a stern and determined stature. Her piercing eyes are commanding and Her lips are inviting. She also goes barefoot through both field and deep woods and wears bangles around Her ankles.

El Bee Kanobe is the Dean of Religious Studies at the College of Occult Science, a member of the board of directors of Oak Spirit Sanctuary, a founding member of the Council of Alternative Spiritual Traditions and long-time Priest and Elder of Yarrow Coven of St. Louis.

Frau Holle

Frau Holle is a Goddess of ancient origins, known throughout the ages in different variants across different countries. In Her beginnings She was the supreme Goddess of the early Germanic peoples, crossing the years, intermingling with the pantheons that developed and changing as migration and civilization took hold. Amongst her many names, She has been known as Frau Perchta/Berchta, Frau Holle and Frau Herke/Freke/Gode/Wode depending on the region. Her legends and tales predate most of the Germanic pantheon.

Frau Holle is a Goddess with many associations, though she is most well known for her connection to classical women's work in the home. She was seen as governing the spinning and the domestic chores, but she also oversaw the lives of the women, from childbirth to their crone years. At the birthing of a child, midwives would place mugwort (a sacred herb to Frau Holle) in the hand of the laboring woman. Runes were drawn on the midwife's palms, which she would place upon the mother and invoke the aid of the idis, the female ancestors of her line. After the birth, the midwife would lay the child upon the earth, and ask for the blessings of Frau Holle. [*Witchcraft Medicine*, Storl. Wolf-Dieter.]

Motherhood was sacred, young maidens would bathe in pools and waters in the hope of a blessing to be healthy and fertile. In a woman's crone years, she would turn Walriderske (hedge-rider). The woman would sit at the hedgerow, to communicate with spirits and Frau Holle. Milk or a small portion of porridge was a common offering. Here she appears as the Goddess of Witches. Her followers would sacrifice a goose in her honor, and rub the fat infused with mugwort onto them to aid in hedge riding.

Aside from her aspects governing the domestic lives of

women, She was known as both Queen of the Elves and Witches, and Queen of the Dead. As Queen of the Elves She is associated with many mythological beings, including dwarves, elves, huldrefolk and more. In some legends the story of Her procession with Wodan during Zwolften (the Twelve days of Christmas/Yule) includes the many faerie beings that fall under Her protection, racing across the land bestowing blessings. During medieval times the beliefs of faeries changed them from supernatural beings to the souls of unborn children or children who died before naming. This leads on to the belief that in Germany it is Frau Holle (known as Frau Wode in those regions) who leads the wild hunt procession of the dead, during the same Zwolften as the previous tale.

As the Goddess of death She was associated with winter, and the darker nature of the wilderness. Small white figurines of the Goddess could be found alongside graves, in the hope she would assist the person in moving on to the afterlife. The Totenfrau (women who cared for the dead) would put good new shoes on the deceased so they could manage the long walk with Frau Holle to her realm. Holda, as Queen of Death, was not feared, but rather looked on as a loving figure assisting people in their final transition. She appeared as either a crooked old woman, or a beautiful youth dressed in white.

Frau Holle throughout Teutonic mythology has been seen as a beneficial deity of nature. She is the rain-giving clouds, the wind, and the sun that grants prosperity to the fields. She was linked with Dunar (the Germanic interpretation of Thor) as the spouse of the sky God. She was seen present in many bodies of water, such as bogs, ponds and wells.

In later mythology she was linked with Wodan, and the pair would lead the mighty procession through the land known as the wild hunt. The procession would start benignly, as a blessing and later turn into the frenzied chaos of frightening beings and howling wolves. Frau Holle was honored at Modraniht (Mother's

Night, held on the same day as the Winter Solstice) along with the idis she oversees.

She was seen as the wise virgin riding a growling bear in spring, a forest Goddess on her stag or flower-covered sun bride in the summer months, a plump farmer's wife at harvest time, and the old grey witch in the winter. [*Witchcraft Medicine*. Storl, Wolf-Dieter.] Her holy tree was the elder. Elder trees were known to house spirits of many kinds, and were a threshold to her realm as well as the realm of the fae.

In modern days, we have lost much of our respect and reverence for those domestic duties that were held sacred by our ancestors. As such, a large aspect of this Goddess would be seen as irrelevant to many who come upon her. However, as stated, she is so much more than a home and hearth deity. She is the motivation when struggles become too much to bear on our own. She can be called upon in all aspects of home management and life events. The followers of Frau Holle invoke Her for blessings upon their gardens, homes, and aid in dealing with the local land spirits. As a deity of witches She can be called upon for guidance in potion making, knot magic and astral shape shifting, amongst other things encompassed in a witch's practice.

Her common modern correspondences for connecting to her are: ice, snow, winter, wolves, geese, mugwort, pastel blue and the color white. All of these can be represented on an altar to Her, which should be located in the kitchen.

Frau Holle is a Goddess whose associations and relevance spans time immemorial. As she was in ancient times, she is honored and cherished today by those who work with and worship her. Her relevance never dies, as she is a Goddess of life, which continues on through the eons.

Rosalie Nilsonhaus is the owner of Grove of the Wildstars, a Pagan writer and lifetime devotee of Frau Holle.

Freyja

Freyja (also Freya) is the Goddess of fertility, sensuality, love, beauty, music and childbirth and is known as the *Bride of the Vanir*. Freyja (meaning Lady) is sister to Freyr (Lord), and daughter of Njord of Vanaheim. She is famed for her beauty, and her counterparts are Venus and Aphrodite. She is also known as a sorceress as she is skilled in magic, especially that of Seidr.

Freyja is young and full of life. Although brimming with love and energy, she is also a battle Goddess with much strength. Associated with war and death, Freyja claims half of all battle-slain warriors with Odin, half going to Valhalla and half going to her own hall.

She is married to the God Odr (although she has many lovers). There are claims that Odr and Odin are the same god and that she and Frigg are the same Goddess, but there are other claims to dispute this.

Freyja has a magical cloak of feathers, which allows the wearer to change into a falcon. She is linked with the boar and mare. Two cats drawing a chariot, a gift from Thor, accompany her.

Kevin Crossley-Holland ably retells the Norse myths in his book *Norse Myths* (Penguin, reprint edition 1993). Perhaps the most familiar are those of how Freyja came to join the Æsir, and the Necklace of Brisingamen.

In the first tale, Asgard and Vanaheim were at war. At first it was the Vanir who gained ground with spells to reduce the walls of Asgard to rubble. The Æsir fought back and caused as much damage to Vanaheim. Soon it was realized that neither side was gaining ground. The Gods grew weary of the constant warring. Peace was agreed with an exchange of gifts as proof of their good intentions. Vanir Njord, his son Freyr and daughter Freyja were accompanied by Kvasir, wisest of the Vanir, as part of the trade of leading figures. In exchange, the Æsir sent Homir and Mimir to Vanaheim.

Although the Æsir disliked the fact that Freyr and Freyja were conceived by Njord's own sister, they accepted them. Njord and Freyr were appointed as priests to preside over sacrifices, and Freyja was consecrated as a sacrificial priestess. She soon taught all her skills in witchcraft to the Æsir.

In the later saga of the Brisingamen necklace, we learn that one night Loki followed Freyja, who had set out on foot from Sessrumnir. At daybreak, Freyja came to a large cavern and within it found a smithy. Diligently working away were four dwarves: Alfrigg, Dvalin, Berling and Grerr. Dazzled at first by the furnace, it took her a moment to see the breath-taking necklace of woven gold. She had never seen anything so beautiful or desired anything so much.

Freyja was willing to pay anything for the necklace, but the ugly dwarves were not interested. Freyja was forced to make a bargain that in exchange for the necklace she would agree to lie with each of them for one night. Freyja kept her part of the bargain and the dwarves theirs.

Loki watched the unfolding events and reported to Odin what he has seen. Odin, consumed with jealousy, ordered Loki to retrieve the necklace.

With skill, Loki first turned himself into a fly and again into a flea and was nimbly able to steal the necklace and take it back to Odin.

Waking to find it gone, Freyja ran to Odin and cried tears of gold, but Odin would not agree to give it to her telling her she would never see it again, except under one condition. She must stir up hatred and war, and find two kings of Midgard and have them meet on the battlefield with twenty vassal kings. She must use charms to bring life back to the dead and each time a warrior fell, he must stand up unarmed and fight again. They should have no choice but to rip each other to pieces. Freyja agreed and asked for her necklace.

According to Snorri (*Prose Edda*), it was Freyja who brought the practice of Seidr with her when she joined the Æsir and taught them to Odin. Seidr was a shamanic divination ceremony presided over by a woman (*völva* or seeress), although this can also be a man. Generally the *völva* sat on a high platform and wore a special costume and headdress made of animal furs. Spirits were invoked and the *völva* would pass into a trance. The spirits would reveal hidden information to her. The *völva* then passed this prophecy to an individual or advised the community.

Accordingly it appears that the practice of Seidr, and also divination, originated with Freyja.

Modern Seidr practice differs from individual shamanic journeying and hedge riding in that it involves more than one person. Up to three seers/seeresses are used for each session. These are frequently dressed in robes and veils or headdresses. The seer/seeress is helped into a trance often by group chanting. Someone works as a mediator between those asking the questions and the seer/seeress; though on occasions, the questions are asked direct with someone keeping watch on and guiding the proceedings. If the seers/seeresses tire, then the session is brought to an end and they are carefully directed out of the trance by the mediator by chanting or, as with shamanic journeying, by retracing the steps taken to enter the trance.

A popular form of divination The Elder Futhark Runes are also linked to the Vanir Gods. The twenty-four runes are divided in to three lots of eight runes called *aetts*. The first aett is ruled over by Freyr, brother of Freyja, though many prefer to attribute them to both as they are likely to have both been skilled in all forms of magic and divination. And it was Freyja who introduced Odin to magic in general.

The rune Fehu from Freyr's aett (Cattle – letter F), is generally linked with Freyja, Freyr and their father Njord. Fehu means won or earned wealth, prosperity, good fortune, and fertility.

Harmonia Saille is an author and Hedge Witch who holds workshops on spirituality, divination and other subjects both locally and at international spiritual events. She is the author of *Pagan Portals: Hedge Witchcraft* and *Pagan Portals: Hedge Riding* and lives in Ireland.

Frigga

One of the most popular Goddesses in the ancient Norse religion was Frigga, who was also called Frigg, Fricka, and Frija. It is from Frigga's German name that we get the name for our fifth day of the week, Friday, or Frija's Day. Her name is probably from a word that means "beloved" and, based on how widespread her worship was, she does seem to have been a beloved Goddess.

Frigga was the wife of Odin, the leader of the Æsir (the Norse Gods) and mother of Baldr. Often called the queen of the Gods, Frigga is a Goddess who may represent the principle of sovereignty. This would make sense as she is both the pre-eminent Goddess of the pantheon and also as a daughter of Fjorgyn (Earth) she is connected to the earth and could represent the right to rule. She is a wise Goddess who can see the future and is said to know the fates of all men. Frigga is also associated with the home, domestic order, and spinning, and could be described as a Goddess of housewives; she was also historically called on to aid in childbirth. Interestingly, her connection to spinning and weaving may also relate to her association with knowing the fates of people, since spinning was sometimes a metaphor for creating fate and may also be associated with acts relating to prophecy. It is said that Frigga has twelve handmaidens, all Goddesses in their own right, who serve her. Frigga also has her own hall in Asgard, the home of the Æsir, called Fensalir, whose name is related to marsh or swamp, and might indicate a connection between Frigga and such natural locations.

Frigga has many myths, but perhaps the best known is her quest to protect her son Baldr. Baldr began having disturbing dreams and so Odin sought to find out if there was any deeper meaning. After consulting a seeress he was told that the dreams foretold Baldr's death. Trying to protect her son, Frigga traveled the world getting everything she met – each plant, animal, and stone – to swear not to harm Baldr. She left out only the mistletoe, which seemed too small and harmless to be a danger to anyone. However, later the Gods were celebrating Baldr's invulnerability by throwing all manner of weapons at him, each of which fell harmlessly aside until someone threw a mistletoe dart at him. The tiny dart killed the shining God.

In another story relating to her role as a Goddess of sovereignty, Frigga's husband Odin goes off on a journey. When a long time has gone by and he has not returned she eventually takes both of his brothers, Vili and Ve, as her lovers and they take over ruling the Gods in Odin's place. Eventually Odin returns and takes back his wife and proper place leading the Gods. This story may represent Frigga's place as the giver of kingship, and show her significance in maintaining the proper order.

The Norse people remained Pagan longer than many others, converting to Christianity 1,000 years ago, and so the Norse Gods stayed, perhaps, closer to the surface of folk memory and folklore than some other Gods. Frigga, as Frea, appears in the *Historia Langobardorum* in the 8th century. In this, she tricks Odin into favoring in battle a group of people who have prayed to her over his own choice. Frigga appears in the 13th century collection of stories and poems written by Snorri Sturluson called the *Prose Edda* and *Poetic Edda*, as well as the 13th century *Ynglinga Saga*. During the same time period Saxo Grammaticus wrote about her in his *Gesta Danorum*. In the 19th century she would appear in a very different form in Wagner's operas *Der Ring des Nibelungen* under the name Fricca.

Many modern people who honor Frigga associate the colors blue and white with her and images or artwork of Frigga might depict her wearing these colors. Birch trees are also often associated with her and the rune Berkano, which is related to the birch and new beginnings, is sometimes called Frigga's rune. Her symbols are the distaff and keys, and some modern followers of

Frigga will wear keys to represent her; keys also represented a woman's power within the home. When called on during childbirth, Frigga was asked to use her keys to unlock the woman's womb or limbs in order to ease the birth and so some modern practitioners will wear a key for Frigga during labor and delivery.

Norse Pagans (also called Heathens or Asatruar) celebrate some different holidays than other Pagans, and for many Norse Pagans Frigga is honored just before the winter solstice on a holiday called Mother's Night, or Modranecht. This holiday honors female ancestors and also often includes honoring Frigga; Norse Pagans may also choose to honor Frigga at any time they feel like doing so throughout the year. Offerings to Frigga can include milk, water, handmade items – especially those sown, woven, or spun – or baked goods. Because of the association with her hall, Fensalir, and swamps, it might be appropriate to leave offerings to Frigga in swamps or bogs.

Frigga is a Goddess of sovereignty and of fate, but most of all she is a Goddess of the home. Domestic order and success are her purview and honoring her is honoring the importance of home and family in our lives. Welcoming Frigga into our lives is an opportunity to understand the value of home and family.

Morgan Daimler is the gythia of Stormlight Kindred, a member of the Troth, and a Druid in the Order of the White Oak. She has had her poetry and prose published in five anthologies, Circle magazine, and Witches and Pagans magazine. Morgan is the author of the book *By Land, Sea, and Sky, A Child's Eye View of the Fairy Faith, Where the Hawthorn Grows* and *Fairy Witchcraft*.

Gerða

*...As she raised her hands to unlatch the door in front of her, a
beautiful light shone from them both so that earth and sky and sea
were brighter for it...*
[*The Poetic Edda*]

Gerða or Gerð (usually anglicized to Gertha or Gerda) is a
mountain giantess who is a member of the Norse-Icelandic
pantheon and her name appears in both the *Poetic Edda* and *Prose
Edda*, which date from 13th century Iceland. Whilst she is a little
celebrated Goddess, she is probably best known for being the
wife of Freyr, one of the most important Gods of the Norse
pantheon, who presides over harvest, abundance and fertility.
She is also named as being a one of the Asyniur, the Goddesses of
the Æsir pantheon who reside in the world of Asgard, one of the
Nine Worlds from Norse mythology. Gerða is also mentioned in
Snorri Sturluson's *Inglinga Saga* where she appears as the wife of
Freyr, named there as the King of Sweden. Between them they
have a son named Fjollnir which means "manifold". She is also
listed as having been a sexual partner of the God Odin. Although
Gerða is not mentioned in any of the Anglo Saxon texts, Freyr is,
so it is possible that she was also known in the British Isles
during the Saxon period as well as throughout Scandinavia.

The most famous story in which she appears is the *Skirnismal*
or Lay of Skirnir. After spying on her from afar and falling in love
with her great beauty, Freyr sends his messenger Skirnir to woo
Gerða for him and to bring her back to Asgard. Freyr's love for
Gerða is such that he gives Skirnir his magical horse and his
sword to complete the task. When Skirnir arrives at Gerða's
father's hall, he offers her precious gifts if she will consent to be
Freyr's wife. When she is not moved he threatens her, which she
also finds unimpressive, saying:

For no man's sake will I ever suffer,
To be thus moved by might...

Finally Skirnir resorts to casting a terrible curse, which calls madness, rage and longing upon her if she will not acquiesce. Gerða then gives in, saying that she herself loves Freyr, and agrees to meet him nine days hence in the forest of Barri where their union takes place. Skirnir carries the news to Freyr who is overjoyed by the news, but devastated that he must wait nine nights for her.

It is difficult to know how Gerða was honored historically as very little of her lore remains. As the wife of a fertility God, and a mountain giantess, she is often associated with the earth and fertility and may have originally represented the cold of the winter earth being coaxed to life by the warmth of the sun, which is closely associated with Freyr. There are certainly elements of the ancient dynamic of the union of earth and sky about their marriage. Yet, such explanations may be overly simplistic and Gerða's guarded response to Skirnir's wooings, despite her own love for Freyr holds important clues to her nature. Those who work with her in a modern context generally agree that she is a Goddess of reserved temperament who hides hidden depths and passions that she does not reveal easily. She is often described as wearing brown and earth-colored gowns which cover her completely with her hair in a long dark plait that reaches to the floor.

Further indications of her nature can be found within her name. Gerða in Old Norse means "fenced in" or "to guard" and she is often associated by modern devotees with the concept of *Innangarð*, meaning "inside the enclosure" – that which is tamed or safe sanctuary, and *Utengarð*, meaning "outside the enclosure" – that which is wild, dangerous or chaotic. These two concepts most frequently refer to physical spaces, but may also be used to denote cultural, psychological or social states too. Gerða is often associated with the peace and safety of Innangarð, holding the sanctuary of sacred space, and as such she may be called upon for healing.

Gerða's close association with the earth, healing and the guarded enclosure has meant that she has come to be associated with walled gardens, particularly herb gardens. Planting and tending an herb garden is a way to honor her and she may enjoy offerings of herbs, teas, or essential oils.

However, her name may more accurately denote her as a Goddess of the physical boundary or barrier that divides the inner and the outer, rather than of the spaces themselves. As such she can be seen as the boundary between the wild and the tamed, keeping the balance between the two, which makes human society and culture possible. Humanity has always sought to moderate the environment in order that existence may be more viable or comfortable. We seek out new modes of agriculture, medicine and technology, build libraries, and fly to far flung corners of the globe, but there must be a balance. In seeking to overly control our environment, separating ourselves from nature, we risk damaging or changing it beyond recognition and compromising our own survival at the same time. This may be seen not only in humanity's relationship with the environment, but in our personal relationships too. In working with boundaries, Gerða can teach us how far we can or should push this fragile balance in order to obtain what we need.

Gerða and Freyr represent the meeting of two very different peoples, the Giants and the Gods, between whom there is often fighting and disagreement. Consequently, as a couple, they are often called upon to bless marriages between people for whom being together is difficult, perhaps coming from different religious or cultural backgrounds, or opposed by family or friends. Their love shows us that there can be harmony between two seemingly opposing worlds, but that this needs to be negotiated and considered with care.

Nell Griffiths-Haynes has been working and studying within the British Pagan community for the past fifteen years. Working as a trustee for The Druid Network, and as a priest, teacher and celebrant, her magical practice is a fusion of Druidry and Heathenry focused predominantly on the Gods and stories of English and Germanic mythology. She can be found blogging at theanimistscraft.wordpress.com

Hathor

The Goddess Hathor's worship in ancient Egypt is one of the oldest among the Egyptian pantheon. Evidence for her worship can be found in the earliest dynastic period. There is a modern belief that Hathor's worship predates the earliest dynastic social structure in Egypt. This belief cannot be supported by archeological evidence because so little is known about pre dynastic (pre written record) Egypt. It is based on the observation that her worship seems well established in the earliest recorded period and therefore might predate it. Those who support this idea suppose that her worship began as an earth/Nile/fertility Goddess cult and later she became associated with complex social structures, dynastic life, and the pharaoh. In this way she may be approached as a primary divine mother.

Hathor or Het-heret's main worship center was at Dendera where a temple to her still stands. It is possible to visit her temple at Dendera, though the temple suffered damage due to the effects of war and other destructive elements.

She is primarily described as the daughter of Ra and the partner of Horus, though these relationships are flexible. She has also been described as the mother of Ra, the wife of Ra, the mother of Horus the Younger and the wife of Horus the Elder. In this way she may be worshiped as the eternal Goddess and Horus the changing God in modern Tameran Wicca practice.

It is difficult to pin down what sort of Goddess Hathor is in relation to the modern categorizing of mother, maiden, crone, lunar or solar, water or earth Goddesses.

As the daughter of Ra she is a maiden, though as mother of Ra she can be accepted as an all-mother figure. Her worship made use of music and dancing (a common element still today). She is closely associated with the systrum, a musical instrument. She is a Goddess of happiness, merry-making, and the sacredness of sex. She played a role in easing childbirth for new mothers, protecting both the mother and child. As the seven Hathors she is like the Fates or other feminine controllers of human destiny.

As lady of the western horizon she takes part in the funereal rites of ancient Egypt. In this aspect she is a dark maiden or crone figure. While she is associated with all the traditional feminine arts (dance, song, adorning with makeup, musical instruments, beauty in all forms, flowers, and perfume), she also is associated with astrology and other hidden arts for which she can be engaged today in modern practice.

She is depicted as a celestial cow figure or a woman with cow's ears and solar disc. She has a tie to the stars of the Milky Way. As Goddess of the eastern horizon she is a solar Goddess, though in modern times she has been categorized as a lunar Goddess. Perhaps that is because of her association with the River Nile, and bodies of water. As a Goddess of feminine arts and particularly of make-up, she is associated with malachite, chrysocolla, and turquoise, which could be ground into a powder for cosmetics.

Many aspects that were later associated with Isis were first associated with Hathor, especially those of her solar aspects and close link with women, and all stars. She is referred to as the Cosmic Mother, just as Isis. Hathor also has a leonid (lion) aspect which is illustrated in her most famous myth which also depicts her tie to the Nile.

In the myth that dates to the Middle Kingdom, Ra, associated with pharaoh, has been ridiculed, shamed, or annoyed by humanity who have lost respect for him. In one version humanity is making too much noise, in another they have openly scorned the God Ra. Ra then speaks to the other Egyptian deities about what should be done with humanity. Who will avenge Ra for the scorn human beings have exhibited for him? Finally, Hathor as the Eye of Ra says she will bring justice to those who have scorned or annoyed him.

Hathor exacts her revenge. In this aspect she may be viewed as a Goddess of divine justice or revenge. She becomes violent to the point of bloodlust. She either shapeshifts into the lion-headed Goddess Sekhmet (in most modern tellings of the myth) or in some other way Sekhmet is engaged as a darker aspect of Hathor. Working with her in this aspect has been useful for women to express their anger or to invoke justice. In Goddess-worship circles and especially in feminist witchcraft Sekhmet-Hathor is viewed as the Mother of mothers and assists women in all stages of life. They may be viewed as sisters or two sides of the same Goddess. Sekhmet as the lionheaded Goddess of vengeance frightens Ra and the other deities. The primary fear is that Sekhmet-Hathor knows no limits. She may destroy all of humanity with her anger.

In order to calm her and keep her from destroying humanity, Ra and the other Gods devise a plan to get her drunk on the Nile River. They mix some red pigment, generally believed to be a red clay with as much wine as can fill the Nile. Seeing the red Nile, Sekhmet begins to satisfy her thirst for blood on it. She drinks up the entire Nile River full of wine and red clay. She gets drunk and is satisfied. She then becomes Hathor again. In this way Hathor is associated with merry-making/drunkenness or ecstatic experience of all kinds and changes in consciousness.

Hathor is quite a versatile Goddess. In modern practice she can be viewed as the Cosmic Mother figure, as a fertility Goddess, as a solar Goddess, as a maiden, a Goddess of love, sex, marriage, women, childbirth, children, and health. She can also be a Goddess of justice in her Sekhmet-Hathor guise, a Goddess who assists the dead in their transition to the otherworld, a dark maiden, a crone, and much more.

Hathor SilverRiver contributed to *Paganism 101*. She has been a dedicant to Hathor, from whom she derives her craft name, for over six years, relating to her as Cosmic Mother with a dual nature illustrated in Sekhmet-Hathor.

Hecate

Hecate, or Hekate, is a triple Goddess, the keeper of keys, the carrier of the torch, and the one who stands at the crossroads. While her form has often been found in Greek art and sculpture, she is thought to have originated in Anatolia, or what is now Turkey. In Hesiod's *Theogony*, it is said that Hecate was the daughter of the Titans Perses and Asteria. Further along her family tree, some scholars have stated that she was a cousin of Artemis. In other sources, Hecate is said to be a daughter of Nyx and Erebus, while other texts name her as the daughter of Zeus and Hera. She is also linked to Hades, and some believe they were married while other texts purport she was a virgin by choice.

While Hesiod's poem, composed in 700BC, would have many believe Hecate to be a larger Goddess figure, this is not an agreed upon fact. There is much thought given to the idea that Hecate was a household deity, a Goddess who supported the daily lives of the people. At the same time, it is clear that Hecate held some importance, as the findings of d'Este and Rankine in 2009 note that her image was used on coins, along with the image of Zeus.

Researchers have uncovered sculptures of Hecate from Roman times, including The Hecate Chiaramonti, which depicts her as a triple Goddess, through a copy of the original from the Hellenistic period. During the time between the 2nd and 8th centuries, some scrolls have noted these heads may have been a dog, a serpent, and a horse, while others have suggested a cow and a boar head.

As a pre-Olympian earth Goddess, Hecate emerges as a Great Goddess in Anatolia, though it is unclear if she is truly Greek, as many have stated her beginnings to be. Her followers began to spread into Greece, where she may have been moved into the Greek pantheon.

According to *The New Book of Goddesses and Heroines* by Patricia Monaghan, Hecate is accompanied by sacred dogs and carries a torch, often in the dark of the moon. Her worship was widespread in the Classical Ages, with private suppers and public sacrifices.

During the Middle Ages, Hecate began to be known as the Queen of the Witches, a title that has continued to modern times.

Today, her followers are spread throughout the world, often carrying on the traditional methods of worship and ritual. During the dark moon, some devotees to Hecate will gather for a supper, often with honey and lamb, and sit outside in the darkness of the hidden moon. When the supper is over, the leftovers are placed at a crossroads or outdoors as an offering to Hecate and to her dogs.

According to the *Dictionary of Greek and Roman Biography and Mythology*:

At the close of every month dishes with food were set out for her and other averters of evil at the points where two roads crossed each other; and this food was consumed by poor people. (Aristoph. Plot. 596; Plut. Synmpos. vii. 6.) The sacrifices offered to her consisted of dogs, honey, and black female lambs. (Plut Quaest. Rom. 49; Schol. ad Theocrit. ii. 12; Apollon. Rhod. iii. 1032).

While Hecate is linked with a number of symbols, the keys, torch, and crossroads are the ones that continue to be used in modern ritual. Trances to crossroads may be done on dark moons or at Samhain, as Hecate is also linked with the underworld. She is often seen as the one who helps those who are taking journeys, and the one who can guide the way.

Worshippers of Hecate might place statues of her triple Goddess image in front of their house, or in the entryways to help protect the home, and to ward off ghosts and apparitions.

According to Patricia Monaghan in *The New Book of Goddesses and Heroines*:

> And Greek women evoked Hecate for protection from her hosts whenever they left the house, and they erected threefold images at their doors, as if to tell wandering spirits that therein lived friends of their queen, who must not be bothered with night noises and spooky apparitions.

To celebrate Hecate today, in addition to her suppers, followers might look too the Deipnon for inspiration. This was a day celebrated by the Athenian Greeks, during which a large meal was eaten at the end of the day and a meal was served to Hecate and to the unsettled dead during the night of the invisible moon. It was said that this meal would settle the dead and the restless souls. And during this time, it was ideal for households to clean and to settle any unfinished business before the new moon.

Queen of the Witches, Hecate lights the way with her torch in the darkness when all seems lost, and inspires us to know we are not alone on our journeys.

Irisanya is a Witch, a priestess, a Reclaiming teacher, a dreamer, an often-vegan, a shapeshifter, and a Sagittarius who is devoted to Iris and Hecate. She has been published in *Paganism 101* and makes her living as a writer. www.irisanya.com.

Hel

When one thinks of Norse mythology, many deities come to mind: Freya, Odin, Thor, but what about Hel? What about the Goddess of the Helheim? Do people know of this place? Do people *want* to know of the Lady who oversees the Nine Worlds? How did she come to be there? Who is this place for? Why is it important in Norse mythology when everyone is trying to get to Valhalla?

Helheim is the lowest of the Nine Worlds in Norse myth. It is located in Niflheim and surrounded by the great river Gjoll. Presiding over this place is the Goddess Hel, daughter of the wily God Loki and giantess Angrboda. This often overlooked Goddess is terrible in appearance, with half of her body being flesh and the other half being black and rotting. The queen of Helheim's name means "one who hides" or "one who covers up", and who can blame her, with her hideous appearance? This visually terrifying lady came to her hall in Niflheim due to fear from the Asgardian Gods. It was prophesied that the children of Loki would bring about Ragnorok, the fall of the Gods, so she was banished by Odin to Helheim. However, she was not charged with simply living a lonely existence in the farthest reaches of the Norse universe.

Hel was given her hall as a place for the dead. She was tasked with keeping the souls of those who didn't die in battle. In her cold hall, she kept the souls of children who died, as well as those who became sick and too feeble to wield a battle axe or sword. There the souls were doomed to an eternity of misery in the cold and damp as she, with much indifference, listened to their wails of sorrow and grief.

This Goddess, and her place within the mythology, became necessary. The Norse, above all, feared her. They feared her realm. If one did not die in battle, then one must not have fought long enough or hard enough. If one did not die upon the battle-field, then it was not a glorious death to be both celebrated and mourned. If one was not struck down by combat with the enemy, then neither Odin nor the Valkyries had any interest in that soul and there would be no eternal warmth or feasting. The only soul to ever enter and escape Helheim was Hermod, in his bid to free Baldur from there and avert Ragnarok.

Baldur, the son of Odin and Frigg (or Frigga), was much loved among the Æsir. Throughout both the *Poetic Edda* and *Prose Edda*, there are numerous references to his death. These reference his death as being both a tragedy and omen for ushering in Ragnarok, the Norse end of days.

The legend goes that Baldur saw his death in a dream and, in an effort to postpone Ragnarok, Frigg went to every object in every realm and made it promise not to harm her son, every object except the mistletoe, which she saw as harmless anyway.

Loki then fashioned a magical spear (sometimes recounted as an arrow) from the mistletoe and hurried to Asgard where the Gods were engaged in hurling objects at Baldur, their favorite pastime. Loki gave the spear to Hod, Baldur's blind brother, who threw the spear and killed Baldur. And so, Baldur did not die in battle, therefore he had to "ride the road to Hel."

From this grief, Frigg ultimately sent Hermod to Hel to retrieve her son. Hermod told of how great the weeping and grief of the Æsir was and to him Hel responded, "If all things in the world, quick and dead, weep for him, then he shall go back to the Æsir; but he shall remain with Hel if any gainsay it or will not weep," according to the *Prose Edda* of Snorri Sturlson and translated by Arthur Gilchrist Brodeur (1916). All things wept for Baldur, all but the giantess Thokk, believed to be Loki in disguise. So, Baldur had to stay in Hel until after Ragnorok.

Within a modern pagan construct, Hel is not a Goddess who is mentioned or even often known outside of those who practice some kind of paganism surrounding the Norse pantheon. There are few, if any, hymns written in her praise. There are few, if any, groups dedicated to her service. Were it not for the translations of the Norse myths, Hel may have been lost completely to history. However, like many dark Goddesses, she has her place when one chooses to work with the Shadow Self and aspects of the Underworld.

This terribly ambivalent Goddess of myth may welcome modern practitioners who are brave enough to travel the "road to Hel" and gaze upon her terrifying form. She seems to be slightly aloof, as though challenging the practitioner to keep her attention. If the practitioner cannot do this, she sends him or her away with nothing gained. However, if the practitioner *can* grab her attention and keep it, Hel will impart some bit of wisdom and give him or her something to carry back. This something always depends upon the person, so it could be a bit of paper with a drawing or a bauble of some kind.

Hel is an interesting Goddess within the Norse construct. She is the antithesis of all of the things the Vikings sought after. She was, to the Norsemen, what Satan is to contemporary Christians. She was something to be feared and loathed. Her presence was part of a necessary dichotomy in their religious and cultural structure. She certainly wasn't interesting or beautiful, yet she had her part to play, just as all of the Gods often do. However, in modern paganism, Hel can be seen as another dark Goddess who can transform the Shadow Self in unique ways that other, more popular Goddesses, may not be able to.

Jennifer Gentis / Kalldrea Ash is a First Degree Priestess of the Southern Delta Church of Wicca-ATC in Lake City, Arkansas and has been studying Craft for nearly 15 years.

Inanna

The Goddess Inanna, "The Queen of Heaven and Earth", is the most important Goddess of the Sumerian pantheon in ancient Mesopotamia. In a different variation of her name, Ninnanna, the meaning changes to "Queen of the Sky". She is said to be the daughter of the Sky-God An (but also of the Moon-God Nanna) and daughter of the Moon-Goddess Ningal. Her sister is the Underworld Goddess Ereshkigal and her brother is the Sun-God Utu. She is the Goddess of sexual love (but not marriage), fertility, grain, and war.

She was known as the keeper of emotions which ranged from loving to jealous, grieving, joyous, timid, passionate, ambitious, and generosity. Her symbols include the Moon, Venus, the eight-pointed star/rosette, and the serpent. With wings and serpents on her shoulders you can see a bit of the Neolithic Bird and Snake Goddess. Because Venus would disappear behind the Sun and then reappear on the other horizon, some cultures recognized her as two separate entities, the morning and evening stars. The erratic movements of Venus and Inanna relate the two. Inanna has frequently been shown as standing on the backs of two lionesses. Inanna is connected with extramarital sex and sensual affairs, prowling the streets and taverns for sexual adventure and then treating her lovers badly. In the temples where Inanna was worshipped, sacred prostitution was commonplace. Inanna was known as a fickle woman who attracted men to her and then rejected them. She can be seen as a lavishly dressed woman or completely nude.

She stirs confusion and chaos against those who are disobedient to her, and battle itself is sometimes referred to as "the dance of Inanna". She would be at the very heart of battles and could make brothers who had lived in harmony together fight savagely against each other. Important sanctuaries of Inanna

were in Uruk, Zabalam, and Babylon. The Akkadians called her
Ishtar. Many stories and hymns are found depicting Inanna, the
most popular are those which describe her coming of age and her
descent into the underworld. During Inanna's coming of age, she
acquires her throne and bed, queenship and motherhood. She lets
go of her primitive, grasping, human aspects so that she is
deserving of her throne and bed. Inanna truly earns her
queenship of her city.

Before traveling to the underworld she takes a consort and
makes him king, and also becomes a mother. When in her aspect
as the Goddess of war, Inanna is shown in a man's armor and
armed with bow and arrows. When Inanna traveled to the under-
world/realm of the dead, she claimed to be its ruler. Her sister,
Ereshkigal, actually ruled there and sentenced Inanna to death.
When Inanna died, nature died with her, nothing would grow
anymore. The God Enki stepped in and ruled that Inanna could
be reborn if another person took her place. So, given this choice,
Inanna chose her consort Dumuzi to rule the underworld half of
every year. In this way vegetation is dead for half of the year and
during the other half is reborn. Yearly, during the New Year's
Festival (the holy marriage of Inanna of Dumuzi) which brought
fertility and growth again, Dumuzi returned from the underworld and made love to Inanna again, bringing the land to life
once more. It represented the yearly beginning and ending to
vegetation in our world. Sacred prostitutes of both genders were
used to ensure the fertility of the Earth and the continued
prosperity of the surrounding communities.

Ultimately, she was playful, passionately erotic, feminine,
powerful, independent, self-willed, ambitious and regal. Inanna
is also a part of the Mesopotamian early creation myth of the
Huluppu Tree, which is likened to the Tree of Life in the Garden
of Eden. This tells of the courtship and marriage of Inanna with
the vegetation God, Dumuzi. Inanna is traditionally likened to
the Goddess Aphrodite because of her great beauty and sensu-

ality. The myths of Inanna were created sometime between 3500 BC and 1900 BC, and possibly even earlier than that. In spite of her power as a Goddess of almost everything, Inanna becomes a wanderer and takes a leave of absence.

Most of her powers slowly dissipate during this time. Inanna provided a many-faceted symbolic image of wholeness, as she combined earth and sky, matter and spirit, earthly bounty and heavenly guidance. She was Goddess of gentle rains and terrible floods. Eventually Inanna was known by many different names (Ishtar, Isis, Neith, Metis, Astarte, Cybele, Brigit, to name a few), those in later times being described as having less power than those used before. Being the favorite of Anu, Inanna will make the ultimate comeback where she will wreak havoc in a manner that cannot be imagined. The Great Goddess can be expected to kick ass and take names... but in a good way.

Ginny "Ravenfire" Dearth has been a practicing Witch/Wiccan for more than 25 years. She is the leader and ordained minister of the Circle of Light Society.

Ishtar

Queen of Heaven. Ishtar is the name or form that Babylonians and Akkadians gave to the Sumerian Goddess Inanna; Goddess of love and war, sexuality and fertility. She was worshiped mostly in North Mesopotamia and she had temples in numerous cities, Uruk being the most important. In the Mesopotamian pantheon, she is the Moon God Sin's daughter and the Sun God Shamash's sister, but she also has been considered both daughter and consort or sacred hierodule of Anu (the Heaven God). She has an astral or stellar aspect that relates her with Venus, as the morning and evening star, and she forms a stellar triad with her father and brother. We can see that in Mesopotamian stelae where she is represented as an eight-pointed star.

Known worldwide as the Whore of Babylon due to her sexual aspect, her worship in temples would implicate ecstatic dance, orgiastic rites, men dressed like women and sacred prostitution. Every year, as every woman had to do once in their life, women would prostitute themselves in temples with the first foreigner who threw them a coin in the new year (spring, Easter). People would go in procession to celebrate the joy of the sacred marriage, the hierosgamos.

However, this wasn't her only aspect and everything wasn't all about sexuality. As a warrior Goddess, she was described as the lady of the battles, the one who rules the fighting and piles up her enemies. Brave, bellicose and fearless.

Some myths connect her with the Tree of Life and wisdom Goddesses. In fact, her priestess, the Akkadian poet and princess Enheduanna (2300 BCE), is the first person in the history of literature who joins an author's name with their work. Her poems, dedicated to Ishtar, portray her as a deity that sometimes brings happiness and sometimes brings mayhem and disaster on Earth.

The mythology surrounding Ishtar gives us a good idea of her personality. For example, in the Huluppu Tree, we see how she takes the only tree that was planted at the Euphrates riverside. This tree was swept away by the water. Ishtar takes it to Uruk, where she planted it in her sacred garden, planning to make, within its trunk, a throne to sit in and a bed to lie on. Nevertheless, a serpent, the Anzu bird and Lilith occupied it, making the Goddess cry. Then, the warrior Gilgamesh forced them out of the tree and shaped it as a throne and a bed, becoming Uruk's hero. In spite of this, in the *Epic of Gilgamesh*, she takes revenge on him because he refuses her advances. She sends him the Bull of Heaven and curses him.

Other myths tell how she gets the Me, or civilization, attributes in Eridu. Her uncle Ea (Sumerian Enki) gives them to her as he was intoxicated, so she takes them and runs away to present them to Uruk and the Sumerian people.

The story continues with the Sacred Marriage, where her brother Shamash suggests that she takes Tammuz as her consort. Tammuz, who is a shepherd and Ea's son, tries to gain her heart and demonstrates to her that he is good enough to be her husband. It is a myth rich with erotica; the lovers speak words of desire. The shepherd gives her cream and she prepares and decorates her body with oils and lapis lazuli beads. The Sacred Marriage between Ishtar and Tammuz brings the seedtime and plant growth, the lush garden and the joy of the people.

And finally, there is the popular tale of descent. The moment when, from the great above, she directed her thoughts to the lower world, the land of no return, the land of darkness. In the Babylonian version, Ishtar descends to the underworld to save her husband, Tammuz. She manages to enter, because she threatens the gatekeeper with breaking the doors and bringing the dead up to eat the living. Ereshkigal, her sister, grants her the access. Every time she goes through a door she has to leave a pledge: her crown, her earrings, her necklace, her breast ornaments, her girdle, her spangles and her loin-cloth... she passes the seven doors, arriving naked to confront her sister Ereshkigal and the seven anunnaki judges that sentence her to death. Three days later, her brother Shamash cries for the loss in the face of Sin, and Ea, who was present. He sends a eunuch for Ereshkigal's amusement so that she would absolve Ishtar.

In the Sumerian version, Inanna takes revenge on Dumuzi because he occupies the royal throne in her absence, she sends him to the underworld to take her place. Dumizi's sister tenders to replace him for six months, giving the origin of seasons.

Nowadays, thanks to the Goddess revival and the interest in feminine spirituality, Ishtar's cult is back on the scene. She sexually liberates women, considering the vulva as something sacred, she makes them descend, in a journey of self-discovery, to the land of darkness. Self-made, independent, emancipated women. Warriors and lovers. Meanwhile in Iraq, the land where the old Ishtaritu priestesses would dance and enjoy the pleasures of life, women live oppressed by their own culture. Ishtar's devotees learn to work with their bodies and minds to bring the Queen of Heaven back to the Earth.

Rosa Laguna is a devotee of Inanna/Ishtar. She is a Spanish tattooist and artist resident in London.

Isis

From the humble beginnings of a mourning queen, her influence surpassed the boundaries of Egypt and swept through the entirety of the Hellenistic world. Her role grew, transformed, and melded with the powers of other deities throughout the millennia, but she remained the embodiment of the perfect wife and mother, a powerful healer, and an unwavering protector of her people. Her name is Isis, Queen of the Heavens, and she is arguably the most important deity to rise from Egyptian antiquity.

Worshiped first in the Nile Delta, perhaps as far back as pre dynastic times, Isis was one of the nine deities of the Heliopolitan Ennead. Born from the earth God Geb and the sky Goddess Nut, Isis was the sister of Set, Nephthys, and Osiris. It was from her role as the sister-wife of Osiris that the story of Isis began. Numerous accounts recall the tale of Isis and Osiris, and although the details vary, the core of the story remains unchanged. Osiris, killed by his jealous brother Set, was torn into pieces and spread throughout the land of Egypt. Isis, so grief stricken that her tears caused the Nile River to overflow its banks, searched for the body of the slain king. With the help of Nephthys and the God of wisdom, Thoth, Isis was eventually able to resurrect Osiris and conceive a son.

It was in the role of a funerary Goddess that Isis first appeared in the written record of ancient Egypt. From the fifth dynasty, Isis became linked to the burial of the pharaoh. Her name appeared over 80 times in the Pyramid Texts that adorned the tomb of the dead king. Not only was she portrayed as the assistant to the deceased pharaoh, she was also one of the four Goddesses that protected the canopic jars that contained the king's organs. In the Middle Kingdom era, the protection of the Goddess Isis would grow to include nobles and even commoners. By the New Kingdom, Isis had acquired hundreds of titles and attributes.

Known for her great cunning, Isis was able to trick the great God Ra into revealing his secret name. This knowledge bestowed upon Isis immeasurable power. She became the Goddess of magic that did not fail, medicine, healing, and wisdom. She taught the women of Egypt to grind corn, make bread, spin flax, weave cloth, and how to tame men. She brought reading, agriculture, and the basic building blocks of civilization to her people. She protected the rich and poor alike, spreading her appeal beyond Egypt and throughout the ancient world.

As the mother of the God Horus, Isis became inextricably linked to the pharaoh. Egyptian kings saw themselves as the human vessel of Horus and, therefore, a child of Isis. The ancient Egyptian name for Isis, Aset, meant simply "throne". In this way, many believed that the power of the pharaoh was given to him through the Goddess Isis. Many artifacts still exist that depict the pharaoh sitting upon the lap of the Goddess. Just as she was portrayed as the perfect wife, Isis was also the apotheosis of the ideal mother. She became the Goddess of children, mothers, and childbirth. Again, her power filtered down from the royal family to the very lowest of Egyptian society. The love and protection of the Goddess Isis was available to any who sought her.

Because of her strength, power, and universal appeal, the cult of Isis grew unlike the worship of any other Egyptian deity. She was so revered in the land of Nubia that her temple at Philae was still active long after the Christianization of Egypt. Temples sprang up in her honor from Afghanistan to England. Large centers of worship grew in Dendera, Egypt and Byblos in Syria-Palestine. The Greco-Romans merged Isis with the Goddesses Aphrodite and Demeter. Her cult eventually surpassed that of her husband and rivaled the fledgling Christian church throughout the Hellenistic world. Isis became the archetypal Goddess, encompassing the attributes of Goddesses before her and inspiring future Goddesses throughout myriad cultures.

Although there would be many centuries when the followers of Isis would be forced to hide for fear of persecution, the worship of Isis has continued into the present day. In the late 19th century, the Hermetic Order of the Golden Dawn recognized Isis as a triple Goddess of great importance. In the early 20th century, Gerald Gardner again perpetuated the story of Isis through the foundation of Gardnerian Wicca. Modern Kemetic groups often focus on the trinity of Isis, Osiris, and Horus. The worldwide group known as The Fellowship of Isis has worked to spread the worship of the Goddess since 1976. Throughout the world, countless pagan and Wiccan groups have chosen Isis as their patron Goddess. She is especially popular among those looking for a Goddess-oriented system, such as in Dianic Wicca.

Today's adherents of Isis meld traditional Egyptian rites with conventional rituals. Isis is called upon to assist with magic, aid in childbirth, and to protect and heal in times of need. She remains as vast and varied today as she did in ancient times. She is the focus of large covens and of the solitary practitioner working quietly alone. She continues to surpass the limitations of culture, uniting people from all walks of life in her grace and timeless allure.

Personifying the doting mother, loyal wife, powerful sorceress, and compassionate queen, Isis transcended the land in which she was born. Isis remains as relevant today as she was five thousand years ago along the Nile Delta. She is a reminder that all boundaries can be surpassed through love, compassion, and the unquenchable thirst to grow and evolve.

Laurie Martin-Gardner is a reiki master-teacher, author, and artisan as well as a lifelong student of myth and magick. She currently has two books available and frequently writes for several spiritual magazines.

Kali

The Hindu Goddess Kali is, perhaps, more misunderstood than any other deity. Whilst Kali is not a comfortable deity, she is certainly not evil and has never been seen as such in Hindu thought. The name "Kali" is the feminine of "kala", which means "time". Another possible meaning of "Kali" is "The Dark One" or "The Black One" as she is usually shown as dark blue or black in color. Her association with time and change leads naturally to the idea of Kali as a Goddess of death.

Some believe that worship of Kali in some form stretches back into the Stone Age and this is certainly possible. Whatever her origins may have been, the first clear appearance of Kali in Hindu scripture dates from around the 6th century BCE where she is called "Kalaratri" (Dark Night). She appears first in dreams to the Pandava soldiers and finally appears fighting among them on the battlefield (*Mahabharata* 10.8.64). The most famous story about Kali concerns a battle between the Gods and the demon Raktabija ("Blood-seed"). The Gods are unable to defeat the demon as each time his blood touches the ground it generates clones of himself so that the harder they fight the quicker they overcome. According to some versions of the story, Kali springs fully formed from the brow of the Goddess Durga as she frowns in frustration and attacks the demon. She drinks the blood from each fresh wound before it can touch the ground, quickly weakening and defeating Raktabija. However, she becomes drunk on the blood and falls into a trance, continuing her dance of death until it seems that she will consume the entire universe in her blood lust. Shiva, her consort, places himself in her path in an attempt to stop her and she forces him to the ground and dances triumphantly on his body. At this point she realizes what she is doing and stops her destruction.

This gives rise to the most common murti or image of Kali,

standing with one foot on Shiva's body with a scimitar raised in one hand and a dripping head in another. Her other two hands may hold a skullcap bowl used to catch blood and a trident, or they may be raised in the mudras (hand signs) of fearlessness and blessing. She is naked apart from a girdle of severed arms and a garland of heads or skulls, and her red tongue lolls out down her face.

Tantric Hinduism, dating back to at least the 10th century CE, seeks to reach enlightenment through intense meditation and visualization leading to the realization that the one who meditates and the object of meditation are one and the same. When seen in this light the frightening aspects of Kali's appearance take on a new significance. The girdle of arms, for example, reminds devotees that by showing us things as they really are, Kali aims to free us from the effects of karma (action) which traps us in the cycle of birth, death and rebirth. The severed head represents the destruction of the ego and her nakedness shows us the true nature of reality freed from maya (illusion). She is the Shakti (energy) of Shiva who represents pure consciousness. Without her dynamic force, however, he becomes shava, a corpse. This concept that together Shiva and Kali represent the union of consciousness and matter, or Purush and Prakriti, is central to this philosophy and explains why they may be shown in copulation or as two halves of a single being.

The *Kalika Purana* describes Kali as the "Adi Shakti" or fundamental power who is beyond time and space. She is, by her nature, formless and infinite. According to the *Nirvana Tantra* the individual Gods, including Shiva, "Arise from her like bubbles in the sea – ceaselessly arising and passing away leaving their original source unchanged." She alone is eternal. Shri Ramakrishna, a well-known 20th century mystic and devotee, wrote of her:

My Mother is the principle of consciousness... indivisible

Reality Awareness and Bliss. The night sky between the stars is perfectly black; the waters of the ocean depths are the same. The infinite is always mysteriously dark. This inebriating darkness is my beloved Kali.

An important aim of Tantric devotion to Kali is to confront the terrifying image of the Goddess dancing in the cremation grounds and so confront our own fear of death. Her gift is to show us life and death as they truly are and to enable us to accept them. This is an idea that appeals to many western Pagans who have chosen to include Kali in their practice.

There are many other reasons why Kali has become popular in modern Paganism. The image of her dancing on the prone form of her consort has obvious feminist appeal, although it should be mentioned that this is not its original context. She is a warrior who refuses to conform to the usual conventions of womanhood and for this reason many women find her empowering and liberating. Shiva's consort traditionally appears in three aspects, Durga, the beautiful warrior who defeats all suitors who demand her hand; the compassionate mother Parvati or Gaudi and the dark and mysterious Kali who is associated with death. It is easy to assimilate this with Pagan ideas of the Triple Goddess who appears as Virgin, Mother and Crone.

Finally, one of the defining ideas of Tantric thought is that the material world is real (and not an illusion to be overcome as suggested by the more well-known Advaita Vedanta school of Hinduism) and that the Divine is best approached through the natural world rather than through renunciation. This idea fits well with the Pagan view of nature as divine. For many Pagans, as well as Hindus, however, the enduring image of Kali is as the Dark Mother who gives life and takes it, in whom we have our beginning and our end and whose gift is true knowledge and understanding, however bitter it may seem.

Jennifer Uzzell holds an MA in world religion and is a

specialist in the religions of Vedic India. She is a senior examiner with a major UK awarding body and spent over twenty years as a head of Religious Education in the 11-18 sector. She is currently a director of an alternative funeral home in County Durham.

Kwan Yin

The Bodhisattva of Compassion Kwan Yin seeks to assist us individually in achieving pure bliss, known as Nirvana in Buddhist thought. She is uniquely qualified for this task because she walked the journey ahead of us. Telling her story is challenging. Which one? So many seem contradictory. That is part of her power as a shapeshifter. She appears as she must to better help our souls stuck in the muck of human experience. She is a survivor of child abuse, domestic violence and murder. She is a martyr to marriage and the pyre. She is maimed and killed to heal her father who then repents his harsh judgment of his daughter. She is a wife, a noble lady. She remains a virgin and lives as a contemplative. She is shipwrecked. She lives in a community with women. She is a healer. She is a musician blessed by song birds. She is a miracle worker. Her stories are told so we know she survived and found enlightenment through a painful life. She reached transcendence with intervention from the spirit world. We can too.

Her colors are the ones of the heart chakra, pink and green. Her emblems include the lotus, a vessel of oil, a sun and bird, a moon and rabbit, a bow and arrow, a willow branch, a rainbow cloud, grapes, and a mirror. There are 42 of them all together. Some of her images show her with as many hands, each holding one emblem. She is depicted riding a dragon, elephant or tiger. Because of her goodness, she is assisted by birds and beasts when she has need.

Although connecting with Kwan Yin as the Divine Feminine is an obvious choice, her roots include a male persona. Avalokitesvara, the compassionate one in India prior to the 12th century, appeared as a man. His name translated to Chinese is Kuan Shin Yin and appears as Kuan Yin. These are the same souls as best as I can understand them. His appearance around 100

BCE is androgynous with the same soft round face and graceful hands. The source book for the bodhisattva, *The Lotus Sutra*, gives them 33 different personas only seven of which are feminine. Current practice separates the male and female Kwan Yin. In fact the Tibetans see him in the Dalai Lama. Because his and her stories all begin as a human born on earth, the parentage varies. Their stories took on national flavors. Kwan Yin as the Divine Feminine is adored throughout India, China, Japan, Southeast Asia and beyond. The homeland of Kwan Yin is now counted as the Chinese island of P'u-t'o in the China Sea partway to Japan. Her temple situated there goes back a scant 200 years.

Her mantra is *Om mani padme hum*. There are many translations the most common being *How beautiful is the jewel in the lotus*. Teachers say each syllable walks us through enlightenment. *Om* is divine bliss. *Ma* reunites the Gods and man. *Ni* infuses us with love. *Pad* sparks our intelligence. *Me* releases selfishness. *Hum* supports nonviolence and pulls us up out of the gutter. Together the parts create universal compassion. I approach the mantra in a tantric non-Buddhist view. I find the jewel of the lotus as the clitoris in the labia. Heresy for sure to the flesh-denying ascetic traditions, but luscious and fully feminine to the Lady herself.

Is Kwan Yin a Goddess? Strictly speaking no, she is a Bodhisattva. She will not reach Divine status until we all do. However, she is a powerful intercessor in human affairs. She is a spirit. She answers prayer. She performs miracles. She sacrifices herself, dies and rises again. Outside of having ordinary human parents and multiple lives filled with a world of trouble, she is all a Goddess ought to be. On the other hand, so are we, at least potentially. One of her purposes is to reflect to us in deep meditation that we are also divine, that we are spirits having a human experience, that we will ascend.

Because she is part of the Buddhist tradition, Kwan Yin has been revered without interruption from before the common era. She found her way to the West through migration with people from India, China and Japan. My personal experience began in the Metropolitan Museum in NYC. I was rushing through a series of rooms to reach a Tiffany exhibit when she caught my eye. There she was, a small porcelain figurine riding a tiger. She stopped me in my tracks. One small figure in a crowded display case held me captive. I slowed down and looked for her image throughout the Buddhist art display.

A slowly blossoming comprehension insinuated itself in my heart; I had known these spirits before. As I made my last turn to complete the last room I faced a larger-than-life statue maybe 20 feet tall. My heart swelled. I had been called. I walked slowly to her, eyes locked. She was no stone entity, but the pulsing flesh of a living spirit. I left a blue crystal at her feet.

We may not be miracle workers, well not big miracles anyway, but we can offer comfort, share whatever we have and help people become unstuck without becoming unglued. Bold, brave, understanding, Kwan Yin asks us to embrace this bodhisattva stuff. If it means we return for 100 more lifetimes because people need common sense and courage along with their miracles, then we need to sign up for it now. How many lives will it take? Who's counting?

Dorothy L. Abrams, co-founder of the Web PATH Center in Lyons NY, has taught eclectic Wicca and shamanism for over 20 years. She is the author of *Identity and the Quartered Circle: Studies in Applied Wicca*; Moveren the Sea Queen, collected in *The Faerie Queens*, and *Cawing Crows and Baying Hounds*, an e-novella about love with the Gods.

Lakshmi

The Hindu Goddess flies across the sky on the back of Garudo, a man bird that symbolizes the wind and the devourer of evil men. She is accompanied by her husband the preserver God Vishnu. Together they maintain the Earth with the creator God Brahma and his consort the Mother Goddess, Saraswati, and the God of destruction, Shiva, and his partner Mother Nature, Parvati. These energies reflect the cycle of birth (creation), life (preservation) and death (destruction). Vishnu and Shiva are opposing forces and Brahma is the balance between them.

According to the *Rig Veda*, the earliest sacred writings dated from around 1700 BC to 1800 BC that consisted of more than a 1,000 hymns describing creation and the achievements of the early Hindu deities, Lakshmi was born when the Gods and demons decided to churn the ocean of milk so they could obtain Amrita, the elixir of immortality. The churning pole was the World Mountain that rested on the bottom of the ocean. The motion was so great that the planet was in danger of disintegrating so Vishnu transformed himself into a giant tortoise and took the pole on his back to steady the motion. Wonderful treasures came from the ocean including the beautiful Goddess Lakshmi who rose out of the foam seated on a lotus flower, the symbol of the womb, immortality and spiritual purity. The heavenly musicians and great sages began to sing her praises and the sacred rivers asked her to bathe in their waters. The sacred elephants that held up the world poured the holy water of the Ganges over her.

Lakshmi in Sanskrit is derived from the root "laks", meaning to perceive or observe. It is symbolic of maternal benevolence and is the universal mother who bestows abundance and contentment on her devotees. Everyone wishes to possess Lakshmi, but no one can keep her for long before she flits away to a new cause. The Goddess is usually portrayed bestowing coins of prosperity while flanked by elephants signifying her divine position. She is related to the chakras of the solar plexus and the heart. Ancient Indian rulers in an annual ceremony would go through a ritual of marrying the Goddess as Lokamata, the mother of the world, to ensure fertility and good fortune throughout the land. Lakshmi distributes good fortune around the planet – not necessary fairly to those who deserve it, but to those who take her fancy – giving out beauty, happiness and prosperity at her whim. She is constantly reborn as the consort of Vishnu each time he was incarnated into his different guises.

Lakshmi is celebrated religiously in the Hindu faith, the world's oldest religion still in use with around a billion followers and third largest after Christianity and Islam. The ethos of Hinduism is to transcend the chaos of the world in order to find enlightenment – Nirvana. It is a philosophical dogma rather than a rigid set of beliefs based on Karma, the cause and effect of the soul, and Dharma, which upholds the order of the universe. Hinduism began in the Indus Valley region of North India more than 5,000 years ago based on divine truths or laws that have always existed. One of the main celebrations in the Hindu calendar is the Festival of Lights at Diwali. This festival celebrates the Hindu New Year and symbolizes the victory of good over evil. Diwali begins on the new moon closest to the end of October and lasts for five days during which rows of lighted lamps or candles are placed in windows and around courtyards in the hope of attracting the attention of the Goddess Lakshmi to bring good fortune to the household. The festival represents the reaffirmation of hope and focuses on friendship and goodwill. Another festival celebrating Lakshmi's honor is the Kojagir Purnima held on the full moon day of Ashvin (September/October) marking the end of the monsoon in India. Her worshippers offer food and sweets, chant her 108 names and sing devotional songs.

Away from the Hindu religion, Lakshmi is mainly an

unfashionable Goddess in the western world today. However, her energy is still used in mantras, a Sanskrit word meaning "divine speech". The mantra uses the greatest creative force in the universe; the power of sound. It is the language in which to invoke the God and Goddess energies. For prosperity and abundance, Lakshmi can be beckoned with the mantra "Om Shrim Maha, Lakshmi Yei Swaha". A continued use of the mantra generates a subtle change in the fabric of time and space that allows the spirit of the enchanter to change also.

Does it work? A friend introduced me to this Lakshmi mantra when I was feeling lost after being out of work for a long time. I found I was chanting the mantra quietly to myself while I walked along the cliffs on Portland. Sometimes I was conscious of what I was after from Lakshmi, other times I just enjoyed the sound of the words while watching the waves crash against the rocks and feeling the sea wind on my face. A month later I accepted a job working with nature. Coincidence or divine intervention?

A simple spell worth trying to bring happiness into your life, another of Lakshmi's qualities requires the wearing of as much gold colored adornments that can be attained and hanging a gold colored lantern in a window so that it can be seen from outside. Light the candle inside while calling to the Goddess: "Lakshmi, you confer happiness at your will: will your happiness to fall on me." Continue the ritual every evening for a month until the attention of Lakshmi has been attracted to you.

Namaste and be happy.

Scott Irvine has honored the Goddess for a number of years writing about her in the pagan magazine *Chronicles*. A vignette on Druidry was published in *Paganism 101* and his articles are regularly published in the local free paper Free Portland News.

Laverna

The trickster is a character who seems to appear within every culture and every pantheon. Whether Loki, Gwydion, Coyote, Mr. Fox, Ananse or Brer Rabbit, these tricksters generally play a catalytic role within mythic and folk traditions, acting as a kind of fulcrum around which change takes place.

The Goddess wears many disguises, and it's no surprise to find her appearing, too, as just such a trickster. The tale of Laverna, an obscure Roman Goddess of thieves, is recounted in Leland's *Aradia*, considered to be one of the primary sources for the modern Witchcraft revival.

In the story, Laverna disguised herself as the priestess of some Goddess or other, then approached a priest, offering to buy an estate from him in order to build a new temple on it. She swore upon her own body that she would pay him in full for the land within a year. With that assurance, the priest transferred the land into her ownership.

Within a very short space of time, Laverna had sold off everything. Crops, cattle, poultry, timber, the buildings, the whole lot, until there was nothing left that was worth even a couple of sesterces.

However, a year having passed, and the day for Laverna to hold true to her promise and pay the priest for his land having come around, she was nowhere to be found.

At the same time as she perpetrated that fraud, Laverna also went to a great nobleman and played much the same trick, swearing upon her own head that she would pay him in full within six months. Of course when the payment was due, and Laverna having sold off every stick and stone of the noble's former estate for profit, she had disappeared.

Both the priest and the nobleman, realizing they had been cheated, appealed to the Gods for help. When the assembled

Gods demanded to know why Laverna had broken her oath to the priest, having sworn on her own body, she made her body disappear leaving only her head visible, saying, "Behold, I have no body!" And when they put to her that she had broken an oath upon her own head, in the case of the nobleman, she made her head disappear so that only her body remained, saying, "Behold, I have no head!"

Consequently Jupiter himself appointed her, from then onward, as the patroness of all rogues, whether thieves or dishonest tradesmen.

Laverna is thus represented as a mistress of cunning, a deceiver, and an immoral twister of words. But I suspect that the real Laverna is even darker, much darker. She probably originated as an Etruscan Goddess of the Underworld. The Romans, linking Underworld darkness with furtiveness and thieves, adopted and adapted her when they came to overwhelm and absorb the Etruscan culture. We know little else for certain about her place in the Roman pantheon, other than that there was apparently a shrine dedicated to her on the Aventine Hill in Rome, close to the Porta Lavernalis (Gate of Laverna); and that she also had a sacred grove on the Via Saleria, a highway that linked Rome to the Adriatic coast.

What's left to us beyond this is speculation, at least so far as the historical picture of Laverna can be drawn. But we can perhaps sketch out some general outlines for her continued role and relevance.

Relevance, because the truth is that life can be harsh, and even cruel. It often seems as though the Otherworld is playing tricks upon we mere mortals, tormenting us and deceiving us. The Lady of Thieves reflects these unpleasant realities in her own nature.

Yet there are situations – particularly, situations where the demands of survival may override questions of abstract morality – when particular aspects of the trickster and the thief, such as the capacities for deception and camouflage, are both useful and appropriate. Even thieving itself can be justifiable. For example, if the only way you could feed your children were to steal food for them, would that be wrong? Was it immoral for the Robin Hood of folklore to steal from the rich in order to give to the poor? Is it wrong to steal the dangerous and revealing secrets of the powerful?

At the same time, and as importantly, Laverna is among those Goddesses who may set obstacles and challenges on the Path, and one who teaches the vital lesson that everything has its price, even (or especially) when it comes to relationships with Goddesses. For instance, if Her assistance is sought for some nefarious venture, She will always demand Her cut of any ill-gotten gains. She may also lay traps, trip us up in the shadows, or play any number of devious, and even downright malicious, tricks to divert and confuse the unwary, the foolish and the naïve.

In the end, Laverna's characteristics, and her roles, however uncomfortable at times, are born out of necessity. The Goddess of Thieves, with all her deceptions, is an equal and essential player alongside the maidens and mothers in Goddess traditions.

The influence of New Age "philosophies" on modern Paganism has tended to obscure the influence of darker powers alongside the light. The consequence is often a tipping of the balance to a point that the spiritual path is perceived as being always a gentle, easy and straightforward one. In fact, it can also be challenging, testing, fierce and even cruel. There are Goddesses (and Gods) who will set the tests and demand real sacrifices.

This is vital. On any spiritual path, and most especially on one that is simultaneously a path of magical practice, our real progress and growth is measurable largely in the capacity to pass the challenges that are set before us. The easy parts of the journey are not the most important.

Philip Kane is an award-winning poet and author, storyteller in the oral tradition, and artist. His books include *The Wildwood King* and *Unauthorised Person*. He is also a practicing Pagan, martial artist, and a founding member of both the London Surrealist Group and of Wolf's Head and Vixen Morris.

Lyssa

Lyssa is the sweet name for the Goddess many of us would like to ignore and repress, for she is the Goddess of anger, rage, madness, hatred and fear. The Athenians knew her well and were very wary of her powers over men and animals alike. They named her Lytta; it is believed that the Romans changed her name to Lyssa, meaning "rage" and as you can imagine she appeared in the deepest of Greek tragedies. Lyssa had the power to drive men mad, she was used by the Gods to inflict rage and madness on those who displeased them. Her likeness can be found on a Greek vase-painting, depicting her smiling as she induces hunting dogs to such a rage that they tear apart the hunter known as Aktaion.

Today, Lyssa is so very misunderstood. Over and over again she tells those willing to listen that she does not want to impose her power of anger and rage on to people or animals. In the 5th century BC Greek tragedy *Euripides*, Lyssa (Madness) appears from above. When she and Iris are seen the men become fearful and panic. Sent from the wife of Zeus to claim revenge, Iris threatens to send Herakles into a maddening rage so fierce that he will kill his own children then live in everlasting shame. Lyssa then explains that she does not want to do what she is being bid to do to Herakles: "I seek to turn your steps into the best path instead of into this one of evil." Iris does not want to hear this news and retorts: "It was not to practice self-control that the wife of Zeus sent you here Lyssa."

This mirrors the true nature of the emotion of anger in all of us, for anger is misused and so very misunderstood. Lyssa lives in the dark shadow side of our psyche. As such most of us fear her lessons, repressing her true message to us. We are often so quick to use her power to impose our will onto others in order to *win* in a situation, any situation where we feel like a victim. When we have released the anger and rage onto someone or something else, we may then be left with shame, remorse and regret. Lyssa is not a warring Goddess. She does not want to be used as a weapon to hurt and manipulate people and situations. If called upon in a respectful way she can help people to set boundaries, assert themselves and to keep themselves safe without having to go to war.

Lyssa: "Of noble parents was I born, the daughter of Nyx (Night), sprung from the blood of Ouranos (Uranus, Heaven); and these prerogatives I hold, not to use them in anger against friends, nor do I have any joy in visiting the homes of men; and I wish to counsel Hera, before I see her err, and you too, if you will hearken to my words."

Lyssa is in fact the shield of the victim. As soon as we become defensive we fall into a victim mind set, feeling that we have no choices. She comes to us to support us at this moment. Of course we always have a choice, even if it is only to change the way we think about a situation, but Lyssa will arise from our depths in order to alert us that our boundaries have been crossed and we feel unsafe. Honoring this powerful Goddess involves looking towards our anger and rage. It means that we have chosen to behave in this way because we believe it will keep us safe. Then, we can open ourselves up to the possibility that we are in fact losing our own power, self-esteem, dignity and energy. Whatever it was that we wanted to win, we may find that we lose much more.

According to neurologists, it take us a nano-second to become defensive and all humans in the world can feel defensive at any time. When you consider the exponential times we are living in, how many of us are crying out for peace on Mother Earth, Lyssa may be considered to be giving us the chance to smash the glass ceiling of our higher consciousness. She asks us to begin with us, look at the way we communicate with ourselves and then to each other. Lyssa wants us to own our own non defensive magnificence!

Christina Hunt works as a spiritual counselor, Non Defensive Communication therapist, writer and wild flower artist in Dorset. She studied with OBOD (Order of the Bards, Ovates and Druids) and walks an Elemental path.

Macha

Macha is a powerful Irish Goddess of the Tuatha de Danann – Children of the Goddess Danu. Her stories and aspects are rich and varied, some of which we will explore in this essay. In brief, She is a Goddess of fertility, the land, horses, battle and sovereignty. Her name, which means "plain", "pasture" or "field", is the key to Her essence as a Goddess of the Earth and to Her shifting moods. The land can be abundant, fertile and peaceful, or dark, deadly and wild, just like the different faces of Macha.

Most commonly in modern paganism, we associate Macha with being part of the trinity of Goddesses who make up the awe inspiring Morrigan. Together Macha, Badb and Anu (or Nemain depending on the tale) represent the three main guises of the Morrigan, and even though all three are called "Warrior Queens", they each represent different aspects of the complex divine feminine – Celtic style!

In the *Lebor Gabála Érenn* (the Book of Invasions), Morrigan, Macha and Badb are stated to be daughters of the Mother Goddess Ernmas. It is a theme in Celtic lore that sisters were often portrayed as different aspects of the same Goddess. To complicate things further, Macha also has three roles, or guises, of her own; the life of a Celtic Goddess is rarely dull! She appears in one tale as Goddess, in another as Mortal Warrior Queen and in another as a Faery Woman. In all these roles, however, She displays Her deep inner strength, passion, and sovereign right to rule.

Despite some of Her more fearsome habits, such as collecting the heads of fallen warriors, known as "Macha's Masts", and helping the Morrigan pour blood and fire on to the battlefield to test the army's bravery, there are many tales of Macha which show Her to be a champion of fighting for what you believe in, loving fiercely and nurturing that which truly matters. Macha's strong energy allows us to journey and change; She can be called upon in times of deep transformation.

Macha is mainly associated with Ulster, and there are several sites in Northern Ireland which bear Her name. "Emain Macha" is Ulster's legendary seat of Kings and modern-day Armagh comes from "Ard Macha", meaning Heights of Macha.

The story of Macha in Armagh is a brief but tragic one. In this tale the Goddess is married to Nemed (meaning "Holy" or "Sacred"). Arriving in Ireland together, Nemed clears a plain and dedicates it to Her. Upon seeing the land She has a terrible vision of the bloodshed in the forthcoming Táin Bó Cúailnge – the Cattle Raid of Cooley, and promptly dies of a broken heart. Nemed then takes Her to be buried at Ard Macha. Her death, however, is not permanent, and perhaps Her severe reaction to this vision relates to Her deep connection to the fate of the land and the people of Ireland.

Emain Macha is one of my favorite places in Ireland; it is an ancient site of pagan and archeological importance, as well as a sacred space of awesome, ancestral energy. Now called Navan Fort, Emain Macha is the home of two epic Macha tales.

The first story portrays Her as a mortal Queen with fiery red tresses, named Macha Mong Raud. When Her father King Aed is drowned, Macha, as his only child decides to claim Her right to rule as Queen. The other heirs to the throne don't take too kindly to this news, stating that they "would not give up kingship to a woman". Probably not the best thing to say to a Goddess! Of course, Macha goes to war with them, wins and becomes Queen.

To add insult to injury She enslaves the sons of a rival King and forces them to build a seat of power for Her. Taking the brooch pin from Her neck, She clears the land and marks the space required. The seat of power which is created there is Emain Macha, which in this case means "Brooch Pin of Macha".

The third and most famous story of Macha gives a different twist to Emain Macha, stating that the name means "Twins of

Macha". This story begins in typical faery tale fashion, but soon escalates into a major precursor for the Táin.

Crunniuc mac Agnomain is a rich widower who falls in love with a woman who runs inconceivably fast and cleans his house for him (Macha). He quickly takes her as his wife and all goes splendidly well until he visits a fair organized by the High King of Ulster. At this event he ill-advisedly boasts that his wife, who is at this point nine months pregnant, can run faster than any of the King's horses. This boast angers the King so much that he orders Macha be summoned to race his best horses. Macha appeals that She is about to go into labor, however the wrathful King cares little for this, stating that if She doesn't do this he will kill Crunniuc.

Macha goes into labor as the race begins, She runs through this excruciating pain, still managing to beat the Kings horses. Collapsing at the finishing line, She gives birth to twins, hence the name, "Twins of Macha".

With Her last breath, however, She reveals Her true power and curses the men of Ulster with the pains of a woman in labor when they are most needed to fight. With this curse upon them, they are all rendered helpless when Queen Maeve of Connacht's army attacks at the Táin, leaving only the semi divine hero Cú Chulainn able to fight.

Cú Chulainn himself has quite a love/hate dynamic with the Morrigan, which in turn leads to his downfall.

These colorful stories may conflict and confuse, but in essence they portray a powerful and uncompromising Goddess who can awaken the fiery warrior spirit within us all.

The Celts believed that the cycles of life, death and rebirth were linked, and not to be feared. Macha's stories reflect this belief and by calling upon Her we can be more aware of the shifting cycles of our own lives.

When I visualize Macha, I think of the land. In my mind's eye I see the rolling green hills of Emain Macha and feel the warm summer sun upon my face. I hear the sound of galloping horses beating the earth like a drum. I see Her there in the herd, red hair blowing wild in the breeze, and I feel a deep call to run with Her, fearless and free.

Laura Daligan is a witch, artist and writer, who paints, holds workshops, conducts readings and has her own internet program, Witchcraft Diaries (www.youtube.com/lauraredwitch). Her work has been published in numerous international publications. She loves animals, visiting sacred sites and dancing with fire.

Meretseger

Within the vast treasures housed in the Museo Egizio in Turin, Italy, lies a small, rectangular slab of limestone. It's an odd-shaped piece with the figure of a Goddess carved into the right side of the stone. She faces left, an unusual position for deities. The Goddess stands before an offering table laden with lotus blossoms. Two of her three heads bear plumed crowns. Above her, the stone bears her names: Lady of the Sky, Mistress of the Two Lands, the Peak of the West. Seventeen columns of hieroglyphs adorn the remainder of the stelae, a hymn to the Egyptian Goddess of vengeance and mercy, Meretseger.

Carved by the draftsman, Neferabu, in the middle of the reign of Pharaoh Ramses II, the stela was once set in a small cave sanctuary dedicated to Meretseger and the God Ptah. Many small chapels once lined the pathway that ran southwest from the village of Deir el-Medina to the Valley of the Queens. It was in that village, among laborers and artisans, that Meretseger would emerge as an important, although vastly unknown, Goddess.

Within walking distance of the Valley of the Kings, Deir el-Medina housed the men that labored each day to craft the numerous tombs and pathways of the ancient necropolis. It was difficult work, wrought not only with the dangers of working underground, but also with the inherent dangers of life in the desert. Scorpions and poisonous spiders hid among the shadows, and deadly snakes struck without warning. Near the village, the pyramid-shaped peak, Al-Qurn, towered above the valley. From its highest point, a plate of rock juts out, invoking the image of a cobra's hood. The peak was once sacred to Hathor, but in time would transform into the dwelling place of the Goddess Meretseger. From the top, she would watch over the tombs and their creators, dealing out punishments to the wicked and forgiveness for the penitent.

Often depicted as a cobra, Meretseger emerged from the desert as a Goddess to be both revered and feared. In his stela, Neferabu acknowledges that he has committed a crime and angered the Goddess. He writes, as recorded in *Ancient Egyptian Literature: Volume II* by Miriam Lichtheim, that he "was an ignorant man and foolish, who knew not good from evil", that he disobeyed the Peak, and that "she taught a lesson to me". Neferabu goes on to detail the suffering he experienced after angering the Goddess, comparing it to the pains of childbirth.

As a cobra Goddess, Meretseger did not only inflict pain on transgressors. She spat venom into the eyes of those who harbored evil intent, blinding them instantly. Her physical manifestations – spiders, scorpions, and snakes – sought out those that had given false oaths. As the protector of the necropolis, Meretseger was quick to strike tomb robbers and was especially vengeful to those workers who desecrated the sanctity of the tombs by carving secret passages through which they stole treasures and offerings to the Pharaoh.

However, Meretseger was an unusual Egyptian Goddess. Just as she delivered pain and suffering to the wicked, she also blessed those who repented of their wrongdoings. Neferabu writes, "for the Peak of the West is appeased, if one calls upon her." For those who earnestly sought forgiveness, Meretseger would alleviate their afflictions. Those once blinded by the venom of the Goddess would find the veil lifted from their eyes. Those poisoned by the creatures of the Goddess would find relief and healing. It is this notion of sin and forgiveness that is highly unusual in ancient Egypt and sets Meretseger apart as a unique deity in the Theban pantheon.

Unlike other Egyptian Gods and Goddesses, Meretseger did not move from the peak of Al-Qurn. She remained there, guardian of the necropolis, while other deities spread throughout the Egyptian empire. As the Valley of the Kings fell out of use, and the workers moved from the village of Deir el-Medina, the cult of Meretseger faded into memory. She had been the divine guardian of the craftsmen, a Goddess with whom they crafted a personal relationship in an era of impersonal Gods. Ptah may have been the God that guided their hands, but Meretseger had been the Goddess that protected them.

Considered by many scholars to be a minor Goddess, much remains unknown about Meretseger. What is known has been gleaned from the records and offerings of the men of Deir el-Medina. Although her reign was brief, her influence is beginning to emerge again among modern-day pagans. Just as in the New Kingdom, she remains a personal Goddess and does not garner large groups of followers. Those who seek her out usually do so alone. Just as she once stood guard over the tombs of pharaohs, she is often called on to be a protector. In a world constantly bombarded with noise and chaos, some have begun to seek Meretseger, whose name means "she who loves silence", as a quiet escape from the commotion of everyday life. She has transformed from a vengeful Goddess to a guardian of quiet, sacred space. As the world continues to grow louder, more may seek out repose under her protection. For now, however, Meretseger remains a Goddess overshadowed, but not forgotten.

Laurie Martin-Gardner is a reiki master-teacher, author, and artisan. A lifelong student of myth and magick, she currently has two books available and frequently writes for several spiritual magazines.

Minerva

Sometimes cited as being motherless, sometimes mentioned as the daughter of Metis, and often understandably compared to, or completely transmuted with, the Greek Goddess Athena, Minerva was born into the Roman Pantheon through her father Jupiter's head. Despite being born fully grown and dressed in the full armor and helm of a military leader, brandishing a spear, the Roman Goddess of war was worshipped as such only in Rome itself. Throughout the whole of the Roman Empire, and the many stories of its mythologies, Minerva was revered in a number of ways akin to Her many attributes. She often comes across as the jealous type and this may shed light on why She remains without consort or offspring. Indeed, She is often referred to as "the Virgin Goddess." Her main festival was held during the Spring Equinox from 19th-21th March while Her minor festival took place on 13th June. Minerva is one of the Capitoline Triad formed with Jupiter, Her father, and His wife Juno, the chief Roman Goddess of war. Her sacred animals are the owl, which embodies Her attributes of wisdom and warfare, and the spider, which symbolizes Her attributes of creativity, inventiveness, and teaching.

The colors that correspond to Minerva and her attributes include emerald green, orange, and royal blue. Sacred plants of Minerva include the olive and mulberry. The olive tree was created by Minerva during a contest with Neptune. She won the contest when the Gods determined that Her gift was more useful to man than Neptune's gift of the horse. The slow, purposeful growth of the buds of the mulberry caused the ancients to consider it "the wisest of its fellows." The combination of this "wisdom" with its widespread medicinal use makes it ideally suited to the Goddess of wisdom and inventor of medicine.

Minerva is a Goddess of wisdom and knowledge. The Romans

credited her with creating both numbers and medicine. She even helped Prometheus steal fire from the Gods for man. Minerva shared how to make thunderbolts with Vulcan and Cyclopes so that Jupiter could use them to defeat the invading giants. Throughout Her history, Minerva, though prone to jealousy, was never quick to punish. She constantly offered patient counsel to those who derided Her, Her attributes, or Her worshippers. This quality shows just how great Her love of sharing knowledge is.

Minerva is a Goddess of creativity. Being especially adept at spinning and weaving, she crafted the clothing of the Gods with the Graces. In one of Minerva's more infamous tales, the Goddess goes head-to-head with gifted, but haughty and obtuse mortal Arachne. Minerva created the first flute but threw it down to the Earth when Cupid made fun of the face she made while she was playing it. She is credited with building the first house.

Minerva is a Goddess of war, though, typically, she concentrates on defensive strategy. In a way, Her jealousy is an act of warfare. Minerva transformed Arachne into a spider destined to spin and weave throughout her lifetime because of her prideful insubordination and the quality of her work. To defend Her beauty, she transformed the equally beautiful Medusa into the Gorgon who turns those who gaze upon her to stone. In ancient Roman tales, Minerva aided Ulysses in many ways, including helping him seek his vengeance for being sent away.

Minerva's relevance has not diminished over time even though Her cult may have. Her image is often used in official awards and seals, such as the Medal of Honor of the military of the United States of America and the official state seal of California. Minerva is one of the deities revered by the infamous Illuminati. As a wise and knowledgeable teacher, Minerva encourages us to expand upon what we already know while we open our minds to new theories and information. She admires our love of learning and wants us to share what we know with others. She helps us to encourage the studious pursuits of others while walking the walk and talking the talk, as the saying goes. Calling on Minerva for assistance with our creative process is a wonderful way to introduce ourselves to Her as long as we are mindful of our attitude – we do not want to be like proud Arachne and fail to heed Minerva's counsel! In her warrior guise, Minerva encourages us to fight for the just causes of our fellow beings. She helps us set solid boundaries when necessary and strengthens our resolve not to be victimized. We can honor Minerva through tutoring a pupil, by supporting a student during their academic adventure, or by applying what we know to help our planet and its inhabitants coexist. Minerva encourages Her worshippers to continue acquiring education through Her patient counsel and careful study. Knowledge gained is to be knowledge shared. It is through this sharing that Minerva is truly known.

A.C. Kulcsar has been a practicing solitary witch for more than twenty years and a cat lover her entire life. She currently works with Bast while caring for her children, a grumpy old house cat named The Pauper, and a colony of feral and stray cats.

Mnemosyne

Little is written about Mnemosyne, who predates the Hellenic pantheon. Her origins begin with the dawning of creation. In the beginning was Chaos, and all that existed was a mighty chasm. From this chasm arose Ge (Gaia), Earth, as did Eros, Love, the most beautiful, and from it also flew Nyx, Night, on raven wings. Others, too, arose from the chasm: Tartaros, Deep, and Erebos, Darkness. These were the First Ones, "The Protogonoi" Hesiod calls them, birthing with themselves the Cosmos itself.

Nyx and Erebos mated and brought forth Day, and Aether. They also let loose the forces of destruction, disorder and death, and their gentler cousins, sleep and dreams. Ge brought forth Ouranos, Sky; the mountains Ourea that reached up to their brother, and Pontus, the Divine Sea. Then Ge and Ouranos mated, and brought forth Hekatonkheires and Kyklopes, and the twelve Titans: Okeanos, Koios, Kreios, Hyperion, Iapetos, Theia, Rhea, Themis, Mnemosyne, Phoibe, Tethys, and Kronos.

As the Protogonoi are the creative forces, so the Titans are the energies who shape the created world. Each Titan represented a fundamental aspect of the universe, or human interaction with it, as understood at that time. These include the ocean, the great stream that surrounds the world, and subterranean waters; heavenly prophecy and divination; the constellations; the heavenly lights; mortality; motherhood; time; natural and divine law and fate, and in the case of the beautiful Mnemosyne, memory, language and inspiration.

The fact that Mnemosyne is the offspring of one of the primordial deities demonstrates how important her gifts of memory and language are in the shaping of Creation. She is the one who discovers the uses of reason, who gives every object a name, and who makes communication itself possible:

... and in addition to the gods you mentioned I must call upon all the rest and especially upon Mnemosyne. For practically all the most important part of our speech depends upon this goddess ...
[Critias to Hermocrates. Plato, *Critias* 108d.]

Her gift of memory was seen as paramount:

... If you had no memory you could not even remember that you ever did enjoy pleasure, and no recollection whatever of present pleasure could remain with you ...
[Socrates to Protarchus. Plato, *Philebus* 21c.]

Mnemosyne has chthonic aspect. She presided over a pool or river in Hades, which had its counterpart in Lethe, the river of forgetfulness. Whereas dead souls drank from the river Lethe, to forget their former existence before reincarnation, initiates into the Orphic Mysteries did not have to drink from Lethe, but could drink from the River Mnemosyne so they would retain all they had learned in their previous lives. She also presided over the Oracle of Trophonius on Boeotia, and those who visited were made to drink alternately from springs called "Lethe" and "Mnemosyne".

As with the other Titans who produced children who were more defined aspects of their qualities (Hyperion and Theia – both aspects of Light – produced Helios – Sun; Selene – Moon; and Eos – Dawn) so too Mnemosyne became differentiated in her children.

Seduced by her nephew Zeus who was disguised as a shepherd, she lay with him for nine nights. In due course she gave birth to the Nine Muses who are, in order of birth: Kalliope (epic poetry), Kleio (history), Melpomene (tragedy), Euterpe (music), Erato (love poetry), Terpsikhore (dance), Ourania (astronomy), Thaleia (comedy) and Polymnia (hymns). Memory, language and inspiration play a vital role in all these arts.

There are no further tales recording other deeds. She is not widely known and only recalled in the word "mnemonic" derived from her name yet, despite this, Mnemosyne is one of the Great Goddesses: so great, so all-pervading in fact, that we take her for granted and only notice when she is gone.

Mnemosyne in her manifestation of memory was crucial in the pre-literate era for a cohesive society; laws and history were learned and kept alive by bards and poets who carried the tribal identity in their memories, to pass on to new generations. With the advent of writing, another manifestation of her gift of language, the importance of memory has diminished, and yet when we write, we do so we in order that we will remember, as did Herodotus: "These are the researches of Herodotus of Halicarnassus, which he publishes, in the hope of thereby preserving from decay the remembrance of what men have done..."

The gifts of Mnemosyne are still important today, and not just for ordinary everyday things like remembering where you put your keys. On a personal level we cannot know who we are if we do not have memory to place us in context, and this is just as true spiritually as it is in the mundane world. Mnemosyne and her daughters can be invoked to give inspiration in many forms for ritual and magical practice as well as other creative endeavors.

More importantly, Mnemosyne herself can help us walk the Path of Return. When we have drunk the Lethe waters, and have forgotten who we are, Mnemosyne's river can reverse these effects. Her inspiration can keep us going in our quest, and help us reconnect with our true selves once again.

We are in a world that has forgotten how interconnected we are with each other; how reliant we are on her mother, Gaia, for everything we need to exist, and that we are, in fact, made of the same materials as the stars. We can become as the Gods, but only if we remember that we are already divine beings. It is time to remember who we are, and Mnemosyne, who remembers all things, can help us. It is time to remember Mnemosyne.

Sr.Q.Q.D.A.M. Magical Order of the Aurora Aurea, contributor to *Commentaries on the Gold Dawn Flying Rolls* (2013).

(The) Morrigan

The Morrigan, the Goddess Morrigan, Morrigu, Morgane, or Morrighan, is a Goddess who is a part of a trinity of Goddesses (Macha and Badb) of war and death in ancient Ireland. However, it is still disputed about how these Goddesses are related or were related, or if one was more powerful or more distinguished. Her name translates from Irish as "Great Queen," indicating her sovereignty and queenship as the key aspects of her power.

The Morrigan arrives in history as the Irish Goddess of magic and death. According to the *Book of Leinster*, as relayed within *Goddess Alive!* by Michelle Skye, "Morrigan was born to Ernmas the she-farmer and bountiful mother, and Delbaeth, son of the love and beauty god Angus mac Og."

The Morrigan offers Cú Chulainn her love, but he does not recognize her and rejects her. She quickly turns into a black bird and flies to a nearby tree. He is devastated by what has happened, saying he would not have treated her the way he did if he had realized who she was. But it is too late and she reminds him that she is the one who guards his death and she tells him that he will die in battle.

According to *Goddess Alive!*, Cú Chulainn meets an old woman who is washing clothes in the river, and he asks her what she is doing. The washer is the Morrigan and she is a crafty one. She offers him dog meat, which puts Cú Chulainn into a difficult situation in which he has to break a geas (or curse) of never refusing hospitality and never eating the flesh of his namesake (the hound). When he does so, he seals his fate in an upcoming battle.

Similar stories link the Morrigan with Dagda, the Irish God, saying he found her by the river washing her yoni on Samhain, and then they slept together. Together, they complete the cycle of life and death.

The Morrigan continues to be found as a figure in the Ulster Cycle and the Mythological Cycle, though it is not necessarily stated that she is ever a Goddess, according to some researchers.

She is the warrior and the dark one, a shapeshifter, often showing up as a black raven or crow to those who see her out of the corner of their eye. While she is associated with war, it is clearer that her connection to the land and to sovereignty may be the impetus to her fierceness.

The Morrigan is named as one of the Tuatha de Danann (the tribe of the Goddess Danu). By blowing a fog over the land, the Morrigan could discourage enemies with the lack of visibility.

She has also been linked to the Arthurian legends, as Morgan Le Fay, but this is widely disputed by scholars as being a forced connection instead of being grounded in facts.

The Morrigan is widely celebrated today, and has been found in public places such as the Stone City Pagan Sanctuary in California and as the deity celebrated by Coru Cathubodua (the Gaulish name for the Morrigan), a modern-day priesthood.

Solitary or single worshipers of The Morrigan may find themselves confused by the vast amounts of information about her – sometimes contradictory. But while she may not show up in traditional mythology, her energy is something that has become crucial to modern culture.

Her worship may look like preparing for battle, girding one's loins for the fight of a lifetime. Some of those who honor her practice sword fighting and battle tactics, while others focus this fierceness in the direction of caring for the land and its inhabitants. Still others may use the energy of the warrior to support them in everyday battles, where the opponents may not easily reveal themselves.

To step into the shapeshifting of The Morrigan, some choose to wear raven feathers or crow feathers, and then move as a bird from the human form. By stepping into unordinary reality, one can step into the movement of one form to another form.

Stepping into an ecstatic state can help to drive this shapeshifting, while trance work can also encourage deeper connections with the Morrigan.

Some will offer blood and urine to The Morrigan, and women especially can offer menstrual blood as a connection to the Goddess. Suggested offerings, as detailed in *Celtic Lore and Spellcraft of the Dark Goddess*, by Stephanie Woodfield, include red wine, whiskey, water, elderberries, dragon's blood resin, hazelnuts, crow feathers, and oak.

The Morrigan is the Irish Goddess of death, magic, sovereignty, waters, and fertility. She is dark and fierce and she is the one that fights when necessary. When you are called to your own personal battles, she can show up to lend you strength and the ability to shift your perspective if you're not sure of your direction.

Irisanya is a witch, a priestess, a Reclaiming teacher, a dreamer, an often-vegan, a shapeshifter, and a Sagittarius who is devoted to Iris and Hecate. She has been published in *Paganism 101* and makes her living as a writer. www.irisanya.com.

Nehallenia

Wherever you go, there she is. This is the essential nature of Nehallenia and is as true today as it was at the height of her worship. For a Goddess who has been watching over practically everybody for 3,000 years, Nehallenia is none the worse for wear. Perhaps she is more relevant than ever.

Inscriptions in stone and other archaeological hints place the historical center of Nehallenia's influence in the modern Netherlands, specifically at the mouth of the Rhine River. Beyond what has been recovered in the Rhine delta, the origins of Nehallenia remain a mystery. Wherever Nehallenia came from, she was a Goddess revered and worshipped by Romans, Teutons, and Celts – three distinct groups that often came into conflict with each other.

Nehallenia embraced basic human interests and concerns that affected the daily lives of many people. Foremost, Nehallenia was a patroness of journeys, specifically sea voyages. In the depictions of the Goddess found in shrines near the coast, she is often portrayed standing in the front of a boat. Here anyone preparing to travel made an offering to Nehallenia, often of apples or bread.

Here is an example of an inscription that represents a popular sentiment: "To the Goddess Nehallenia, on account of goods duly kept safe, Marcus Secundinius Silvanus, trader in pottery with Britain, fulfilled his vow willingly and deservedly."

And Marcus was by no means alone in requesting metaphysical protection.

In addition to ships and apples, shrines to Nehallenia feature her with a loyal dog at her side. The dog is not a totem that is often coupled with the sea, but in this case, Nehallenia's dog can represent home and the hearth, the promise to return from our journeys.

The central idea is the union of Norse/Teutonic and

continental Celtic cultures (that is, not from the British Isles) symbolized by the shared Goddess Nehallenia. She was especially popular in this area as the Roman Empire declined. The devout invoked Nehallenia for safety in travel, for fertility, and as a general mother figure.

Most traditions are driven by a particular focus. In the Nehallenic Ways, the emphasis is on the continuing improvement of the self as well as reaching out to others to help them reach their fullest potential. Many Nehallenics become teachers for the general population.

Aside from Nehallenia, deity is represented by the Goddess Dagmar and the God Alaric. These are special to this tradition and have not been taken from legend or lore. Nehallenia is representative of totality.

The Nehallenic Tradition promotes three specific points of concentration:

Teaching: There's been lots of talk about the relative ignorance of new Witches/Wiccans/Pagans. Instead of complaining, why not teach?

Spirit: More and more it seems that the spirit of our ways gets lost behind the flashier side of spell work. Nehallenics emphasize the spiritual aspect.

Interfaith: Each Nehallenic is an ambassador of our faith to the world beyond our path. Nehallenics seek to take this to a new level and be excellent representatives.

The Nehallenic Way is practiced in groups, although there's no reason a solitary couldn't adapt group ritual for private practice. Working clothed, the Nehallenic chooses ritual wear according to the work being done. There are times when special robes and accoutrements lend a magic of their own to ritual, and then there are times when simple street clothes will suit. This tradition observes Full and New Moons as well as the eight traditional

Days of Power.

As much as Nehallenia protected her devotees on physical journeys, she is a guardian of all journeys – in mind, in life, in growth, and in development. In this aspect Nehallenia is most relevant to us today. Think of her as a guide on the path of life, gently nudging us forward and offering gifts of her wisdom. This is Nehallenia of the Ways.

Nehallenia is the focus of several groups in the modern Pagan community, an example being the Temple of the Ways. In the 1970s, seekers living in Philadelphia, PA, of Breton, continental Celtic, Dutch, German, and Norse descent came together to compare their traditions. They discovered they all had a great deal in common philosophically. They also all shared a common Goddess of seafarers and journeys, Nehallenia.

This group stuck together through the years. Finally, in 1985, a priestess established the Nehallenic Tradition. Aldsvider Loar Nevez became the first Nehallenic "lodge" or coven, and it is the center of this tradition which weaves these cultures together. On the Fall Equinox of 2003, the lodge was reincorporated as the Temple of the Ways.

The Nehallenic Way is a religion of spirit and magic, giving the spirit precedence over the magic. Groups exists to celebrate the universe with the joy of the spirit. Magic is a part of that, but it is by no means the main focus.

On the subject of magic, Nehallenics do not believe that magic is black, white, or gray. Magic is clear. It is the intention of the practitioner which defines the magic. Nehallenics work positive magic, but it is up to the individual what magic they may practice on their own. The act of binding is forbidden, as it preys upon the free will of others.

Nehallenics serve in three prominent roles. They are teachers of the Nehallenic Way, of other traditions, and of other areas of knowledge. They are Nehallenia's ambassadors to the rest of the world. They are activists for causes which better humanity and our earth.

A temple of Nehallenia was built based on archaeological evidence to replicate an ancient temple near the lost town of Ganuenta. This fresh and modern tribute to Nehallenia opened in Colijnsplaat in August, 2005.

Emilie Conroy is a legally recognized Pagan clergywoman currently serving on several interfaith councils in Philadelphia, PA USA. In addition to her work with a number of local groups, Emilie is a published author. When not acting in the service of the Goddess, Emilie is a writer, editor, and creative consultant.

Nemetona

Historically, little is known about this Celtic Goddess. In Europe, mostly in the area of modern Germany, a handful of epigraphs have been discovered. In Bath, England, another inscription links her to the Romano-Celtic Mars-Loucetious (a hybrid of the Roman God of War and Agriculture and the Celtic God of Lightning) although it is unclear as to whether he was widely considered her consort. Any mythology that might place flesh on her historical bones is sadly lost to us.

The limited information about her qualities and worship has not proven to be an obstacle to modern Pagans. Her name has gifted us with a clue as to how she might be approached: Nemetona comes from the Celtic word "nemeton", commonly believed to refer to the groves of trees once used as temples. This link has resulted in Nemetona's manifestation as a personification of the Grove and Goddess of Sacred Space. Modern devotees are building an intimate connection to her and, by their efforts, the once sparsely inhabited landscape of Nemetona's realm is coming to life and a deeper, richer and more complex character is revealing itself to us.

As Goddess of Sacred Space, she is seen as Patron of the modern Pagan Sacred Circle. We understand this circle as a layered Mandala of change. It includes our Wheel of the Year, Lunar month, our day and night, and acts as an holistic, vibrant, spiritual map of the spiraling cycles that bring movement and transformation, reflected not only in the macrocosm of the natural world but also in the microcosm of our own lives. As Lady of Sanctuary, she holds and supports us through the unfolding journey of these cycles, but she is both the circle's core and circumference, paradoxically moving with us whilst embodying the still center at its heart. Nemetona anchors us whilst opening us to the mystery of change. The butterfly is a powerful symbol of her gift to us, reminding us that nothing is lost, only transformed, as we move around her Wheel. Through her we acknowledge both the eternal, indestructible mystery of life and the ever-changing expressions and cycles that articulate and manifest that mystery. Within Nemetona's embrace we are enabled to ride the changes, engage with them more fully, whilst never losing sight of the eternal soul within.

She can be understood as a Goddess of Mindfulness; of being fully connected to the moment. She centers and grounds us in her peace, encouraging us to open to and embrace the sacredness within and without. She is the meeting point between the two and we engage with her whenever we build intimacy with self, other and nature. Through her the ordinary becomes extraordinary; her holding opens us to the wonders of life; her circle a lens that brings into sharp focus a wider, deeper, more sanctified view of the world and ourselves.

As Goddess of the Sacred Circle, by extension she rules over ritual and ceremony. As such, she is a patron of celebrants – those who create and perform rituals for others – aiding them in the holding of space to enable participants to mark important rites of passage. She is the priest/ess within all of us, helping us to create words and actions rich with meaning, ones that guide us deep into a space where the sanctuary of our being widens to inhabit the sacredness of the earth. She is the Goddess of Making Sacred and through her eyes we are able to witness the spirit that illuminates matter.

As Goddess of Sacred Enclosure, she can teach us a good deal about boundaries, not only of place but also of our own bodies. She is the shell of our skin, of our personal space, the line at which our inner, hidden world touches the world outside. She can teach us to set healthy boundaries that are both flexible and strong, encouraging us to be aware of our limits, and to respect these in others. Through an engagement with her we learn to sense and be sensitive to the contracting and expanding of our edges, finding a balance between protection and openness.

She dwells where we feel belonging. Many see her as a Goddess of hearth and home, where we live and feel rooted acting as a form of temple where the Divine may enter and be experienced.

This said, her sacred spaces are not rigid or set in stone. Wherever we draw a circle she can be found; she resides in every spoken or unspoken moment of prayer. Her temple walls are decorated with the wild hues of ocean and shore; the corn gold of summer fields, even a city park will offer up her presence. But it is the green peace of a forest grove where many find it easiest to engage with her. As her name suggests, she is intimately connected to trees. She can guide us to build relationships with them, deepening our understanding of their individual wisdom and healing powers. When we think of the peace of her Grove, we cannot help but ponder Her connection to the breath of life, the rhythmic exchange of oxygen and carbon dioxide that we and the trees depends on for existence. This dance of breath can calm or enliven us and in breathing in its inspiration, we are able to breathe out our own unique voice as a gift to the world. In this sense, Nemetona is a Goddess of the Druidic concept of Awen; engaging with her can create a receptiveness that allows the flowing spirit of the Divine to move through us.

Ultimately, Nemetona is the Goddess of Sacred Belonging. When we feel cut off from our center and the wonders of life, she offers reconnection and a profound sense of our place in creation. In deepening our relationship with her, we come to understand that the boundary of Nemetona's Sanctuary is as vast as the blue sphere of our planet and as intimate as the space of our own hearts.

Maria Ede-Weaving is a Druid/Wiccan hybrid and longstanding member of the Order of Bards, Ovates and Druids. She has published articles in *Sage Woman* and *Pagan Dawn* and essays for various Pagan anthologies. A regular contributor to Philip Carr-Gomm's blog, she is also the author of *A Druid Thurible* blog.

Nicnevin

Nicnevin with her nymphes, in number anew
With charms from Caitness and Chanrie of Ross
Whose cunning consists in casting a clew
[Alexander Montgomerie, *Flyting Betwixt Polwart and Montgomery*]

Nicnevin (sometimes Nicneven or Nicnevan) is a queen of the fairies or Queen of Elphame within Scottish folklore. She rules the unseelie court of Alba, unusual creatures, spirits and nymphs. She is very much an otherworldly deity associated with witchcraft and necromancy and she has been connected to several other deities with similar attributes.

Her name derives from the Gaelic surname *Neachneohain* meaning "daughter(s) of the divine" and/or "daughter(s) of Scathach". *NicNaoimhein* meaning "daughter of the little saint". The use of the name was first recorded c.1585, in Montgomerie's *Flyting*, and also given to a woman condemned to death for witchcraft: Kate McNiven. [*Scotland: Myth, Legend & Folklore*, Stuary McHardy, Luath Press, 1999.]

"This name, generally given to the Queen of the Fairies, was probably bestowed upon her [Kate McNiven] on account of her crimes." [Pref. to Law's Memor. xxviii, N. *Supplement to the Etymological Dictionary of the Scottish Language: Volume Two* by John Jamieson.]

Nicnevin has been conflated with the Gyre Carling, Black Annis, The Cailleach, Habetrot and has also been called the Scottish Hecate. We can infer from these connections that her domain is primarily magic, witchcraft and her role as queen of the fairies as well as being connected to the realm of the dead and necromancy. She is known as a hag and giantess; however, both the Cailleach and Habetrot have been known to transform into younger, more beautiful, versions of themselves, and it can be said Nicnevin also has the power of shape shifting into a young and beautiful form. She is a Goddess who moves between the worlds:

> She has been called the Bone Mother. She is among those who take part in The Wild Hunt. Nicnevin flies through the air accompanied by flocks of honking geese, and geese are among those classed as psychopomps.
> [Judika Illes, *The Weiser Field Guide to Witches*.]

By examining some of those we will gain a much better understanding of Nicnevin's domain. To begin with there is the Gyre Carling. "Gyre" possibly originates from the Norse gýgr meaning "ogress" and "carlin/carling" is used in both Scots and English and translates as "old woman". So the Gyre Carling is understood to be a crone-like figure, an ogress/giantess. The word "carlin" has also been used to describe a witch, a link to the supernatural. She is much maligned as a giant hag with a taste for the flesh of good Christian men as mentioned in *The Flyting of Dunbar and Kennedy* (1508) and the poem The Gyre Carling mentioned in the Bannatyne MS.

It is interesting to consider that the terms Nicnevin and Gyre Carlin were both used to describe a senior witch, so this may not simply be a description of cronehood, but representative of rank and power within a witch cult. As mentioned by Sir Walter Scott in *Letters on Demonology and Witchcraft* (1830): "After midnight the sorceress Marian MacIngarach, the chief priestess or Nicneven of the company."

> [Mother Nicneven] This was the name given to the grand Mother Witch, the very Hecate of Scottish popular superstition. Her name was bestowed, in one or two instances, upon sorceresses, who were held to resemble her by their superior

skill in "Hell's black grammar."
[Sir Walter Scott, *The Abbot*, 1871.]

Nicneven has been called the Scottish Hekate in the works of Sir Walter Scott, and he often uses the terms Nicniven and Hekate interchangeably as though they are one and the same. Scott uses these terms to describe the head of a Scottish covine (coven) of witches practicing necromancy in Letter V of his *Letters on Demonology and Witchcraft* (1830).

Hekate is widely known as the Greek Goddess of witchcraft, the crossroads, and the night. She also has connections to the fairy realm and realm of the dead – attributes also associated with Nicnevin – so it's not surprising she is referred to as the Scottish Hekate.

Nicnevin has also been aligned with The Cailleach, and both are Scottish deities described as giantesses and hag-like. It has also been suggested that Nicnevin means daughter of [Ben] Nevis, as Nic means "daughter of" and Neven is linked to Nevis, thus linking this Goddess to The Cailleach as Ben Nevis is her seat of power. [Sorita d'Este and David Rankine, *Visions of The Cailleach*.]

It is said Nicnevin does have a consort, but no name is given, and I've found no historical content of this nature. It is possible that this is a modern concept to fit in with western witchcraft and of the Goddess/consort duality.

In modern practice Nicnevin is believed to ride out on The Wild Hunt at Samhuinn Eve as The Queen of Elphame with her spirits and mysterious creatures, whereas others say her sacred days are 9th and 11th November. Yule, or Midwinter, is also said to be sacred to her. Nicnevin can be called upon for aid in otherworldly travel, communicating with spirits, protection at night, and pretty much everything within the domain of witchcraft.

I've found no specific places or sites sacred to her, although there is a folkloric belief that one of her sacred sites is

Tomnahurich Hill, on the outskirts of Inverness. However, I feel as she is so closely associated with the Cailleach, Gyre Carling and Black Annis, then their sacred sites can be attributed to Nicnevin also. It is worth considering all these deities may in fact be one and the same and their names have changed throughout the duration of history. Another place of interest linked loosely to Nicnevin is Kate McNiven's Stane which is a solitary standing stone believed to once be part of a stone circle, found at Knock of Crieff, [Stuary McHardy, *Scotland: Myth, Legend & Folklore,* Luath Press, 1999.]

From what we have examined it is apparent Nicnevin is a multi-faceted deity with a far-reaching domain and yet she still exudes so much mystery, for not only is she a Goddess but also a fairy queen. She is a Goddess of transformation and all things in the realm of witchcraft. She is queen, she is hag, she is beauty and she is power. Her mysteries are waiting to be explored, and perhaps if you look to the skies from the safety of your home on Samhuinn Eve, you will be lucky to see the Queen of Elphame ride out with her party.

Pamela Norrie is a witch and priestess residing in Dundee, Scotland. Her interests include writing, divination, foraging, folklore, and reading. Some of her work include articles published in *Pagan Dawn* and *Witchcraft & Wicca* magazine, and her essay Cliodhna: Faerie Queen and Potent Banshee was printed in *The Faerie Queens.*

Night Queen

...the divine is not separate from the beast...
[Lenore Kandel, *Hard Core Love*]

How should I write of the Night Queen?
She is a fleeting shadow in our dreams, ineffable, touching our world in the darkness, the light of distant stars caught in Her cloak and in Her hair.
How should I write of the Night Queen?
She is a Goddess like no other, and yet She is all Goddesses. She is ecstasy. She is Rapture. She is the creative essence of all that has been, that is, that will be.
How should I write of the Night Queen?
She is.

The Goddess known simply as the Night Queen is at the heart of a little-known method of sex magic called, at least in modern times, Amg Ada. The method was initially developed – reputedly on the foundations of much older material – during the 1960s by Jane Hurley, who was a practitioner of traditional Chinese medicine alongside her diverse interests in the occult arts. Others, since, have made a point of stripping away any accretions from Chinese medical practice, and of studying more deeply with the inner contacts of the Amg Ada system, so that working with it now brings us closer to the original source, to the Night Queen Herself.

Because the Night Queen *is* Amg Ada. The method uses ritualized sexuality in order to bring the practitioners into direct contact with the Divine, which is manifested through dream and through contact with the Night Queen in the realm of dreams.

Of the Night Queen as a "character", as an individuated deity, little is written. She may take on many visible forms. It has been said that Her truest form, Her "self" as it were, is as a dark woman with long black hair and jet black eyes. But She is a deity who must be directly *experienced*, a Goddess who is in a genuine sense a Mystery, and hence She cannot be understood intellectually. Like the experience of sex itself, writing or talking about it, and actually doing and feeling it, are two very different things!

This experiential nature of the Night Queen is reflected in the practice of Amg Ada's rites, in which the use of normal language is considered a breach of sacred space, and ritual communication must be by way of various chants, physical gestures, the physical senses and the intuition of the participants.

> *How should I write of the Night Queen?*
>
> *She is not of the classic trinity of Goddesses, She is not the Maiden, She is not the Mother, She is not the Crone. Yet She is all of them.*
>
> *How should I write of the Night Queen?*
>
> *She is the Goddess of desire and lust and pleasure. She knows and nurtures the divine animal that is restless within each and every one of us.*
>
> *How should I write of the Night Queen?*
>
> *As a poet, for as with poetry Her innermost truths are hidden and not hidden, in the spaces between the words.*

Perhaps the most powerful insights into Her true nature are contained in a lengthy series of poetic verses that have been preserved within the Amg Ada corpus. Attributed to one of the Night Queen's known, otherworldly and discarnate, attendants, *The Songs of Volvizia* constitute both praise and wisdom teaching.

They can function as a set of keys, for those whose desire may lead them to the very outermost gates of the Night Queen's realm. They may work as the seeds of meditation, and as pathways that can be followed in the creative imagination.

Perhaps you have heard my footfall in the forests?
I sing among the alders and the may.
The Chant of Spring!
The Chant of Spring lives within the rocks, the soil.
The murmuring forests of the Dark Age.
Distant abandon!
The cry of a broken mare!
You have heard me, yes?
You understood?
Many men have heard my song but who in his heart
sings the song of Spring as the rocks and soil?
There are inner songs.
Songs from the inside of Being.
Caught in the Rapture of Being!
A thousand years ago a temple stood, or the memory of a temple, a
temple of flesh, a temple of light, a temple of dreams, a temple filled
with violent sobbing, filled with anguish, filled with ecstasy, purple
robes, white robes, scintillating shadows crossing between you and
I. A thousand years before a thousand years ago, in a memory, in a
hushed whisper in the winds, she stood here, standing naked,
crying, making signs of lust and wonder.
There is an ancient path for us to follow,
into the lost worlds,
worlds forgotten,
worlds condemned.
We are together there forever.
In my dreams I meet you there.
On a cliff.
I undress for you.
On the edge of an abyss.
[Lines excerpted from *The Songs of Volvizia*.]

Philip Kane is an award-winning poet and author, storyteller in the oral tradition, and artist. His books include *The Wildwood*

King and *Unauthorised Person*. He is also a practicing Pagan, martial artist, and a founding member of both the London Surrealist Group and of Wolf's Head and Vixen Morris.

Nut

As part of the Ennead, or the Nine Gods of Heliopolis, the Egyptian sky Goddess Nut, daughter of Shu, God of the air, and Tefnet, Goddess of moisture, and sister and wife of Geb, the earth God, is critical to the Egyptian creation myth. The Ennead is composed of Atum (God of Heliopolis, at times also Ra, the sun God), who created Shu and Tefnet; Nut, Geb, and their four children, the deity twins Osiris and Isis, and Set and Nephthys. According to mythology, Nut and Geb embraced so tightly that they could not be separated and nothing was able to exist between earth and sky. Nut was unable to bear her and Geb's children, so Shu separated the two and, with assistance from other Gods, Shu held Nut high above the earth so things could live in between the earth and sky and breathe air. [Peter Bentley, *The Dictionary of World Myth*.]

In another version of the creation story, Nut and Geb were twins, and Nut's husband was Ra (or Re), the sun God. Nut and Geb slept with each other, which angered Ra, so he separated them with the help of Shu, who supported Nut and forbade her to bear children during the year. In this version, Thoth, the moon God, pitied Nut and, by gambling with the moon, Thoth won one seventy-second of the moon's light, which he made into five intercalary days before the Egyptian new year, during which Nut bore one child each day: Osiris, Horus, Isis, Set, and Nephthys. [Anthony S. Mercatante, *Who's Who in Egyptian Mythology*.]

Nut is unique in that she is the only known female sky deity, since the Egyptian word for sky is feminine, and sky is masculine in most other cultures with known deities. Nut is usually represented as a nude woman with her body stretched across the sky, with only her fingers and toes supported by the earth. As the sky, it was said that Nut swallowed the sun each night; the sun passed through her body and was reborn each morning.

Sometimes Nut is represented as a sow and Ra, the sun God, represented as the calf that she bore daily. Some accounts state this representation is because she wanted to swallow all her children (possibly all the stars), and a sow is known for eating its young; other versions simply say she was the Celestial Cow; a sow with stars covering (or inside) her body [Bentley]. Susan Tower Hollis, in Women of Ancient Egypt and the Sky Goddess Nut, explains that, unlike masculine sky deities, Nut does not simply support the sky [*Journal of American Folklore*]. Nut also served as a mother Goddess – she gave birth to deities and, whether represented as a sow or a woman, she gave birth to the sun and stars each morning. It appears, based upon different versions of stories and various forms by which Nut is depicted, that Nut served different purposes at different times throughout ancient Egyptian history.

In *Egyptian Mythology*, Veronica Ions states Nut was a universal mother-Goddess to early Egyptians, and mother of the sun, Ra. Hollis and other sources also support this, noting inscriptions in pyramids attesting to the belief that Nut was mother to Ra and bore him daily. In addition, states Hollis and others, Nut served as a protector of the dead and provided air, meat, and drink to those in the underworld. Inscriptions of her image have been found inside royal tombs and coffin lids. According to Anthony S. Mercatante in *Who's Who in Egyptian Mythology*, Nut's image in Egyptian art is often a woman balancing a jug on her head, holding a papyrus scepter in one hand and an ankh, a symbol of eternal life, in the other. Ions states that the jug is also thought to represent a womb, reinforcing the image of Nut as universal mother.

From pre-dynasty times to as late as the 19th dynasty, reference to Nut is found in mythology, in tombs, on papyrus, and on royal sarcophagi. Though Hollis references the cult of Nut, she acknowledges few sacred structures or priests of such a cult, stating any offerings likely were as a Goddess of the dead;

however, Pascal Vernus, in *The Gods of Ancient Egypt*, notes that trees often were believed to be inhabited by Gods, because they bore fruit and provided shade. He alludes to Nut being associated with a tree (depicted in front of a tree) in two representations of Nut offering food and drink to the dead. Mercatante expands upon this, stating the sycamore was sacred to Nut, citing a text that reads, "Hail, thou sycamore of the Goddess Nut! Grant thou to me of the water and of the air which dwell in thee." (110). He suggests that Nut's sycamore tree, under which travelers sought refuge from the shade, might have evolved to the sycamore under which the Virgin Mary rested en route to Egypt with Joseph and the infant Jesus. There seems to be no revitalization of Nut, or modern veneration of her, though, as a mother-Goddess and associated with aspects of nature – the sky, its stars, and the sun – what Nut represents has and will continue to be of great importance.

Vita Castellana has lived in Alaska for 15 years. During that time, she has contributed to the University of Alaska Southeast's student newspaper as editor, production manager, and writer, the *Juneau Empire* as a writer, and her poetry and short stories have been published in the journal *Alaska Women Speak*.

Pandora

You've all heard of Pandora. You've all been told the story of the silly girl whose curiosity released all the ills of the world. She has the distinction of being the second-most-blasphemed Goddess in human history (after Eve – Mother of All Living, of course). These "just-so stories" may even have some common origin – both are still used remorselessly as misogynistic propaganda. In my local high street, Pandora has been turned into a shop selling expensive bling. And just about every hack journalist in search of a cliché will open up "Pandora's Box" before long. Computer games pervert Her into a Goddess of calamity and deceit. A more appropriate recent tribute is that Her name is used for the idyllic planet portrayed in the 2009 film *Avatar*.

The usual tale derives from the 7th-century BCE Hesiod whose works could be considered the "party line" of Greek mythology. Perhaps a lost play by Sophocles would have given us an alternative. A few hints from other ancient writers remain. The birth of Pandora was represented on the pedestal of the statue of Athena situated at the Parthenon on the Acropolis in Athens – hardly the location for a sadly moralistic fable. Nearly all websites and reference books will just repeat the same nonsense of Pandora as being "the first woman" – indeed, for me, their approach to Pandora is a good test of their intellectual value. A few do suggest that the difficulties of mortal life are a more worthwhile challenge than easy comfort.

Jane Ellen Harrison's classic *Prolegomena to the Study of Greek Religion* is the primary presentation of a somewhat different perspective. She castigates Hesiod as "pessimistic" and "bourgeois" and as having "ugly malice". I believe her analysis is unchallenged. Wikipedia can give you a good introduction to all this. Charlene Spretnak's *Lost Goddess of Early Greece* has a very nice modern retelling.

Pandora never had a "box" – the 16th-century writer Erasmus mistranslated the Greek word "pithos" (a large storage jar) as if it had been "pyxis" (box). Just about every artist since then has reproduced the mistake – lovely pictures but not much help when it comes to understanding Her. (Except maybe that the word "box" is sometimes used as a euphemism for female organs...) This has been a very sticky error – one even finds Goddess-worshiping Pagan writers caught up in it. A pithos is basically the sort of Grecian urn one finds in garden centers nowadays for people to make into water features. This is not an inappropriate use. The flowing, and ever-cycling waters are a good invocation of Pandora, for She is the One from Whom All Gifts Flow, and to whom all returns.

"Pandora" means "the all-giving". It's neither an Olympian jest nor a sarcastic euphemism. Harrison shows clearly, from the evidence inscribed on ancient pottery, how "Pandora" is a title of the Earth Mother, in Her "Anodos" – as Koré, the Maiden Uprising. Another name inscribed by Her image is "Anesidora" – "sender-forth of gifts".

As well as for storing the physical gifts of the Earth, the pithos was also used for funerary purposes – a practice possibly associated with the canopic jars of Egyptian rites. Pithoi were often partly sunk into the ground. So the pithos is also the grave. The belly of the jar is the Womb of Pandora. Images on surviving Greek pottery show pithoi as containing the "Keres" – not "demons" but the souls of the dead that are in Pandora's care. The Keres are depicted as little winged beings – She sets them free. It's possible a ritual enactment of this was by breaking the pithoi with hammers. Or perhaps the hammer-strikers free Pandora Herself from the earth.

The hubris exhibited by Hesiod is quite breathtaking. He has transformed the Mother of the Gods into their created plaything, a foolish, disobedient girl. He has turned Her Gifts into things of fear and contempt. He has turned our Mother into a vengeful curse upon humankind – "a woe for men who live on bread." And he clearly doesn't approve of curiosity – of asking questions. All of this is a perfect example of what Robert Graves calls "iconotropy" –the re-interpretation and perversion of ancient religious images in the service of a contrary dogma. (Poor Eve has much the same problem with Her Tree, Her Snake and Her Apple of course!)

Fascinatingly, the ancient Greek word for "pot" relates not only to ceramics, but also to chasms and fissures in the Earth, just as in the English "pothole". Springs, the waters of life, flow from such pots. (Even the phrase "gone to pot", meaning ruin and destruction, translates similarly.) We know that Persephone, the Koré, descends through such a place and returns thereby in Her ascent, Her Anodos. So the jar is not just the holder of Pandora's gifts – it is also Her embodiment and Her gateway into epiphany.

I first made my own dedication to Pandora many years ago. Back in the Typewriter Age I published a magazine entitled *Pandora's Jar*. I wrote then that the reclaiming of the truth of Pandora is a good metaphor for the task we face. It is even more urgent now. Instead of dominating, fearing and cursing the Earth (and women), our society needs once again to live in harmony with the gifts She so freely provides. We also need to understand that the creatures that we find inconvenient or which bring us sickness are Hers too, older than We. The great gift of life is matched by the gift of surcease, of death, that we may live again, renewed in vigor.

Pandora, Anesidora, Koré,
Crowned With Flowers,
First of the Graces,
You that bestow all things necessary to life.
From your never-emptying Jar
Come all the Gifts of Earth in season.
May Your Hope Uprise Within Us.

Rufus Brock Maychild is founder and hearth-holder of the Fellowship of Isis Centre of Pandora.

Pomba Gira

In Brazil, an angry woman, especially if she goes berserk and starts shouting and screaming, is often described in common vernacular as "having the pomba gira." It is used too to characterize women who behave erratically, who talk, laugh or swear loudly, or appear to be out of control. These are all simplified, distorted representations of the Pomba Gira, detached from their original meanings but having, as will become clear, a basis in truth.

In the Afro-Brazilian cults of Umbanda and Quimbanda, it is believed that we each have a Coroa, a crown of spiritual entities who influence, shape and protect us. These consist of three types: (a) the Orixa; (b) Guardian Angels; (c) the Exu and Pomba Gira.

The Orixa are the most elevated and are similar to the planetary influences in an astrological chart, each Orixa affecting different aspects of our personality in varying degrees, with one being closer to us than all the others. The Guardian Angels are similar to spirit guides and angels, offering protection on a day-to-day level and within spiritual workings, especially mediumship and healing. The Exu and Pomba Gira are families or legions of spirits who are the closest of the Coroa to the material world, standing at the crossroads between the physical and spiritual realms, between life and death. The Exu are the male counterparts of the Pomba Gira, and they are often portrayed as consorts, representing the interconnected male and female energies within us all.

There are Exu and Pomba Gira of both the light and the shadows, and we can draw them to us through service, healing and selfless acts of kindness, or by using, abusing and hurting others. They do not judge, and it is their ambiguity, along with their association with cemeteries, death and darkness, that have led to them being thought of as negative or demonic influences. If we wish to sink into a mire of depravity, they will help us to achieve this, just as they will help us to become a force for goodness and positivity, if this is what our heart desires. We always have a choice, and too often the lure of the forbidden is too great a temptation to resist. They leave us to face the karmic consequences and do not take responsibility for our actions.

"Pomba Gira" literally means "swirling pigeon" or "swirling dove", and when a Pomba Gira takes possession of a medium, she arrives in a spinning dance with a cackling laugh that sometimes resembles the calling of a bird. Nicholaj de Mattos Frisvold has linked the name to the Bantu "mpungo" and "nzila", meaning "spirit of the road", again linking back to crossroads.

All Pomba Gira have separate identities and complex back stories, with certain consistent characteristics: an essentially good woman who becomes corrupted, descending into a life of excess and debauchery that leads to her degradation and eventual ruin. She's a woman who has suffered, empathizing with and understanding those who struggle through life, making her a champion of the downtrodden, the distressed and the poor. This doesn't stop her, however, from having a good time. She may be seeking a form of redemption through helping those in need, but she doesn't intend to do so quietly, dancing into the room in a whirl of red and black, looking for a glass or bottle of cheap rum, something to smoke and someone to flirt with. She likes to tease, to sing, to joke, to be the center of attention. She is often lewd, funny, brazen, mischievous and unpredictable.

In Pomba Gira, we find a personification of female sexuality and womanhood at its most unrestrained. She is passionate, capricious, seductive and unashamed. She is fiercely independent and can be owned by no man. She is the archetypal femme fatale, Siren, enchantress, goodtime girl or fallen woman, depending on her aspect. Yet she is more than all of these, a complex and at times perplexing and contradictory figure (who is concurrently both singular and plural), mercurial, ambivalent and wise. She comes through to lift the spirits in times of adversity, but is also a muse, inspiring poetry, art and song, a healer and a teacher, forcing those who engage with her to become better people through whatever means she deems necessary. It is important to have a good degree of self-knowledge before starting to work with her, as she'll bring out your darkest secrets whether you like it or not.

As a teacher, Pomba Gira enables men to understand the complexity of women whilst offering women the opportunity to realize the true meaning and potential of womanhood. She demands loyalty and honesty, reciprocating with generosity and devotion, becoming a Pomba Gira of the shadows to those who fail to treat her with the respect that she deserves. Men who dishonor her will experience her as a banshee, haunting their dreams, manipulating and obsessing them, whilst women will be seduced into a degenerate and chaotic lifestyle that may well end up destroying them. This isn't done out of malice or to punish, but in order that those who are subject to her darker side will learn the error of their ways and become better people.

In psychological terms, working with our Pomba Gira enables us to understand and accept our baser instincts, our passions and our lower aspirations. It is a form of self-development that forces us to look upon the darker aspects of ourselves, acknowledge them and let them go. The Pomba Gira offer us the opportunity to co-exist in harmony with the paradoxical and antithetical polarities within ourselves, and without this we are in danger of our Pomba Gira running wild, becoming a screaming harridan who causes mayhem, discord and destruction in every facet of our lives. We will never control our Pomba Gira, just as no person can ever truly control another, but we can live peacefully and productively with her, learning the lessons she has to offer and paying homage to her in return.

Shaun Johnson has been a student and initiate of the Mysteries for many years and has previously been published in *Mandragora, Esoterica, AMeTh Lodge Journal* and *Paganism 101.*

Prydeinia

This Goddess first came to me under the above name during a meditation I'd been drawn to do one evening. At first, she appeared as the Goddess Don, a familiar figure to me (see bio below), but during my time with her, I was given to understand that she had once been known to the people of the Islands of Britain as Prydeinia, or Prydainia. This name came from the ancient name for Britain, Prydein.

Prydeinia is the tutelary Goddess of the Islands of Britain. She was once known as Britannia, but the image we have from the old British coinage of a warlike Goddess with shield and weapon is very much corrupted. Prydeinia is an aspect of Gaia, Goddess of the Earth, and as such, her energy is gentle, warm, and incredibly loving, because she is, first and foremost, a Mother Goddess.

The way we humans tend to experience love is clouded by our conditioning, but the love that emanates from the Mother is truly unconditional and offered to all her children, without bias. If, when you approach Prydeinia, the feeling you get is different from what you experience from your own mother, or even towards your own children, this will be why.

Having Googled the name, I discovered that it is not yet "out there" on the internet. My feeling is that this is a very ancient name for our British Goddess, and one that has not been used in many hundreds of years. All the information I can give about her, therefore, has come to me through my personal contact with this Goddess.

I can't tell you what she looks like, in a physical sense. My meetings with her have been mainly through sensing, although at our first contact I saw her simply as a beautiful ball of light – white, with strands of pastel colors such as lilac, pink, primrose yellow, sky blue, and pale green moving through it. Of course, all deities have the ability to appear in any guise they choose, but perhaps, having spent so long in the background, she currently has no favorite material form; or perhaps she has ascended beyond needing one.

In attempting to describe her energy, the words written on the base of the Statue of Liberty came to mind, which I remembered as, "bring me your tired, your poor, your hungry..." However, on discovering the actual words on the plaque, parts of it seem even more relevant:

> Not like the brazen giant of Greek fame, with conquering limbs astride from land to land; here at our sea-washed, sunset gates shall stand a mighty woman with a torch, whose flame is the imprisoned lightning... From her beacon-hand glows world-wide welcome... cries she with silent lips, "give me your tired, your poor, your huddled masses yearning to breathe free..."

Prydeinia welcomes all who need her gentle, loving energy, with open arms and open heart.

She will guide, support, uplift and nurture any who call on her, and is willing to help them heal from any wound or trauma, if they are truly ready to be healed. She is waiting to connect with any and all of her children, whether British born, adopted, or naturalized; or even those who simply feel an affinity with her land or wish to contact ancestral roots. She has come forward at this time because we need her, now more than ever, to help us find a way to live in peace and harmony with ourselves and with one another.

She can be contacted any time, anywhere, and in any way that works for you, but if you are having difficulty in getting focused enough to find her, any place where water meets land, whether physical or imagined, will have a stronger connection to her energy. Sit or stand quietly and comfortably, and close your eyes. Concentrate on or imagine the sound of water, or the wind in the leaves, and offer her a smile. Even if you don't feel like smiling – perhaps especially if you don't feel like smiling – just that simple act will bring her energy closer to you.

Once you have found her, you may want to simply bathe in her beautiful energy for a while, perhaps over many meetings. The feelings this can bring are so soothing to the soul, you may find yourself releasing old hurt and injuries without conscious volition. It may take some time, but once you have healed yourself, the Goddess asks that you work to help heal those around you, the people of Britain, and the world. In asking her what else I should write about her, she showed me an image of Silbury Hill. I feel this is because she wanted me to know that she was once the consort of King Sil, whom local legend says is buried under the man-made mound. This is a symbolic burial, rather than a physical one, which is why no archaeologist has yet found any evidence of him. I believe that Temple Downs, just the other side of Avebury stone circle from Silbury Hill, was once sacred to Prydeinia.

On searching for information on the ancient name of Britain, Prydein, I came across an article about the early Welsh writings, some which seem to state that Prydein was originally the name of a conqueror of the Island of Britain, some time after it was colonized by Brutus of Troy, and that two generations after Prydein comes Beli, known in some writings as the consort of the Goddess Don. Indeed, it may be that Beli was the first of a new conquering tribe, as there is a suggestion that the "Plant Don" (which the article refers to as the Cymric Gods) had taken the crown by force. If this is so, perhaps the Goddess Don now wishes to make herself known in her aspect of the Mother Goddess Prydeinia in order to heal the pain of conquest the British have held for thousands of years.

Rhianna Nodens is the bardic name of Karen Tucker, under which name she is the author of *Healing the Wounds*, a novel of past-life trauma and present-life healing, and its sequel, *Claiming* *the Pearls*, as well as the Kindle short story series, *Bite-Sized Books*. She has written a number of published articles, reviews and other non-fiction pieces, and is a member of the House of Don within the British Mysteries Tradition.

Queen of Elphame

True Thomas he took off his hat,
And bowed him low down till his
knee:
"All hail, thou Queen of Heaven!
For your peer on earth I never did
See."

"O no, O no, True Thomas," she says,
"That name does not belong to me;
I am but the queen of fair Elfland,
And I'm come here for to visit thee."
[Child Ballad #37, *Thomas Rymer*]

Like a ghost, the Queen of Elphame haunts the pages of the stories and songs written in Her honor. Before the written word, She was remembered and feared by those who knew Her tales. She is sung about in the ballads collected by Francis James Child in his book *English and Scottish Popular Ballads* published from 1882-1898. The most talked about being *Thomas Rymer* and *Tam Lin*. In both, the Queen of Elphame is shown as the abductor and faery lover. She grants True Thomas the tongue that cannot lie and he went on to become a great poet who could make men weep with his spell-like lyrics. In *Tam Lin*, She tries to keep Her mortal lover captive in Her underworld kingdom, only to lose him to his true love, Janet.

Shakespeare wrote about the Queen of Elphame in *A Midsummer Night's Dream*, identifying Her as Titania along with her husband, Oberon. In *Romeo and Juliet* She is Queen Mab, a pesky trickster spirit.

In Alexander Montgomerie's *Flyting* (c. 1585), She is Nicnevin, Queen of Witches. He describes Her as a sorceress:

Nicnevin with her nymphes, in number anew
with charms from Caitness and Chanrie Ross
whose cunning consists in casting a clew.

As Queen of the underworld kingdom of Elphame, Nicnevin is said to lead the Wild Hunt, collecting the souls of the dead. She is often equated with Hekate, the Greek Goddess of the Dead and Witches.

There is not much known about the way the Queen of Elphame was worshiped in ancient times. The Celtic lands kept their lore as an oral tradition. Nothing was written down until the coming of Christianity. Through the ballads and legends, a few modern-day authors have unraveled the secret to Her identity.

In today's tellings, the Queen of Elphame is seen as the Witch Mother and Grandmother of All. Robin Artisson, in his ground-breaking book *The Witching Way of the Hollow Hill*, describes Her as "...the Pale Women lying below the Land, the Queen of Faery, Elphame, Queen of Hel, the Three Fates, or Old Fate." He goes on to define her as "...the Queen of the Dead, surrounded by the Pale People or the Sidh-folk..." In my understanding of his work, Robin Artisson sees the faery and the dead being related and possibly the same in some respects, making the Land of Elphame the Land of the Dead as well. Possible names he gives for the Queen of Elphame are: "Kolyo, Kali, Klotho, Kalypso, Cailleach, Holda/Hulda/Holle and Hel/Hella."

In *The Underworld Initiation* by R.J. Stewart, She is the Dark Queen, "an UnderWorld or under-earth power..." He sees Her as a sexual being and initiator into the Underworld Mysteries. She asks us to explore the inner realms of self-discovery. This is a very complex book that leads the reader on a journey with the Queen of Elphame on the dark, sometimes sinister roads to truth. Using the Ballads of *Tam Lin, Thomas Rymer, The Cruel Mother,* and more, R.J. Stewart has woven the tales of old into a new and stimulating reality, leading us to embrace of the Dark and Formidable Queen of Elphame.

Orion Foxwood takes a different approach to Her in *The Tree of Enchantment*. Here, he shows the Queen of Elphame as "the Weaver-Goddess of Fate". His description of Her brings to mind the poem *Orchil* by Fiona MacLeod/William Sharp. Both are shown to weave the threads of birth, life, and death. In Orion Foxwood's eyes, "She embodies the ancient forces of fate, destiny, interconnectedness, magic, and the patterns of life." She is embraced by the *Guardian*, he who holds the Keys. He is both Her lover and protector.

From ancient times to the present, the Queen of Elphame is always one that challenges. She will snatch you up in an instant, dragging you to Her underworld realm. Leading you on the journey of your life, She teaches you the ways of life and death, of magic and sorcery. In the past, She was feared and mocked. Today, She is still feared, but many are embracing the darkness She brings. From the success of books like those mentioned above, those who are called to take the bonny road to Elphame are rising in number.

By whichever name you call Her, the Queen of Elphame lives on in the legends told by many. She is often seen riding a white horse or accompanied by white animals such as dogs or geese. This may be seen as Her connection to the underworld and death. She has many lovers and is never satisfied for long. When called by Her, be prepared to offer the *Seven Year Tithe to Hel*. You may come back as someone great like True Thomas, or you may go mad like the woman from *The Cruel Mother*. When you encounter the Queen of Elphame, whether by a chance meeting on the edges of the Otherworld or when invoking Her name during ritual, be prepared for a life-changing event. The Queen of Elphame is resurfacing, calling for the witches of today to gather and honor Her.

Vivienne Moss spends her days brewing up trouble with her two daughters, and her nights casting spells. When she's not writing, you'll find her meandering through the enchanted forest with her witch sisters, her cat Marcee, and her dog Paco standing guard. A lover of all things occult, Vivienne dedicates her time to the study of esoteric knowledge. Vivienne's hope is to share the magic of the Otherworlds with fellow seekers of Witchdom.

Raven Woman

This is a write up of Raven Woman as she appears to me, rather than as she is recognized, honored and/or celebrated by any other tradition. I initially present her as I found Raven Woman when I was in my early 40s, and then upon reflection in preparation for this book, I updated her description.

I came to my own analysis through intuition, reflection and visioning, initially inspired by an image created by Sandra M. Stanton in a We'moon calendar about ten years ago. That led me to researching Raven Woman on the internet, and finding images, principally from the Northwestern US and Canadian indigenous communities. I did not find specific writings about Raven Woman until I expanded my research to The Morrigan, the Raven Goddess. But, as I explored The Morrigan, I came to realize that although she is a central Triple Goddess connected to Raven energy, and some of her elements of ritual and action resonate for me, she is not Raven Woman for me.

Other influences in my development of my image of her have included:

- Raven energy in the East, as introduced by Jamie Sams in her Medicine Cards
- *Daughters of Copper Woman*, by Anne Cameron, whose narrative on the ancestral Women's society and warrior women of the indigenous community on Vancouver Island, illuminated my path
- The lyrics, music and lives of Cher and Tina Turner, as anthems to the passion, power and strength of bad-ass, TOUGH women
- Gypsy women everywhere and throughout the ages

Initial impressions: Her energy is that of a Triple Goddess;

Passion with a Purpose.

Through this research Raven Woman, like Morrigan, emerged as a Triple Goddess. Her three aspects are Lover, Warrior, and Keener. She is a woman with strong male energies, but she is fully, passionately, a woman.

She is a playful lover, strongly, even fiercely passionate in love – unbridled wild Passion is her energy in this aspect.

She is a warrior woman, brandishing her sword and shield, driven to battle by righteous anger, to fight on the side of justice. In this aspent, she is passion with a purpose and gritty determination.

And she is also a keener who mourns the dead, particularly those who lose their lives in the course of battle, who die in the fight for justice. It is an intense but brief mourning, giving honor to her fallen comrades, while fueling her determination to battle on, to make their deaths not be in vain. She is also skilled and trained to help with the ceremonies of death, both those to assist the newly departed transition to the greater Cosmos as well as those of comfort for the loved ones who remain behind in the physical world. She is Compassion with a purpose, in this third aspect.

The image I have of her is a woman with arms that are wings, whose vulnerable, soft spots – her heart and belly – are covered by a red, woven shield, and on her head is a bird's mask, a beak mask covered with feathers, that she can drawn down over her eyes and face when she is in battle. And her legs are bare. They are strong and sturdy; they are the foundation for her strength, her passion, her power. And nearby, behind her, is her horse, black, her trusty steed, a reflection of her passion and power. Her hair is auburn, the red and black blending with the heat of passion, with a hint of white/silver at her temples, and flowing down her back from her widow's peak. Her skin is golden, tanned, strong, and healthy.

Dressed in her battle garb, she bows before the leaders of the community in whose name she serves and does battle. Her head is bowed, her right wing folded across her chest, her left wing spread wide out from her side. Her knees are bent, with her right leg a step back from her left, but she is not on her knees. Her breast shield is in place and her sword lies on the ground in front of her, the handle facing her, pointing away, towards the community. Her total energy and demeanor is one of having put her mind, body and soul at the service and command of the community: to do battle for the righteousness of their cause, it is her calling; it is her life; it is what she must do and does so from a place of joy and fulfillment and quiet certainty and clarity.

So she has the capacity to kill, for the sake of justice, with a sense of righteous anger. But not from vengeance, or in response to spurned love or passion; and she does not pick or foretell who will die, nor eat their flesh or eyes upon the battlefield – these are some of the aspects that I have read of Morrigan that do not resonate for me. She is a Warrior Woman, passionate, fierce, strong, determined, but yet always centered in love.

As I sat with Raven Woman for this write up, ten years after first exploring her, and now in my crone years, I brought new eyes and heart to her. I have come to define her "keener" third aspect as a "holder of sacred space" – a convener and celebrant of ceremony, a guide and support at the crossroads (in life and/or death), in the nature of Hecate. She is one who holds our hand and gives us comfort as we mourn and release those aspects of ourselves or others who are passing on, and embrace these transitions and honor new beginnings. In short, "Passion with a Purpose" – my initial definition of her essence – has now matured and deepened into "Passion guided by Heart-Centered Service" – a call that hopefully resonates for all of us in this new age.

Cindy Arnold Humiston/Dreamweaver is a witch descendent of three interwoven ancient feminine energetic lineages and their gifts: the "knowing" of wise womyn of the

Celtic/Druid British Isles, the sacred ceremonies of the Mediterranean region's Goddess Priestesses and the shapeshifting of the North American indigenous. With emphasis in kitchen magick and tarot, she is also a high priestess/ordained minister graduate of the Mesa Moon School of the Divine Feminine and the University of Esoterica.

Rhiannon

Rhiannon is a Welsh faery Goddess whose name means Great Queen. Her name may have possibly derived from the Celtic Goddess Rigantona. This lunar deity plays a central role in three narratives in *The Mabinogion*, a Welsh collection of medieval and mythological stories. Rhiannon's most famous story shows the faery princess in love with a mortal and overcoming a crime she is wrongly accused of committing.

We first encounter Rhiannon out riding one day upon her magnificent white horse, dressed in gold. She caught the eye of Pwyll, her future husband. Pwyll sent his men after Rhiannon to bring her to him, but she rode gracefully away, too fast for their horses. On the third day, Pwyll galloped after her himself. He called out for her to stop. At last she halted, lifted her veil, stared him directly in the eyes, and said, "Since you ask it of me, I will gladly stop." Rhiannon proceeded to tell Pwyll that her family had arranged for her to marry one of her own kind, a man she did not love. Showing how strong willed she was, Rhiannon told Pwyll she would much rather marry him. Pwyll eagerly agreed to this, telling Rhiannon he was wooed the second he set eyes on her.

The wedding was set for a year and a day later. The ceremony was held at her father's castle in the otherworld. During the wedding banquet, Gwawl – the man Rhiannon was supposed to marry – arrived. Rhiannon asked to speak with him outside. Using magic, she transformed him into a badger, tied him in a bag and drowned him in a river. We see later in the story that Gwawl escaped the bag and sought revenge on our unsuspecting Goddess, by stealing her son.

Rhiannon and Pwyll embarked on a life together in the mortal world and Rhiannon bore her husband a son. Here we see the Goddess transitioning from her maiden to mother role. The night her son was born, exhausted from a long birth, Rhiannon was assigned six maids to help her look after the baby. Unfortunately, all the maids fell asleep. Upon awakening they discovered the baby was not in his crib. Terrified of being punished, the maids killed a puppy, smeared the blood over a sleeping Rhiannon and scattered the bones around her bed. The maids then sounded the alarm that the new mother had eaten her new-born.

Pwyll, distraught, did not defend his wife. Rhiannon pleaded her innocence, but the evidence was stacked against her. Pwyll would not see his wife punished by death, but instead he sentenced her to a punishment that tied in with her horse association. Rhiannon was to greet visitors outside the castle, tell them of her heinous crime and then carry each of them up the hill on her back to the castle. Poor Rhiannon knew of her innocence, yet showed great inner strength by agreeing to this soul-destroying penance, believing that the truth would out eventually.

We next visit Rhiannon a few years later, still serving her unjust punishment without complaint. One day a couple and a small boy arrived on horseback. The boy handed Rhiannon a piece of cloth, she recognized it as fabric she herself had woven. When she looked into his eyes, she saw a striking resemblance to Pwyll. The couple went on to explain that they found the boy as a baby one stormy night, abandoned in their barn. When they heard of Rhiannon's plight they made the connection and set out to prove her innocence.

Rhiannon, finally acquitted, could now name her son. She named him Pryderi, meaning "care" or "anxiety" in Welsh. The kind-hearted Rhiannon forgave her accusers, showing us that holding onto bitterness is rarely a viable option. When we keep resentment locked away inside us it can make us malicious and hostile.

Aside from her strong, forgiving nature, other themes associated with Rhiannon are: gracefulness, survival, magic, death, fertility, transformation and triumph.

Rhiannon is more often than not depicted riding her majestic white horse. This horse symbolizes her heroism, bravery and free spirited nature. Rhiannon is often linked to the fellow equine Goddess Epona. The Uffington white horse situated in the UK county of Oxfordshire, is a possible place where a Horse Goddess was worshiped. Many theories surround this huge, Bronze-age white-chalk horse and Goddess worship is only speculation. It is certainly a possibility, however, given its strong resemblance to Rhiannon's white horse. Many people visit this enigmatic spectacle to connect to Rhiannon.

Another of Rhiannon's associated animals is the song-bird. It is said that three of these melodic birds glided around Rhiannon's head and could sing the living to sleep as well as raise the deceased. It was written that Rhiannon had a wonderful singing voice and would sing to anyone who would listen.

This extraordinary Goddess is still remembered today and featured in a song written by Stevie Nicks, entitled Rhiannon. The song was voted #488 in the 500 greatest songs of all time by Rolling Stone magazine. When singing this haunting song live, Nicks lovingly explains that the song is about an old Welsh witch. The song was apparently written in ten minutes, perhaps Rhiannon inspired her to write it!

Although Rhiannon's story is one of isolation and despair, we can take inspiration from the fact that this courageous Goddess never gives up hope. Even though her punishment is one of humiliation, Rhiannon remains dignified and patient throughout. She teaches us to believe in the light even when our situation is bleak and dark. Although the story is set eons ago, the moral is very applicable to today. Rhiannon asks today's women to remain strong and not to become a victim in persistent times of woe. Holding our head high and believing in our truth is something we can all take with us on the path of life. This remarkable Goddess shows us that women of the past and indeed today's women are strong, level-headed and steadfast. Females are undeniably a miraculous gender.

Laura Bell is a professional Tarot reader, writer and artist – specializing in paintings of Goddesses.

Sedna

Sedna is the Goddess of the Sea. She is known as Sanna, Nerrivik, Nuliajuq, or Arnarquagssaq. She was a beautiful young Inuit woman pursued by the hunters of the village. She was vain and rejected them all despite her father's protests. Then one day a handsome man arrived and asked her father Anguta for his daughter's hand in marriage. The stranger hid his true appearance from them. The father agreed, but the man lied to her father, assuring Anguta she would live in a castle and be happy.

Once they arrived on the island Sedna became upset. The man was a bird in disguise and lived in a messy bird nest on a barren rock. He fed Sedna raw fish. Sedna cried and pleaded for her father to return and rescue her from the island. Sedna's father heard her cries on the wind and hurried to rescue her.

As they fled from the island in the kayak, the bird arrived on the island to find his wife gone. He summoned the birds to find Sedna. The birds flapped their wings strong enough to cause a storm to threaten Sedna and her father Anguta and the Inuit people. The ocean waves almost capsized the kayak. Anguta cast his daughter into the sea to appease the bird spirits. Sedna clung to the boat to avoid drowning but her father cut her frozen fingers off. She drowned and as she sank to the bottom of the ocean, her fingers transformed into the first creatures of the sea – seals, fish and whales. Anguta died of grief over what he had done to Sedna.

The sea creatures turned her into the sea Goddess and granted her dominion over them. Sedna became the Goddess of the Sea. She ruled Adlivun, the Inuit Underworld, and when she cried, the sea creatures visited her to console her. Shamans journey to her lair to comb her hair since she has no fingers to comb her hair herself. They depend on her to provide them with food to sustain them. Sedna chooses when to send her sea animals to the surface for the hunters to hunt and kill.

Sedna lives in a home built of whale ribs and stone where she rules over the Underworld. Sedna compels us to journey deep within ourselves. She dwells in the deep abyss of the ocean. We fear to journey deep within ourselves, because we fear what we might discover.

Every hunter who catches fish must put fresh water into the dead fish's mouth to appease Sedna. She is a temperamental Goddess who is loving and cruel, like the ocean. When her hair is combed, she is generous. When her hair is tangled, she is the opposite.

We all have negative aspects of ourselves we need to overcome. We grow as a human being by confronting our fears. Sedna's story reminds us of the necessity of facing our fears and weaknesses.

Here is a meditation to meet Sedna, the Goddess of the Underworld. Prepare yourself by lighting a dark blue candle. Dark blue represents the watery depths of the ocean. The Element of Water symbolizes the power of intuition and the inner self. Burn jasmine incense, which corresponds with Water. Cover your altar with a dark blue altar cloth to represent the Element of Water. Place a few seashells and a lapis lazuli gemstone on your altar. Lapis lazuli aids a person in conscious attunement to the psychic self. Sit, relax, and make sure you will not be disturbed.

Take three deep breaths to cleanse your mind, body and spirit then return to a normal rhythm of breathing, avoiding shallow breathing. With each in breath, inhale positive energy and on each exhale, release negativity; draw in relaxation and release tension; inhale harmony and exhale discord. Know that the Universe will absorb and neutralize all the negativity you release.

Perform the meditation in the evening on a Full Moon. Assemble and place your altar facing the West quarter. Perform the rite on a Monday or Wednesday night. The Water Element flows from the Full Moon. Place a bowl of salt water on the altar.

Be sure to make a small offering to Sedna to gain her favor. As you meditate, visualize that you are swimming deep in the ocean. Bring a comb with you to comb Sedna's hair. When you meet Sedna, comfort her. Be open to any messages you may receive. Sedna is a demanding Goddess. She challenges you to embrace your inner self and the aspects of yourself that you would normally ignore. She is cruel as the sea yet she believes that all people and creatures deserve to be treated with respect. If you are given a message about the aspect of yourself you dread to face, you must take the time to acknowledge and release it. For example, it could be impatience, jealousy or rage. If you do not work on yourself, you won't be whole, like Sedna's mutilated fingers.

When you are ready to end the meditation, thank Sedna for her guidance and blessings. Leave her home of whalebones and swim to the surface. Return your awareness to the room you are in. When you are ready, open your eyes and stretch. Let the candle burn down.

Record the experience in your journal or Book of Shadows. Reflect on what you learned from Sedna. Sedna rules the realm of the dark deep oceans.

Sedna's theme is gratitude, abundance, and nature. Her symbols are water, an eye and fish. She is the mother of all marine life. She is honored in Inuit tribes as the provider of food for the body and soul. Be mindful of the way you treat the earth and the oceans. Adopt a pet fish to invoke Sedna's blessings upon you. Every time you consume seafood, remember to honor Sedna and her life-giving powers.

The ocean represents the power of intuition and our subconscious. She challenges us to see our true selves and have compassion.

Heddy Johannesen

Sekhmet

Sekhmet the ancient Egyptian lioness Goddess, is a great force to be reckoned with. Her name literally means "One who is all powerful". Her attributes can be those of either great rage or wrath, or at the opposite end of the spectrum, a mighty healing force for good. She is depicted with the head of a lioness, and the body of human woman wearing a red dress. The dress often depicts the motif of a rosette; which is an ancient symbol stemming from the pattern of the "shoulder knots" seen on a lion's mane.

The anger of Sekhmet is a legendary tale, it tells of her fury at humanity, because they forgot to adhere to the Sacred Laws of the Goddess Ma'at, whom she loved very much. Ma'at represented truth and justice. One title Sekhmet held (she had many) was: "The One Who Loves Ma'at and Who Detests Evil". Sekhmet became so incensed by humanity, that she ran amok wreaking havoc and vengeance, destroying a huge percentage of humans, with a great blood lust. Finally the Sun God Ra, her father who gave birth to her through the fire of his eye, tricked Sekhmet into drinking beer to calm her down, the trick worked, and when she awoke three days later the calmer qualities had won out.

Another story of the birth of the Great Goddess Sekhmet tells of her creation through the union between the Sky Goddess Nut, and the Earth God Geb. It is said that Sekhmet is a far older Goddess than her father Ra; more ancient than any of the other Gods or Goddesses. Another one of her titles is "The Scarlet Lady", which came about due to her blood lust. The pharaoh himself was believed to be protected by Sekhmet in battles. It is said that she walked besides him, shooting her fiery arrows against all of his opponents. The hot desert winds were reputed to be the breath of Sekhmet.

At the end of any battle, great celebrations that consisted of mass intoxication were held in honor of Sekhmet. One particular Egyptian Queen, Hatshepsut, had an entrance porch of drunkenness especially built onto one of her temples in homage to Sekhmet. Sekhmet became associated with what was known as the "Memphis triad" – this is where her main worship spread from.

Some scholars say that Sekhmet came originally from the Sudan where there were lions. This would confirm her much older roots. Her consort, Ptah, was a potter God of creation and wisdom. Together they had a son, Nefertum, who became the God of sunrise. Elaborate rituals were held in her honor and tame lions were kept in her temples at Leontopolis. Amongst her symbols are the "udjat" (Eye of Horus), along with the ankh (a looped shape which is said to be the key to life) and the cobra. The sistrum (a type of rattle) is her sacred instrument; this is because the sound of the sistrum it is said was most pleasing and soothing to Sekhmet.

Records discovered indicate that tens of thousands of people participated in her festivals. In just one funerary temple, more than 700 statues of Sekhmet were found. Many fine statues are in The British Museum, they are a wondrous sight to behold. Exuding all the great qualities one would expect to find in such a great Goddess in Ancient Egypt, the Priestesses performed separate rituals every single day of the year in her honor, each before a different Sekhmet statue. Modern day Priestesses often comment how particularly powerful a statue of Sekhmet is. It is said that they practically "sing with power" when placed upon an altar or shrine devoted to her. One side of the double-edged sword which is Sekhmet, is a wrathful, vengeful Goddess who bestowed destruction and pestilence upon mankind. Her other side, in contrast, is characteristics of the Lady of Great Magic, a powerful healer and patroness of surgeons.

A well known story within Reiki (energy healing) circles, is that of a Reiki practitioner who decided, whilst visiting a famous temple dedicated to Sekhmet in Egypt a few years back, to hide away from the tourist guides, planning to sleep overnight. Whilst in the dark temple, he had a vision of "Sekhem" Reiki energy; here he saw symbols which reputedly were given to him directly from the Goddess Sekhmet. This information he took out into the world, and as a result these particular Reiki symbols associated with Sekhmet are now being used on a grand scale.

Modern day women/Priestesses have embraced Sekhmet as a tutelary Goddess who serves to empower them. She is a Patroness of all women through the menstruation/blood connection. Many believe that her anger is an energy which can transform the world, by ridding it of the unbalanced system of Patriarchy. The Goddess movement recognizes the injustices which have been created by a male dominated hierarchy, and are enraged enough to protest for the greatly needed changes.

Sekhmet teaches us that after the chaos and madness, a calm and healing process ensues. She is rather like the eye at the center of the storm with chaos all around her. Once the storm disperses, everything gets better. She is akin to Karma in the sense that those who oppose the natural laws of truth, beauty and harmony evoke her wrath. Modern-day adherents understand the transformative powers of Sekhmet; rather like alchemy she continues to change all in her wake.

On a final note, those who wish to deepen a relationship with the Goddess Sekhmet can use a daily chant to connect, bringing her energies closer to them. The Chant itself is: "Sa Sekhem Sahu." This means: Sa = The life breath; Sekhem = Mighty power; Sahu = Empowered human. The chant is said to stem from even further back than Ancient Egypt and is reputed to bring about a transformative, self empowered state. It also honors the Goddess.

Rosie Weaver is a Priestess, artist, writer and activist who resides on the south coast in the UK.

Selket

An Anglicized form of the name of an Egyptian Goddess Serqet, also known, depending on the translation, as Sirket, Serket or Serqit, with the Greek form commonly rendered as Selkis.

The name is formed of "Serq" (and variations) meaning scorpion and "et" (and variations) is determinative for Goddess. The hieroglyph of the name appears in a variety of shapes suggesting a scorpion with which she is often associated. Sometimes her name is rendered as individual letters (for example, inside a canopic jar of Tutankhamun).

In common with many Egyptian deities she sometimes has additional epithets, one of the more common being "hetu", which is often translated as "she who lets the throat breathe", most likely in reference to the paralyzing effect that a scorpion sting has on its victim. In artistic rendering, she is usually portrayed as a woman with a scorpion on the top of her head, and in some instances as a scorpion with a woman's head.

The early records of Selket are few, with the most notable being an image and possible connection on the mace head of King Scorpion, an early dynastic ruler. If this does indeed relate to Selket, then this places her in a significant role of protector of the king. Protection in other areas includes a role in protection of the mother and child during childbirth, leading to continued protection of the child. This also extends to non-mortal child protection; in the tomb of Tutankhamun Selket serves protection of Qebehsenuef, one of the four sons of Horus that guard the canopic jars. How this protective role originated could be as a result of practical observation of the habits of scorpions, which have been known to transport their young on the parent's back.

It is the tomb of Tutankhamun that has seen the return of Selket to some recognition, due to a statue of her being found there. In the pharaoh's tomb she appears with her three sisters,

Isis, Nephthys and Neith, surrounding the shrine that held the canopic jars and acting, unusually, in a funerary role. There is some confusion of the positions of these four statues, as some archaeologists think they may have been placed back in the wrong position when the tomb was restored to order in antiquity after it was robbed sometime after the burial. In this context she is associated with Qebehsenuef who presided over the protection of the canopic jar containing the intestine of the deceased.

Personally I have found that the west position feels the most viable of the two options (the other being east). From working with her for more than 20 years, the association with the west, water and deep emotional mind and dream work, appears to be her area of expertise. These have been borne out with personal experience as well as anecdotal evidence from others I have encountered who have also experienced her presence. There appears to be few who interact with this Goddess in modern times, perhaps this could be due to the difficulty in locating material on this obscure deity.

In any case, the depth of the experience of working with her is borne out and, from personal experience, I've found her very useful in protective roles and that she is actively interested in any child protection situation that is called for.

Another role that Selket has been associated with is healing, and this comes from various medical papyri. Again, this could be the result of the common belief that if stung by a scorpion, eating it will provide its natural antidote. Curiously though, in later periods, Isis assumes control over scorpions and of healing from their stings.

Her relationships, unlike many of the other Egyptian deities, are almost non-existent, although another possible form of her goes by the name of Ta-bitjet. [George Hart, *A Dictionary of Egyptian Gods and Goddesses*, Routledge, 1990, p 210.] There she is noted to have been the wife of Horus. She is said to have had a son, Dedy, in Utterance 385. [R O Faulkner, *The Ancient Egyptian*

Pyramid Texts, Oxford University press, 1969.]

As far as cult centers go, there appears to be little evidence of any, and no temples dedicated to her are so far known. Although, being a Goddess of such a hazardous animal, it is perhaps unsurprising.

Few other instances appear of her; there is a reference in various versions of *The Book of The Dead* in a chapter entitled Transformation into a Swallow, and a reference in the *Lament of Nephthys and Isis* where Isis demands that Selket sends her scorpions to aid Isis in tracking down and enacting revenge.

These scorpions are then evoked by Isis and placed around her in a style that is very reminiscent of a part of the lesser banishing ritual of the pentagram: "Tofun and Bofun before me, Mestet and Mestatef beside me, Potet, Thotet and Ma'atet behind me."

Kevin Groves is the author of *A Path Laid Bare*, a Komyo Reiki Kai Master, teacher of visualization and astral projection, and a regular speaker at Children of Artemis events.

Senuna

The village of Ashwell, near Baldock in northeastern Hertfordshire, features a group of springs which form a beautiful well pool among a shady grove of trees. I first visited in September 1993 with my friend the mystical artist Chesca Potter and Olivia Robertson, a founder of the Fellowship of Isis. We were there at the insistence of another friend who had been inspired by a dream that we should go, that he felt it was 'an important site for the goddess'. The spring's form the source of the River Rhee, which itself is a source for the River Cam, which joins the Ouse and takes the waters of these springs out to sea and around the world.

The waters were dappled by the shadows of the leaves, creating a perfect meditative mood, and as we sat in the sun by the picturesque pool and bubbling springs, we commented that there must have been a nature spirit, a goddess, a *genius loci* associated with this place once, now long forgotten. The spirit of place was palpable. We attuned to her, and we shook sistrums to the unknown and un-named spirit.

Nine years later, in September 2002, a man with a metal detector uncovered a hoard of treasure in a field in Ashwell End, about a mile from the springs. It had been buried. Possibly stolen, possibly hidden from raiders. Whoever interred it had not been able to retrieve it. The hoard was a declared a temple treasure, and sparked great interest. It consisted of plaques, items of jewelry and a small silver statue of a regal goddess, garbed in classical tunic and with her hair in a bun. The votive plaques were no mere lead petitions or curses that are to be found at Romano-British shrines and rivers. These were of gold and silver, and they were finely worked. They named a goddess who had been veiled for over 1700 years: Senuna. Her name was gleaned from inscriptions left by those who had deposited votive offerings in her shrine. There were gems in the hoard too. The Treasures were taken to the British Museum to be cleaned and examined.

Archeological investigations at Ashwell reveal, so far, a complex that covered eight hectares which included an area for feasting and possible accommodation for pilgrims and a bath house. Lying near the Icknield Way, the main East-West route across England, this was an important shrine. A geophysical survey of Senuna's site indicates both Romano-British and Iron Age structures. The treasure had been buried outside a circular enclosure between the settlements. Perhaps this was the *Temenos*, the sacred enclosure. (www.britishmuseum.org)

The shine itself is considered to have been a spring, almost certainly related to the nearby group of sprigs in the village and the source of a river. The votives may have been made and bought and inscribed in workshops at the pilgrim centre on site.

So who is Senuna, and what can we know of her ways? Very little. We can see from the votive plaques that those who made them or bought them here, and had them inscribed, had pledged that they had fulfilled their sacred vows to her. We don't know what those vows were. We know that these offerings were costly, representing a true sacrifice, pious maybe, or perhaps buying favour with the goddesses of the shrine. The general interpretation is that Senuna was an existing British water nymph, well guardian or river Goddess assimilated by the Romans. Like other goddess that the Romans encountered, she seems to have been linked with Minerva. In these Roman twinnings we lose a lot of the unique characteristics of the old British and Gaulish Goddesses, although it is the very act that ensured their survival so that they could emerge centuries later. Minerva is a goddess of wisdom and the arts, of commerce, all suitable qualities for a goddess seated near a river and by the major road across the country. Does her later war aspect fit with a water nymph or river goddess?

There is a certain poetic synchronicity with the name of the river that the Ashwell Springs feed, the River Rhee. The etymology of the Cretan goddess Re or Rhea gives us *discharge, flow,* and also *ground.* Rhea's worshippers used chants and frenetic dances with tambourines and clashing cymbals to induce a state of ecstasy. I was reminded of Olivia raising her arm and shaking her sistrum in invocation to the unknown goddess at the Ashwell Springs. In her myth, the Goddess Rhea sought fresh water in which to bathe herself after giving birth to Zeus, but the streams were dry. She called upon Gaia, the Earth goddess, for help, and Gaia struck a rock and a spring gushed out, just as the springs at Ashwell break through the rock. There is also the phonetic likeness to Ri, linked to 'royal' and 'reign', as in the name of the goddess Rhiannon, meaning Great Queen, but also nymph, and to Rigantona, whose name means High Queen. We were led to the place of Senuna by a dream, and we can dream and meditate and ask her to reveal more of herself, and be careful not to project too much on to her, while ensuring she is not forgotten again.

Dr Ralph Jackson, Roman curator at the British Museum, observed

This is a hugely significant find, of national and International importance... Personal hoards, hidden in some crisis, are reasonably common. To find a hoard of a temple treasure, such as this one, is incredibly rare, not just in Britain but anywhere. To give Britain a new goddess is extraordinary.

All hail Senuna.

Caroline Wise serves on the steering body of The Fellowship of Isis, an international network for those interested in the Goddesses. She runs a Priestess training course within it and the FOI starofelen website. She trains and ordains women and men as priests of Elen of the Ways and runs days on Elen, on the

Floralia, and on Sacred London. She came to the goddess by way of the Earth Mysteries, being associated with The Ley Hunter journal and working as a monitor on their 'Dragon Project' in the early 1980s. She is a former owner of the Atlantis Bookshop and works in esoteric publishing.

Sophia

The Goddess Sophia is not a common Goddess known to us by this name. Sophia's name is Greek for Wisdom. Now, as the abstract concept of Wisdom, we can see a great many Goddess manifestations of Her through time and spanning many cultures: Sia (2600 BCE Egyptian), Athena (6th century BCE Greek), Chokmah (5th century BCE Hebrew/Jewish), Anahita (4th century BCE Persian), Menrva (3rd century BCE Roman/Etruscan), Snotra and Vör (8th century CE Norse). So why focus on Sophia and not one of these other great wisdom Goddesses? Well, because She is uncommon. Wisdom is popular in media references, literary quotes, and Buddhist philosophies about enlightenment. Wisdom is something we humans strive to achieve. However, personifying Wisdom, engaging with this concept (even as a divine feminine) and living by the teachings is very difficult. Wisdom is elusive. Wisdom defies true concrete definition. Wisdom is gained only through experience. Many people are blind to Wisdom. Many people can see it, but have no idea how to incorporate it into their lives.

Let us not regard Wisdom as an IT. Let us regard it as a SHE. She is out there. She is within us. She appears in actions, words, and choices. There is literature about Her dating back thousands of years: some of it controversial, some of it declared heresy, some of it rediscovered and incorporated into new spiritual practices. Specific Sophianic literature and mythology is predominantly based in Gnosticism. Gnosticism draws its literature about Sophia from the Hebrew, Judaic, and Christian Wisdom Literature: Proverbs (1, 4, 8, and 9) and the Apocrypha texts of Wisdom (Wisdom of Solomon 6 through 11) and Ecclesiasticus (Sirach 1, 4, 6, 14, 15, 24, and 51).

It is from these early writings that Sophia came to be a personification of the wisdom of God, His co-creator (which is not exactly a consort though in some texts there is an interpretation that She was the consort of the Hebrew God), and the teacher of mankind in the ways of Her art (the ways of Wisdom). "The Lord possessed me (or brought me forth) at the beginning of his works, before his deeds of old." [*Wisdom's Call*, Proverb 8:22.] In the 2nd century CE, we saw the rise of Gnosticism and the feminine divine principle of Sophia became heresy. Most early to medieval Christians did not recognize Sophia as a Goddess or a feminine principle to God. She fell into the realm of Jewish mysticism. There She (as Chokmah) holds a place in the Kabbalistic Tree of Life and is personified as feminine divine.

The Wisdom Literature became foundational for the development of the Gnostic beliefs. She became part of the Gnostic pantheon of divine beings and concepts. Gnosticism grew through the early middle ages, incorporating texts like the *Nag Hammadi* and developing its Sophia mythos. Rose Arthur, author of *The Wisdom Goddess: Motifs in Eight Nag Hammadi Documents*, shows Sophia in a beautiful verse saying, "I am the first and the last... I am the silence that is incomprehensible... I am the utterance of my name." In Gnosticism, Sophia is seen as one of the Aeons, intermediate deific beings between God and humans. In Gnostic literature, She seems to have several manifestations, some contradictory. At some instances, She is seen as creator, co-creator, teacher, the taught, divine presence, elusive knowledge, temptress, wife, mother, Christ, etc. In the Gnostic text, *Pistis Sophia*, She reclaims her realm of Light, where Light is Gnosis (or knowledge and understanding) through devotion and penitence.

Sophia resurfaces around the 19th century CE (through to today) in feminist Christian studies of the Wisdom Literature and with Russian Sophiologists (those who study the teachings of Sophia, the feminine wisdom of God). Michael V. Fox, a contemporary researcher, wrote an article on Ethics and Wisdom in the Book of Proverbs where he analyzed the Wisdom Literature into three categories: Wisdom as Piety; Wisdom as

Desire; and Wisdom as Obligation. While this was just a study, it shows that Sophia is still a divine concept in people's minds today. There is also a branch of study within Modern Greek philosophy that relates to "The Sophists," stemming from the word *sophistes* (wisdom and learning). The Sophists today are considered those who exercise wisdom and learning.

As for those engaged in current beliefs and practices related to the Goddess Sophia, we return to Gnosticism and feminist spirituality. In the book *Wisdom's Feast: Sophia in Study and Celebration*, we see the evolution of Sophia much as has been described in this essay. We also see how today's adherents of feminist spirituality and Gnosticism have revived their interest and connection with this Goddess of Wisdom. Within the book, Sophia is experienced through ritual, liturgy, celebrations, prayer, bible study, and more. All aspects of Her are studied or engaged with in discussion, meditation and ritual. (See Michael V. Fox's three categories.) Today, there are groups of New Gnostics who follow Sophianic beliefs of Sophia as divine feminine and divine Wisdom. Such groups include: Holy Order of Wisdom; Ecclesia Gnostica; Sophia Foundation; organizations based on Sophianic healing (healing through the path of wisdom); Hagia Sophia; and many more.

Caitlin Matthews, author of *Sophia: Goddess of Wisdom: The Divine Feminine from Black Goddess to World-Soul*, ends her in-depth study of Sophia with: "Open your heart, walk within and find Sophia." This is a reminder to modern adherents that Wisdom is within, much as the Wisdom Literature often explains. That to find Wisdom without, you must seek it first within. This is reminiscent of the Wiccan *Charge of the Goddess* that states:

And thou who thinkest to seek me, know that thy seeking and yearning will avail thee not, unless thou knowest the mystery: that if that which thou seekest thou findest not within thee, then thou wilt never find it without thee.

With the rapid growth of Paganism and Wicca, Sophia offers a broader female divine concept to worship, Wisdom, complete with texts and mythology that can be drawn from early times. Yet she is still not truly definable.

The ways of Wisdom are so prolific that she changes every moment to adapt to all conditions and circumstances. If she embraces all times and space in fullness of her capacity, she will never let the wellspring of her gifts run dry, in whatever situation we may find ourselves. [Hildegard of Bingen, *Book of Divine Works*]

In my own worship, Sophia is both ever-present and ever-changing, like the moon and so the moon serves as a symbol of Her. The moon also serves as a way for me to time my meditations and worship of Her, whether it is to look inward on the Dark of the Moon, or whether it is to bask in the Light as I seek Her wisdom by the Full Moon's Light. While there may be several ways to depict Sophia, I prefer a dark woman, dressed in shining moon-white robes, veiled so I cannot see her face only her lips. She is silent for I can only hear her within my heart. And her charge is *Wisdom's Call*, Proverb 8.

T. Scarlet Jory is a university graduate, she has Bachelor degrees in Classics/Anthropology and in Honors Religious Studies. She is the author of *Magical Blend: Book of Secrets Volume 1* and several articles. She is called a wordsmith by her readers with a calling to teach and to encourage others to love learning. She currently leads Crescent Moon School of Magic and Paganism (since 1995) and writes fantasy fanfiction. She can be found via *scarletcougar* on most social media.

Sulis Minerva

Take yourself to the landscape of 2,000 or more years ago, a natural landscape, a place surrounded on three sides by a river, a river which snakes across a flood plain making the going treacherous. You follow the land to a promontory and from the limestone between two small hills erupts hot water. A place where the bright orange-red mineral rich waters contrast with the mute greens of the surrounding landscape and a dense steam rises from the expelled water – certainly a place of the Gods. This is the home of Sulis, a Celtic Goddess of Britain.

Sulis is a very British Goddess principally associated with the hot springs that surface in what we now recognize as the city of Bath. There are mentions of her in inscriptions across Britain but only one outside Britain, in Alzey, Germany. Much of our understanding of the Goddess Sulis and her relation with the people comes from the archaeological remains and because of the Romans' syncretism of Sulis with their Roman Goddess Minerva.

The fact that the Romans called the Goddess Sulis Minerva is quite interesting, usually the Celtic / local name for a deity would be after the Roman God's name i.e. Minerva Sulis, this then may be a sign of the importance of Sulis to the people. Also the Romans called their settlement Aqua Sulis (The Water of Sulis) and again the local deity's name takes precedence.

The hot springs that surface in Bath are a wonderful geological phenomena and although we now understand the science behind it, it is still amazing, particularly as the water that emerges at the King's Bath at 46 degrees Celsius fell as rain at least 6,000 years ago. Evidence of settlement in the area suggests a high occupation rate from prehistory onwards. There is evidence of Mesolithic hunters as well as Neolithic, Bronze Age and Iron Age settlers in the area. We can only try to imagine how much more marvelous the hot springs must have been to our ancestors.

In his lecture *Fertility, Propitiation and the Gods in the British Iron Age,* Barry Cunliffe discusses the importance of the elements earth, air/fire and water in Iron Age worship and how the archaeological record can be used to glimpse how people interacted with their deities through these elements. Deities associated with water were most often communicated with, petitioned and thanked by depositions in springs, rivers and bogs. The archaeological record from Bath shows that prior to the Roman Baths being constructed there was a rubble and gravel causeway built out to the center of the spring. This was clearly manmade as stakes had been used to stabilize the pathway which ran through an alder swamp to the point of the spring. Evidence of pre-Roman deposition was found when the causeway was uncovered and the mud of the spring was explored and eighteen Celtic coins were found.

Sulis is a Celtic sun Goddess who oversees the waters and as such has been seen as a healing Goddess. For thousands of years the waters from the springs have been used for the treatment of ailments. Through the Roman Minerva syncrisis, it has been inferred that Sulis was also a Goddess of wisdom and decisions. The curse tablets (Roman Era) found in her sacred spring reveals that this wisdom was also coupled with the ability to dispense justice, an interesting contrast to her healing aspect.

An example of a curse tablet reads: "Docimedis has lost two gloves and asks that the thief responsible should lose their minds [*sic*] and eyes in the Goddess' temple." Although there is some debate regarding the root of and meaning of her name (Sulis may mean eyes or sun) it is intriguing to muse that both may be appropriate; a seer's ability to identify the perpetrator and fiery qualities to exact a just and relevant revenge.

It is interesting in today's society, where it is often frowned upon to show "negative" emotions such as anger, how Sulis can help us for if we hold onto these intense energies they can be damaging. Writing a curse on a tablet and giving it to Sulis is very much like journaling or writing a letter and burning it. These are ways that people are able to be really and truly in the moment today with their anger and not hurt anyone while working through it and let it go. By offering it up to the Goddess the petitioner requests the intervention of Sulis who will ensure that a measured and considered response is made.

To connect with Sulis today:

- Take a trip to visit the Roman Baths where Sulis Minerva's temple stood
- Read Barry Cunliffe's wonderful book *Roman Bath Discovered*
- Find out what an amazing phenomena water is by reading *The Water Planet* by Lyall Watson
- Spend some time writing down that which you need to let go of, particularly if someone has wronged you, and give this up to Sulis
- Take a bath or sauna, visit a spa or use a hot shower in your bathroom to create a steam room and allow the warm water and steam to cleanse you
- Visit the coast or a local body of water
- Call on Sulis to aid you in healing ceremonies using water
- Join a local organization or donate to a charity which cares for the waterways in your area
- Spend time meditating with a bowl of water, watch candle light dance on its surface, taste the water, laver your head and body etc
- Drink more water
- Try scrying in a bowl of water

Jo Robson lived in Bristol in till her late teens and often visited the Roman Baths. She now lives in Greater Manchester with her partner and their animals. She contributed to *Paganism 101* and is joint editor of *Cotton, Curry and Commerce: The History of Asian Business in Oldham.*

Tailtiu

Largely forgotten by the vagaries of time, Tailtiu is a fascinating Celtic Goddess. She has never gained the type of renown that other Celtic Goddesses achieved. Yet, the entire Festival of Lughnasad is said to have originally been held in Her honor and the Irish town of Telltown in County Meath is named for Her.

To learn about Tailtiu and gain some sense of her significance, one must dive into the murky waters of Irish history. It is fairly familiar ground to say that the *Leabhar Gabhala Eireann* (The Book of Invasions of Ireland) lists five invasions of Ireland. This book is said to have been written sometime around the 11th century by an anonymous scholar recounting the ancient and mythological Irish past. For the most part, the first few "Invasions" appear to be less battles for staying power on the land than attempts at settlement. The first Invasion was led by a woman named Cessair, said to be the granddaughter of Noah. The second Invasion was led by a Greek named Partholon who arrived many years after Cessair. The third of these Invasions happened right around the time of Partholon's death, led by another Greek, by the name of Neimheadh.

Neimheadh appears to have more of a challenge at settlement, needing to oust a strange race called the Fomhoire who had also arrived and gained a foothold on Ireland as a base for themselves. The Fomhoire were said to be one-eyed, one-armed, one-legged people who were intimately connected with the sea ("Mor"). In myth, they tend to appear as representing chaos and blood-thirstiness. After defeating the Fomorians, the Nemedians worked hard to clear land and create a home for themselves. However, ultimately Neimheadh and many of his descendents died, presumably of plague. The Fomhoire returned and the remaining Nemedians fled.

One of Neimeadh's grandsons, Beothach, fled to the North

and was the forebear of the tribe known as the Tuatha de Danann. Another grandson, Semeon, returned to Greece. His descendents became the tribe known as the Fir Bolg. After many years, five brothers of that tribe returned to Ireland, arriving around the beginning of August. They divided the land between them, creating the well-known five ancient provinces of Ireland. Tailtiu was the daughter of Moghmor of Spain and his Queen, the daughter of the King of the Fir Bolg. Tensions arose with the arrival of the Tuatha de Danann, who also wanted to settle in Ireland. Despite ancient family ties, war was declared.

It appears that a coalition between the Tuatha de Danann and the Fomhoire occurred with the marriage of Eithne (daughter of Fomhoire King Balor) and Cian of the Tuatha de Danann. They had a child, Lugh. Together the Tuatha de Danann and Fomhoire defeated the Fir Bolg. Tailtiu became the wife of a warrior chieftain of the Tuatha de Danann and foster-mother to Lugh, guiding him in His early years and laying the foundation for His later sovereignty. The message of Goddess as bestower of Kingship is clear, with the added element of bringing cohesion of all the disparate lines of the Invaders. She is the mediator, in a sense, between the two opposing tribes and nurtures the resolution of all these energies in Lugh.

What is even more fascinating about Tailtiu is that She is one of the very few Goddesses who dies. Her story ends. One can infer that sometime after having fostered Lugh, She set Her mind to the clearing of a great plain. The clearing of plains was enormously important to the success of the tribe, ensuring space for farming and supplies for building. That Tailtiu takes on this task Herself indicates Her love of the people, Her dedication to doing everything in Her power to help Her people and Her enormous capacity of self-sacrifice. The burden of the task is so great that Her heart breaks under the strain and She dies. The plain She cleared became the town that bears Her name: Tailtiu in ancient times or Telltown as it is currently known.

The most beautiful part of Tailiu's story comes after Her death. The time around the beginning of August had always been significant to the people of Ireland. As mentioned before, it is said that the Fir Bolg arrived in Ireland at this time. It was a time of gatherings, weddings and contract negotiation. Considered the midway point of summer (after the work of cultivating was complete and before the work of harvesting was begun in earnest), it was a time of tribes gathering to set in place arrangements that would hopefully foster beneficial future relationships. It is said that, out of deep love for His foster-mother, Lugh buried Her in a huge chambered cairn on the plain which She had cleared and instituted the tradition of holding games in Her honor: the Aonach Tailteann (Tailtean Games). It is said these games are the oldest in history, predating the Celts and possibly dating back to around 2000 BCE. Not surprisingly (given Tailtiu's feat) these games consisted mainly of sport and feats of strength. They were a way of honoring Her accomplishment and of celebrating the gift which She had given to Her people. We now know this time as Lughnasad (literally "The Fair or Assembly of Lugh"). Though it bears His name, this festival still carries the energy of honoring the Goddess who gave Her life in order to insure the survival and future of Her people.

If you are ever feeling overwhelmed; if you are ever feeling you can't see the forest for the trees; if you ever feel that your own energy stores are waning; if you ever feel over-responsible, overworked or overburdened; remember Tailtiu. Remember the bigger picture of what you are striving to accomplish and hold yourself a beautiful, fun celebration! Nothing of effort, particularly when done with thoughts of the community in mind, is ever done in vain.

Tiffany Lazic is a spiritual psychotherapist and owner of The Hive and Grove Center for Holistic Wellness in Kitchener, Ontario, where she teaches her Patterns of Conscious Living Program, an integrative approach to Western emotional and energetic healing cycles inspired by the ancient festivals and celebrations. She is a member of the Sisterhood of Avalon, Hearthmother to the local chapter and facilitates quarterly Red Tents for women.

Terra Mater

Terra Mater directly translated from Latin is Earth Mother, and She commonly has also the name Tellus. While praying or saying the name Tellus to address Her, it was customary to touch the Earth, according to *A Companion to Roman Religion*, by Jorge Rupke. She is the giver of vegetation and Goddess of the sown field. Terra Mater within Roman culture precedes Greek influence. She was most widely recognized during the empirical period of Rome having images, shrines, and temples. Even then, there were few images of her. The Roman concept was that a statue of earth was not necessary, you had earth with you, near you, or below you, much as there were few statues to Vesta, for how could you represent fire better than an actual flame? It was common to have oaths and vows made to Her, especially prior to war or battle. There are also a few carved epitaphs, which would be carved stone monuments of dedication, with a short phrase to honor the Goddess that stood alone as well.

Fordicidia, on 15th of April, was Her agricultural festival in ancient Rome.

In addition to being called on for agricultural related needs, She was also called to bear witness during stages-of-life events such as births and deaths.

Antaeus was a son of Terra, and had invincible strength as long as he maintained in contact with his mother Earth, according to *Bulfinch's Mythology*. He was defeated by Hercules when lifted above the earth, thereby weakening him. She is pictured on a relief with two children, which I have heard both referred to as Flora and Fauna, representing all plant and animal life, or perhaps Romulus and Remus, founders of Rome.

She is inferred in Horace's hymns both as Terra and as Tellus. Tellus is referred to directly in Virgil's *Aeneid*, which is most likely the most well-known work. According to Julian the

Blessed IV, she is not only the mother of all that comes out of the Earth, but also the mother of the Gods, both mother and spouse of the mighty Jupiter, and source of all the intellectual and creative Gods. The work that is most like prayers we would be used to hearing would be the *Precatio Terrae* attributed to Antonius Musa. Within the *Precatio Terrae*, she is credited with regeneration, birth, overseeing all, giving food, enriching life, and providing healing. The *Precatio Terrae* closes with a petition for health and herbs. Tellus is also very similar to Demeter in Her associations.

The ancient Roman culture recognized their dependence, and the necessity of maintaining connection to Terra Mater, Tellus, as a Goddess and as the Earth itself.

In contemporary times, she does not have the following that many other Goddesses have been experiencing. Some Goddesses get more acclaim for their very direct associations with witchcraft or sorcery. More likely, Terra Mater / Tellus are a bit overshadowed by the Greek Gaia, or other similar Earth Mother Goddesses from succeeding cultures after the Roman Empire fell. In addition, titles like Great Mother, Holy Mother, and similar epithets and title names are used to refer to Mary as well in Latin. While sounding similar phonetically to the Hindu / Buddhist Goddess Tara, there is no substantial evidence of a historical connection.

It is relevant to connect to Terra Mater, and to recognize and make connections with our food, and the sources of our food. In times of chain supermarkets with canned, packaged, modified and frozen foods, many people can and do forget that food comes from somewhere. Try to use fresh ingredients if possible and, if it is in any way possible, try to grow a portion of your own food or herbs. Giving thanks and saying a blessing over your food would definitely be a suitable way to honor Her as well.

While ancients made a variety of sacrifices which would be unconventional today, the idea and intent of sacrifice with the right intent would be favored and has value. Donations to food pantries, supporting actions or groups related to farming or farmers, would be appropriate. Any type of volunteer work, especially to help heal others or environment related would also be appropriate. If you were to practice this in a reconstructionist style, such as cultus deorum, an offering of wine, milk, bread, bacon, sausage, or pork may be suitable.

When outdoors, make intentional direct physical contact with the Earth whether it be by touching trees or going barefoot. This would help you make this same connection, and would be similar to what the Romans might have done.

Most importantly, to honor Terra Mater, think about what it is and means that She is the Mother Earth. That She is the source and the provider from which all of our necessities are provided and come from. Think about your own mother, or your ideal mother, and magnify that times the size of the world. Take this realization or this thought beyond an academic or intellectual exercise, into one that you feel and sense personally.

Robert Scott was a founding member of Church of the Living Earth in Columbus, Ohio, and has volunteered regularly for the Earth Warriors Festival based also in Ohio. He contributes the Moon Lore blog on Moon Books Blog, and is a regular contributor to Circle Magazine.

Tlazoteotl

It's a movie cliché – the person with an angel on either shoulder, one telling you to be good and the other telling you to be bad. The Aztec Goddess Tlazoteotl (*tla sol tay otl*, literally Garbage Goddess) is a bad angel. She leads you into temptation and tells you it is alright for you to be naughty, and then when you realize what you have done, she is there to forgive you, to wash your soul clean of stain and ingest and recycle your sins in her guise as Eater of Filth. If society thinks something is wrong, but it feels oh-so-good to do it, Tlazoteotl is in favor of it. She wants you to do what feels good, but if doing what feels good makes you feel bad, she is there to cleanse your spirit. Ingesting the darkness is what keeps her alive and keeps the world functioning, as she keeps the balance between light and dark, sin and piety. She turns the filth into fertilizer and shows that temptation and forgiveness are part of the same wheel.

Tlazoteotl was originally a Goddess of the Huastec people (who lived in what is now Vera Cruz, Mexico). She was a Mother Earth Goddess who ruled sexuality, fertility, and filth. The Aztecs often adopted the deities of other cultures and fused them with existing Gods, or just added them into the pantheon.

The enfolding of Tlazoteotl into the Aztec belief system may be how she acquired her four aspects, which are of particular interest to modern pagans. European Mother Earth Goddesses are usually three-fold: maiden, mother, and crone. Tlazoteotl is a four-fold Goddess: the innocent flirty adolescent, the sensual young woman, the fertile woman, and the elderly woman; four sisters all named Tlazoteotl, although some people use the Aztec designations of their birth order, from youngest to oldest: Xocotzin (youngest sister), Tlaco (middle sister), Teicu (younger sister), and Tiacapan (first born) to differentiate between them.

Each sister is associated with a moon phase, from new moon,

to first quarter (waxing), to full moon, to last quarter (waning), encompassing new life, death, and rebirth. The full moon is the time of sin-eating and forgiveness as the moon grows round. The two youngest sisters are the sinners, beautiful and sexual beings, and the oldest one, the waning moon, encourages the sinning so she may be reborn.

Tlazoteotl was depicted in several ways in the surviving Aztec codices. Often she has a blackened mouth (from bitumen, used to decorate pottery and people, and chewed like gum), is riding both a snake and a broom, or is shown actively giving birth, and is often completely nude, showing the wrinkled belly of recent childbirth. The red snake represents the menstrual cycle and the moon, the broom her cleansing aspect, and the blackened mouth the temptation of youth (as only unmarried women could chew the bitumen gum) and also the fertile black earth.

The ancient Aztecs only called upon Tlazoteotl once in their lives, just before death, when their time of sinning was past. One of her priests came to the house and took a complete confession of every wrongdoing in the person's life, and even may have given the sinner penance, not unlike the Catholic Church. Modern worshippers of Tlazoteotl usually confess to her as needed, not storing everything up until the end of life. You can use a statue of her, or even a picture reproduced from a codex, as the focal point of the ritual, prayer, or meditation.

When working with Mesoamerican Gods, it is proper to offer a sacrifice. You do not have to kill anyone; that's not how modern sacrifice works. A few drops of your blood or sweat, incense smoke, flowers tossed into running water, crystals buried into the earth, or liquor poured onto the earth, are all appropriate. Although you are feeding Tlazoteotl your sins, you are also asking her for a favor – remember that the ancient Aztecs only called on her once in their lives, at the very end.

In our Circle, we do a spring equinox ritual that calls upon Tlazoteotl. With a statue of her on the central altar, we say, "Let us also start anew (like the year)." On the altar is a representation of the Aztec Goddess Tlazoteotl, known affectionately as Filth Eater. Tlazoteotl is a vulture-like Goddess of karmic cleansing. Give her your wrong doings, your bad thoughts, your sins, and she will eat them for you, leaving you clean and new to start again. Take turns stepping forward and putting your hands on Tlazoteotl. You may pick her up and whisper to her what you wish her to take from you, and she will do it gladly and with love and compassion. The statue is smudged and cleaned after each person gives up his or her sins.

Tlazoteotl was also known as Ixcuina(n) and Toci, and in addition to the attributes listed above, was the patroness of herbs, healing, and midwives, and the protector of women who died in childbirth.

Gevera Bert Piedmont, Shaman of Mayanism, Mayan Reiki Master, Feathered Serpent Initiate, is the author of the *Jaguar Nights* series of Mayan-Aztec calendar books. www.Obsidian Butterfly.com

Vesta

As the virgin Goddess of the sacred flame and the blazing hearth, Vesta, also called the Shining One or the One of Light, was at the heart of every home in ancient Rome. She was worshiped on a State scale, her sacred fire burning at the center of the Aedes Vestae, the Temple of Vesta, and becoming the hearth of Rome itself. There is little written of her story and she was not often depicted in statue or form of any kind. She was protectress of the home and family, keeper of the hearth fire, patroness of bakers, and, in some schools of thought, presided over childbirth. Although there are no temples to Vesta today, her sacred flame can still be found burning at the heart of every home.

All Roman family life revolved around the hearth and the hearth fire. No home was without fire. As keeper of the sacred flame, Vesta was at the center of this life, ever present in the hearth of every Roman family, offering protection, warmth and nourishment to each member of the household. The hearth was considered her altar and each meal began with an offering to Vesta, a morsel of food tossed into the fire. The women of the home called upon Vesta to protect their families and to guard over their homes at all times. It was believed that, should a person come to the door in search of shelter or food, it was ill luck to turn them away as Vesta offered all warmth and nourishment.

Vesta was also present at the center of the Roman State. Her temple, the Aedes Vestae, was located in the Roman Forum and surrounded by a sacred grove. It was a circular structure, with an inner sanctum housing the ever-burning flame in the round hearth at its center, considered to be the hearth of Rome. The door of the temple faced east, the direction of sunrise, symbolizing the connection between the Sun and Vesta's flame as the sources of life. Vesta's fire was tended by six priestesses, known as Vestal Virgins or Vestales, who were chosen between the ages of six and ten and spent 30 chaste years in service to Vesta. These women maintained the fire, ensuring its continual light and warmth for the city and the empire. Vesta's fire was renewed each year on 1st March by the Vestal Virgins. This was an anxious time for the Roman people as they believed the fire to be a symbol of the life of the city and a safeguard of the empire. Its extinguishing was thought to be a portent of disaster.

The inner sanctum of the Aedes Vestae was closed to all but the Vestales except during the time of her festival, the Vestalia, from 7th June through 15th June, during which time only women were allowed within, barefoot, to make offerings to the Goddess. For the festival, the Vestales made sacred cakes from grain, salt, and water from a holy spring. On the last day of Vestalia, the temple was ritually cleansed and the hearth ashes swept out. The ashes were then taken to the Tiber River for disposal. It is believed that the last day of the Vestalia was also a holiday for those who worked with grain, such as bakers and millers. For this reason, Vesta is considered the patroness of bakers as well.

There is little written in myths and stories of Vesta. She is equated with the Greek Goddess Hestia. Most myths seem to focus on Vesta refusing advances made on her by other male deities. It is believed that she was the first born daughter of Saturn and Rhea and sister to Ceres, Juno, Jupiter, Neptune and Pluto. One myth notes that Vesta was given the choice to marry by her brother, Jupiter, but she refused and was granted freedom, to be of and to her own. Vesta is usually depicted as a robed and veiled figure, holding a lamp and scepter. Some artwork shows her with flaming hair or holding a simple flame in her hand. However, it was felt that Vesta needed no statue, no picture; that she was the very flame itself and therefore needed no representation.

And where would Vesta be found in today's world of technological advancements, industrial revolutions, and hectic family lifestyles? One need look no further than their own home. This is her temple now as it was in ancient Rome. Vesta is there, still protecting the home and family, still providing warmth when needed, and still giving nourishment to household members. Her sacred fire is the same flame used to cook daily meals, whether in an oven or on a stovetop. It is the same kindled fire in the hearth on a cold day or the campfire around which people gather. It is the flame of a candle lit in her honor. She is still called upon by homemakers and kitchen witches alike to bless and protect the home and all in it. Vesta can still be honored during the time of the Vestalia by lighting a red candle surrounded by stones, to represent a hearth, and keeping the candle lit for the duration of the festival. Use the time to bake bread in her honor, to cleanse your home and hearth, and to make offerings to Vesta. The Shining One will continue to keep your home fires burning.

Johanna Lawson is a long time eclectic green witch whose work has been published in the anthologies, *Pagan Writers Press Presents Samhain*, *Pagan Writers Press Presents Yule*, and *Paganism 101: An Introduction to Paganism By 101 Pagans* as well as in Circle Magazine. She is also the author of a blog chronicling her journeys on the Pagan path, entitled *Village Wise Woman*, which can be found at johanna-villagewisewoman.blogspot.com/.

White Buffalo Woman

Some young hunters, on an unsuccessful hunt, came upon a dense white mist on the trail they walked. From the mist came a beautiful, nude, young woman. One hunter had lustful thoughts and approached the maiden. The mist surrounded the hunter. When it receded, there remained only a skeleton crawling with snakes. The other hunter, realizing he was in the presence of something mystical, humbled himself. The maiden directed him to prepare a lodge for her in his village. He did as he was told. When the lodge was prepared, the maiden arrived at the village, carrying a bundle containing a sacred pipe.

The maiden invited the village elders into the lodge and taught them the seven sacred ceremonies and how to use the pipe. When the maiden departed, she stepped to the top of the hill over the village, through the mist. On the opposite side, she exited as a white buffalo. Hence, her name is given: White Buffalo Calf Maiden, as described by Joseph M. Marshall III in his book, *The Lakota Way*.

White Buffalo Woman taught multiple lessons, in historical context, to the ancient Native Americans, of the Lakota tribes. She brought the sacred ceremonies and the pipe, which allowed the tribes to become strong through the basis of their religious practices. Arguably, the Lakota were the most powerful people on the early American plains. But, in current context, there are several lessons offered to us by White Buffalo Woman.

The first deals with arrogance. The lustful hunter had full intention of using the beautiful, nude maiden to satisfy his own base urges. White Buffalo Woman teaches us that arrogance is destroyed. In fact, the lustful hunter was covered by the mist (representative of the life force) and devoured. Lesson learned: we treat women (and deity) with respect and reverence, assuming no ill treatment of those we perceive as physically weaker than us.

Next, we are taught that humility is the path to strength and goodness. The humble hunter who recognized the divinity of White Buffalo Woman was given the right to bear the message to his people, preparing for her arrival. Because he was able to humble himself before her, the people received the sacred ceremonies and the pipe that brought their success. This lesson is reinforced through the tales of the Lakota people. Humble men rarely stumble, because their head is lowered toward the earth, allowing them to see what lay ahead. An arrogant man, instead, lifts his head to the sky, expecting praise, and frequently falls.

One of the sacred ceremonies brought was the hunka. It is the ceremony that reminds us that, regardless of our behavior, we are children of the earth. She will always love us. It is, in fact, our responsibility to be generous to her other children and to care for our mother earth, as our practice of giving comes directly from she who gives us all we need. The Releasing the Spirit ceremony is also in keeping with these concepts. The process, often called the Giveaway, is when family and community gather one year post death to feast, pray, and discuss the cycle of life. Then, items are given away to symbolize sharing of emotions between the giver and the receiver. This, of course, is a condensed and simplified version of the processes as discussed in *The Lakota Way*.

The pipe itself, represents the connection and importance of all things, according to Brooke Medicine Eagle in her book *The Last Ghost Dance*. Medicine Eagle goes on to describe another of the sacred ceremonies which emphasizes the interconnectedness of all peoples and things called hunkapi. This ceremony allows those who are not connected by birth to pledge their sacred relationship to another. This is most commonly used in ceremonies of marriage or adoption. However, the hunkapi is a reminder that we are connected to each thing, not just those that we choose.

White Buffalo Woman's lessons are as appropriate, perhaps more so, today than when they first arose in a simpler time – ideas of humility, generosity, connection, sacred reverence, tradition, purity, unity, and peace. And, she warns us of wrong behaviors: arrogance, power-seeking, maltreatment of others, disregard for the earth and its creatures. This Goddess gives us guidelines for morality, ceremony and ritual for practice, a direct connection to the life force and an understanding of the cycle which includes living and death. She is the epitome of the Great Mother Goddess who cares for her children, guides and directs them, and punishes for errant ways. Her ceremonies are still in use by the Lakota people and those who recognize the power of the rites.

Michele L. Warch, MCC, is a solitary witch of mixed Native American and European descent, who practices an eclectic mix of herbology, earth magick, and traditionalist witchcraft. She can be found teaching local to the Mid-Atlantic coast, participating in a circle of like-mindeds (Temple of WomanSpirit), writing her blog (The Witch's Way), and living in accordance with the elements.

Yingarna

In the time before time, all was in darkness and all was without shape. The creatures of the Earth made their way about in the darkness, in the void. And during this time before time there came a flash from the skies, of iridescent color, it came crashing upon the Earth with a mighty, thunderous, roar. Yingarna, the Rainbow Serpent, had arrived. A giant crater appeared in the formless earth where she had landed. She writhed about the land, tunneling under, rising above, displacing the earth, creating form and nourishing all as she went. Her journey across the land created the mountains and gullies, the rivers and lakes. She gave form and shape to that which was once formless. She had brought rains with her, the waterholes filled, rivers ran and new life appeared within and without. She called to the creatures in hiding to come forth and enjoy the new fertility of the land.

Yingarna, an ancient ancestral being of the Australian Indigenous people, is credited with bringing the human form into existence. In her human form she carries a dilly bag full of babies or new spirits to populate the Earth with, in other images she has a large womb full of half formed beings. She is most often represented in serpent form, however. The myth of the Rainbow Serpent is one of the oldest continuing beliefs in the world and continues to be an important part of Indigenous culture today. Cave paintings depicting Yingarna, occurring in the North of Australia, have been dated back some 6,000 years with Indigenous culture dating back 40,000 years or longer. The Rainbow Serpent has at times been given position as the most prominent creator God/dess in Australian Indigenous mythology, but this has largely been the creation of non-Aboriginal anthropologists. There are believed to be more than 200 "tribes" or nations across Indigenous Australia, each with their own variation of the Dreaming and subsequent localized mythos that explain and teach the Dreaming as it is for that part of the country. Another similar error often made by western-educated people, with a cultural stereotype of Greco-Roman myths, tell the Aboriginal stories in the past tense. For the indigenous people of Australia the stories are "Everywhen" – past, present and future, as are we, all interconnected and as one.

In some variations of the myth found in the Northern Territory, Yingarna accompanies the Great Mother as she travels across Australia giving birth to the Indigenous tribes. Yingarna brings the wet seasons of rain and floods to sustain the life brought forth by the Great Mother. In other versions from the Kimberley regions of Australia it is told that it was the Rainbow Serpent who deposited spirit-children throughout pools in which women become impregnated when they wade in the water.

Yingarna is credited with teaching laws of community and its structure, including ethics and respect.

In her more vengeful aspect Yingarna was known to swallow whole other, lesser, ancestral beings or humans who had wronged her; they would then be regurgitated in other forms. These regurgitated forms are believed to have become the rocky formations and escarpments and, in some cases, animals particular to a local geography or region. The stories behind their formation are shared through the oral traditions of the tribes in that area to educate and inform the new generations the lessons learned by the ancestors. In this way Yingarna's laws are passed down and remembered. In its most general sense the Rainbow Serpent is a symbol of both the creative and destructive forces of nature, akin to Mother Nature or Gaia in western cultures.

The energy invoked by calling on Yingarna is a very deep, primal energy, unpredictable yet fierce. Her energy is an ancient one and one not to be invoked lightly. She may be of assistance when working with women's mysteries and healing rituals, helpful during childbirth or in working with weather and primal creative forces. She is often associated with human blood, both the circulatory system and the menstrual cycle. She is considered a powerful healing force and a vengeful protectoress of her people.

Rainbows are the obvious association with the Rainbow Serpent, as is the halo around the Moon that occurs when rain is forecast. Thunder and lightning are said to be signs of an angered serpent.

Clear quartz is often used in ritual work to invoke her, presumably due to its capacity to fragment light and produce rainbows. Opal also works well in this regard with the rainbow captured within it. Both stones are believed to have been laid down by Yingarna in her journey across the lands. Red ochre can be used to anoint the third eye, womb area and hands, depending on the work to be undertaken: third eye for intuition, womb for working with women's mysteries and hands for healing work. Primal sounds such as the drum, clapping or a deep guttural hum from within can be used to focus and call her forth. Dance is a powerful way of drawing forth her energy into the physical realm and can be of particular benefit if the dancer proceeds to attend to healing work afterwards. Particular attention needs to be paid to maintaining a balance or staying partially grounded. This is a powerful, ancient energy at work here.

Rebecca Taylor

Epilogue: Emily, Goddess of Forgiveness

"Em! Emily!"

Emily hears the faint cry ascending from the living room. She sighs deeply, somewhat irritated by the insistence in her mother's voice and the constant interruptions. Scanning the text on her laptop, she takes her time writing the last sentence and saves the document. She slides out from the chair, her legs still tired from her nine-hour shift at the hospital, and makes her way back down the stairs to see what her mother needs.

"I can't find my glasses, Emily," the frail woman whispers, her withered arm grasping at air around the table that sits next to her bed. Emily looks around briefly and spots the glasses perched on the open book in her mother's lap. She leans over the outdated hospital bed that takes up most of the living room and adjusts her mother's blanket. Emily closes her eyes for a moment, remembering when the bed was not such an obstacle in her life. There is very little space to maneuver around to the kitchen; there is just enough room for Emily's two terriers to jump and play, and for Emily to eat at the kitchen table or respond to emails and reviews from her budding health blog.

Emily gently removes the reading glasses from her mother's book and places them on the bridge of her nose. She smiles slightly and props the book so that her mother could continue reading, even though Emily knew she hadn't turned a page all day.

Instead of returning to her laptop upstairs, Emily makes a cup of tea and sits, trying to recover from her shift and wondering how she got in this space, tending to the woman who had been so horrible to her for so many years. With a slight gesture, Emily pushes stray hairs away from her eyes, while grey strands at her temples are still gracefully swept up in a barrette. The cup of tea warms her hands and she sits in silent meditation. Emily wishes she had more time for her growing project that is often dwarfed by the seemingly unending tasks that her mother's illness requires. Several of these, Emily feels, are unnecessary, but for the sake of her mother's failing mind and Emily's growing stress levels, she does them anyway. Thankfully, Emily admits, she doesn't have to chase after children. Babies were never an interest to her and, at this point, are no longer a possibility. Instead she takes comfort in her terriers, who are always happy to see her when she returns from a day at the hospital, covering her face in puppy kisses as a reminder that she is loved without conditions.

With her mother tucked in for the night, her medicine administered and soft music played to lull her to sleep, Emily decides to return to a book on healthful eating. For a minute, her mind wanders and she recalls a memory of childhood dinners, one that wasn't so fondly recalled. The plates were large, but the portions were tiny, filled only with a few vegetables and a slice of meat, not enough for a growing young girl. Not enough for a child. Emily would often stuff her pockets with extra food from the school cafeteria – rolls, fruit, and cakes from the vending machines – and hide them in a shoebox under her bed. It wasn't a lack of money that drove her mother to feed Emily so little; mother didn't want her to get fat. Mother wanted her to grow into a thin, beautiful woman instead of what she saw to be Emily's disgusting, thickening body. Mother was anorexic and didn't understand the danger she was putting her daughter through by refusing to feed her balanced meals.

Emily tried to remind herself that it was her mother's illness that brought on the starvation; not her mother… the illness. She could not be blamed for her actions. But Emily did blame her for the words her mother would sling at her when she didn't slim down.

"How is it possible that you continue to gain so much weight when I feed you these healthy meals? What are you doing to yourself?"

Emily would often say nothing and keep her head down, the words hitting her like little sharp pebbles thrown at her most vulnerable spots.

"Fat."

"Disgusting."

"Lazy."

"You just aren't trying…"

It was at these moments that Emily would slink off to her room and comfort herself with the stash of food she brought from school or purchased from the corner store on the way home.

Mother is so much older now, Emily muses. The cutting words are no longer hurled in her direction, but Emily still feels the lingering sting. Her mother's eyes no longer squint right before she slings an insult in her direction, but Emily knows that the watery, vacant stares are unable to comprehend where she is anymore, let alone find the energy to chastise and mock. Her mother is weak, so very weak now, and now soon she will be free from the torment that was so pervasive in her teens. Now she can tell her mother what her mockery did to her, without fear of repercussions. But she doesn't. Instead, Emily wipes the water from her mother's slippery check and pulls the covers up to her shoulders, warming her.

Emily pauses in her memory and tries to re-focus on her book. Distracted she sets it aside, takes up her worn notebook and begins to jot down more ideas for her blog.

For the next focus of my work, I must reach down deep inside and reveal the seeds of my eating disorder. In the process of doing that, I will be able to counsel more women through the process of forgiveness, for themselves and for those who were instrumental in feeding their pain.

Not all of us had great mothers. Emily remembers talking with one of her friends, at a late afternoon lunch, and the topic turned to the trials of their respective childhoods and how they got to those places they were at now. They met for a rare moment of peace and to talk about the possibilities of growing a business out of their passions: passions that grew out of those troubled years.

"Maybe the business is a long shot, but a worthy one," her friend urged.

To help girls and women become healthy no matter what size, that's what I wanted to do. I want to help those girls feel secure in their body so that they wouldn't feel what she felt, Emily thought.

"Our bodies grow into womanhood," Emily said, "but inside is that hurt, neglected, tired little girl… that teenager who tries to cover up the pain with food. She is still in here, waiting with every passing moment, waiting and hopeful, but also afraid to hope."

"You could really make this into something, you know?" Her friend continued to urge.

"I know." Emily smiled, "but no. How can this be a business? How can I devote more time to this cause? I just can't do it. She needs me now. It will have to remain a labor of love."

Emily sets down her tea cup and sighs. She remembers that moment so well, wondering to herself if she made the right choice for her own life. Reassurance washes over her as she remembers why, years ago, she started to document her path. No matter what it was now, recovery was always the goal.

Emily quietly whispers to herself, "She knows not what she has done. She is also a product of her upbringing and what she has seen around her. If I continue to recognize that, I can bring about my own release." She nods briefly and places the empty tea cup in the sink.

Yes, Emily thinks to herself, listening to the oxygen machine softly hum in the background. Mothering our mothers, giving her the love that she deserved, that we also deserved, but didn't receive. Without guilt and mockery, we can be there for her, even when she was not there for us, and in return we are mothering ourselves as well.

Emily is the Goddess of Forgiveness, forgiveness of others, but also of ourselves, because forgiveness is really about healing. In this light, Emily can be viewed as the Triple Goddess because of the universality of her gifts. She is the maiden simply because she is the daughter figure, still trapped in the memories of her childhood, remembering the pains of her youth and trying to reclaim what she lost. She is the mother, re-mothering her parental figure and mothering herself in the process, trying to rectify the damage that both women caused to each other and to themselves. Emily also mothers in her daily work and with her young pups that give her so much joy. Finally, she is the wise, all-seeing crone. Emily knows what she needs to do, even subconsciously. With her work in the writing projects and reaching out to others who deal with negative body image and eating disorders, she sacrifices her daily life to forgive and to redeem herself and her mother from the agony that grips their lives so steadily.

How did I get to this space? Emily occasionally wonders. Through the yo-yoing of diets and bingeing, trying powders and extreme exercise, starvation, cutting, and counseling, Emily finally had no more energy to push the merry-go-round anymore. It used to be her favorite ride on the playground, as a child, but seeing the motion play out in her adult life just made her dizzy and tired. She got off the ride and started walking, just walking away and occasionally glancing back to see where she had come from.

Emily did not come to this realization quickly or gently. It was years before she could begin to talk with her mother about her own eating disorder and even more time before she could see her mother as someone deserving of love and compassion. Someone who needed forgiveness, for her sake and for the sake of her daughter.

In the mirror, Emily faces her shadow, a vision that she sees every day. The billboards commend her for her narrow lines and the absence of curves on her arms, but she knows the truth. This is not the body she was meant to have. This was what she was forced to create and while her lines cannot change, the image in her mind can. "I am beautiful," she says every morning after rising. "I am what I am meant to be. No one can tell me that I should change my lines, my curves, my face."

And maybe one day, she'll believe them to be more than just empty words.

Margo Wolfe is an educator, Pagan, and member of the Sisterhood of Avalon. She co-ordinates many local events for adults and teenagers, including a Teen CUUPS (Covenant of Unitarian Universalist Pagans) group in PA, working with many amazing young people. Her forthcoming book is entitled, *Turning the Wheel and Mentoring our Pagan Youth: A Curriculum Guide for Instructors of Pagan Teens.*

Community Writing Projects
From Moon Books

Paganism 101: An Introduction to Pagainism by 101 Pagans

978-1-78279-170-6 (Paperback)
978-1-78279-169-0 (eBook)

This is a much-needed book that gives voice to the diversity of ideas and opinions being voiced by contemporary Pagans. As I read it, I felt as if I was sitting in a circle, in a community of like-minded souls, hearing new points of view, challenging ideas, old ideas expressed in different ways. Warmth, humanity, creativity all flow from these pages.
Philip Carr Gomm, Author and Leader of The Order of Bards Ovates & Druids

Witchcraft Today – 60 Years On

978-1-78279-168-3 (Paperback)
978-1-78279-167-6 (eBook)

Sixty years after the publication of *Witchcraft Today*, we have seen Gerald Gardner's vision grow and evolve as it spreads around the globe. *Witchcraft Today – 60 Years On* is a fitting tribute, bringing together authors from different paths within the Craft, each with a unique contribution and insight to inspire those who are practicing, teaching, and strengthening Wicca today and for the generations to come.
Dr Vivianne Crowley, Faculty of Pastoral Counseling and Chaplaincy, Cherry Hill Seminary

Moon Books invites you to begin or deepen your encounter with
Paganism, in all its rich, creative, flourishing forms.